Heavenly Ambitions

Heavenly Ambitions

America's Quest to Dominate Space

Joan Johnson-Freese

PENN

University of Pennsylvania Press

Philadelphia

Published by
University of Pennsylvania Press
Philadelphia, Pennsylvania 19104-4112

Printed in the United States of America on acid-free paper
10 9 8 7 6 5 4 3 2 1

Library of Congress Cataloging-in-Publication Data

Johnson-Freese, Joan.
    Heavenly ambitions : America's quest to dominate space / Joan Johnson-Freese.
        p.   cm.
    Includes bibliographical references and index.
    ISBN 978-0-8122-4169-3 (alk. paper)
    1. Astronautics—Government policy—United States.   2. Space race—United States.
3. Astronautics and state—United States.   I. Title.
    TL789.8.U5J649   2009
    629.4′10973—dc22

                                                                    2009001012

Contents

Acronyms

ABM	anti-ballistic missile
AFSPC	Air Force Space Command
ALMV	Air-Launched Miniature Vehicle
ANGELS	Autonomous Nanosatellite Guardian for Evaluating Local Space
BMD	ballistic missile defense
BMDS	ballistic missile defense systems
CAV	common aero vehicle
CBP	capabilities-based planning
CCS	Counter Satellite Communications System
CD	Conference for Disarmament
CDI	Center for Defense Information
COMSAT	Communications Satellite Corporation
COPUOS	UN Committee on the Peaceful Uses of Outer Space
DARPA	Defense Advanced Research Projects Agency
DEW	directed-energy weapons
DoD	Department of Defense
FMCT	fissile material cutoff treaty
FREND	Front-end Robotics Enabling Near-term Demonstration
FY	fiscal year
GEO	geosynchronous orbit
GMD	ground-based, mid-course missile defense
GPALS	Global Protection Against Limited Strikes
GPS	Global Positioning System
HASC	House Armed Services Committee
IADC	Inter-Agency Space Debris Coordination Committee
ICBM	intercontinental ballistic missile
INW	isotropic (nondirectional) nuclear weapons
ISS	International Space Station
KEW	kinetic-energy weapons
LEO	low Earth orbit
MDA	Missile Defense Agency

MDSEC	Missile Defense Space Experiment Center
MEO	medium Earth orbit
MIT	Massachusetts Institute of Technology
MKV	multiple kill vehicles
NASA	National Aeronautics and Space Administration
NFIRE	near field infrared experiment
NGO	nongovernmental organizations
NIE	National Intelligence Estimates
NMD	national missile defense
NORAD	North American Aerospace Defense Command
NRO	National Reconnaissance Office
NSP	National Space Policy
ORS	Operationally Responsive Space
OST	Outer Space Treaty
PAROS	Prevention of an Arms Race in Outer Space
PE	Program Element
QDR	Quadrennial Defense Review
RAIDRS	Rapid Identification Detection and Reporting System
SBI	space-based interceptors
R&D	research and development
SDI	Strategic Defense Initiative
SDIO	Strategic Defense Initiative Organization
SSA	space situational awareness
THAAD	theater high-altitude area defense
TICS	Tiny independent coordinating spacecraft
TMD	theater missile defense
USAF	United States Air Force
WMD	weapons of mass destruction
XSS	Experimental Spacecraft System

Preface

Analysts who specialize in future studies are not merely playing a parlor game, trying to see whose predictions will one day come closest to reality. In fact, they are not trying to predict the future at all, but to shape it. The question "What will the future look like?" is really only the prelude to a more important question, "What do we *want* the future to look like?" There is little point in simply proceeding on a linear path and reacting to what one finds along the way, allowing idiosyncratic political or bureaucratic goals to dictate direction. Further, there is no reason to be trapped into believing the future is the inevitable result of trends present or past. It is far better to choose a destination and map a path to get there, no matter how improbable a journey it might seem. As University of Hawaii futurist Jim Dator says, "Any useful statement about the futures ought to appear ridiculous."[1] Dator's use of "futures" in the plural is not an error. There are many possible futures, and, though it may seem obvious to say so, we make the decisions that determine which have the greatest chance of becoming reality. Nothing is inevitable.

And nothing lends itself to the imagination and the vision of multiple futures like the exploration and mastery of space, both near and outer. From the battles between the intrepid Flash Gordon and his nemesis, Ming, to the establishment of the noble and democratic United Federation of Planets in *Star Trek*'s vision of the twenty-third century, the future of humankind in space is most often depicted as one in which humanity in general, often led by Americans in particular, emerge triumphant over any number of threats from within or afar.

But the reality of America's future in space is much more uncertain than the triumphant images of the conquest of the cosmos found in the popular imagination (and, truth be told, too often in the overconfident positions of advocates of a kind of American space dominance). There is no magic solution, no sudden discovery of warp drives or phaser beams or ion cannons, that will get us to such a secure future. Instead, we have to think in terms of not only what kind of future we are trying to build, but what kinds of policies we should embrace—especially the incremental policies that today might seem like small steps but tomorrow could result in great leaps. What paths, which futures, will best protect the multiple and critical interests of the United States in space?

Wherever we are headed, any change in course will almost by definition be better than where we are currently. Chapters 1 and 2 provide an overview and analysis of how we reached the present circumstances, which are, quite simply, a mess. The United States has gotten itself into a position where to protect its essential space assets, including military assets and those critical to the economic and social well-being of the United States, it must constantly outdo its own military capabilities—that is, conduct an arms race with itself—in order to stay ahead of the rest of the world's potential ability to thwart those capabilities. Other nations, or at least certain ones that do not feel particularly warm toward the United States or trust its benevolent intentions on faith, in turn feel it is their unavoidable goal to try to undermine America's search for ultimate space security, which of course sets the whole process in motion again and again. The United States has by choice and by overconfidence bordering on folly embarked upon a course that relies primarily on technology, including space weapons, to protect its space assets, rather than diplomacy and cooperation, which had been the cornerstones of U.S. policy until the Reagan administration. Whereas space was once a strong basis of U.S. global "soft power" efforts, it is now increasingly viewed by our friends and enemies alike as just another hammer in the coercive array of hard power weapons in the American toolbox.

Chapter 3 explores the difference between fact and fiction regarding potential space weapons. This difference is often vast, and the possibility of achieving the sought-after capabilities is often slim, at best, despite the fervent belief of many ordinary Americans that such systems are within our grasp. As Arthur C. Clarke pointed out in 1962, "Any sufficiently advanced technology is indistinguishable from magic."[2] The line between advanced technology and magic over the years has become increasingly blurred. There is, however, a line that when crossed takes plans from the realm of engineering into that of magic, and thence to make-believe. To base our national security and economic prosperity on such illusions is not only irresponsible but risky beyond reason. Unfortunately, expert opinion on these issues has fallen victim to the same kind of politicization that has afflicted so many other areas of science policy.

Chapter 4 moves from the realm of technology to the realities of politics, and particularly the dangers of America's recent bellicosity regarding space. The United States does not have a monopoly on either space technology or the intent to utilize space to the fullest extent possible in pursuit of both economic- and security-related national interests, but this has not stopped American policymakers from acting and speaking as though space were a private American preserve. This last point is especially critical, because a recognition of the rights—to say nothing of the capabilities—of other nations in space is the key to a more secure space future not only for United States, but for the other countries of the world as well. The damage done by eight years of chest-thumping rhetoric about American space prowess must be recognized and addressed as part of a new approach to space policy.

The opportunities and limitations of arms control to provide security for U.S. space assets are considered in Chapter 5. There is a terrible irony in U.S. space policy where arms control efforts are concerned. While technical difficulties—indeed, even likely failure—have not been considered sufficient reason to discourage much less cancel costly military space programs in recent years, far smaller difficulties with technical and legal definitions seem enough to derail advocates of those programs from even exploring arms control avenues. In short, highly questionable technologies are able to deflect uncertainty about their viability, but the smallest wrinkle in an arms control proposal is a dealbreaker for further diplomatic efforts. The approach of arms control instruments also matters. The kinds of verbose, tangled, and dense treaties increasingly popular with liberal internationalists in Europe, who favor rules decided upon and "enforced" through international institutions, are unlikely to be accepted in the United States (and for good reasons too, in some instances). Yet other options could provide greater security for the United States while placing minimal restraint on U.S. activity—a key condition that opponents of U.S. involvement in arms treaties insist on but one they continually refuse to recognize as it would compromise their larger (and unattainable) project of U.S. space dominance.

Finally, Chapter 6 explores the realities of globalization and what those realities mean for space security. Globalization is characterized by mutual dependence and a high degree of connectivity among societies, cultures, and economies. Given that space technology is critical for connectivity, deliberately using space policy to create mutual dependence can enhance American security far more than mere space technology and threats ever could. It would again allow space to be viewed primarily as an expression of America's enormous soft power—or "smart power," as the next iteration of soft power is sometimes now being called[3]—thus polishing the U.S. image abroad.

But this repair of both America's space policy and its image in the world will require dramatic changes. Our flawed approach to space is the product not of any single source of dysfunction, but a swamplike mixture of partisan politics, bureaucratic gamesmanship, the traditional pressures of the military-industrial complex, and an unfortunate and blissful ignorance on the part of the American public. Worse, this ignorance is wedded to a kind of American exceptionalism that drives Americans—the conquerors of the Moon—to believe that they have an almost inherent right to declare space as their own, the reaction of the rest of the world be damned.[4]

The hubris which has dominated U.S. attitude and policy has become counterproductive. It is time to change. With the Obama administration in 2009, the possibility exists for a course correction. But in the meantime, we should consider how our current policy developed, where we stand, and where we want to go.

From being regarded as a nation of heroes, even miracle workers, as on that summer evening in 1969 when Neil Armstrong left the first human footprint on the moon, the United States is now regarded in some quarters as little better than would-be pretenders to the evil Galactic Empire of the *Star Wars* legends. We turn now to the origins of our current policy, and how our approach to space over the past two decades has squandered a once-huge reservoir of goodwill toward American efforts in space.

Chapter One
Space
The Final Cold War Frontier

> The Cold War is over, Mr. President, and there is no arms race in
> outer space. Thus, there is no—repeat, no—problem in outer space
> for arms control to solve.
> —John Mohanco, U.S. Statement at the Conference on
> Disarmament, 13 June 2006

Satellites and the multiple services they provide have become indispensable elements of life in a globalized world. Tourists trying to navigate
the streets of New York City using the NeverLost system in a rental car,
mountain climbers in Nepal trying to reach base camp, soccer parents
hurriedly paying for gas at the pump using a credit card, commercial
airliners on transoceanic routes, warplanes firing precision-guided
munitions, and U.S. soldiers trying to identify approaching troops are
all reliant on satellites, particularly the Global Positioning System (GPS)
for assistance. GPS is a U.S. military owned and operated system of
twenty-four satellites, plus four spares, each with several synchronized
atomic clocks on board. GPS is only one satellite system among many.[1]

As of 2007, more than 800 active satellites orbit around the Earth and
more than half of them belong to the United States. The United States
dominates space both in terms of orbiting satellites and financial investments made to develop and support those satellites. Although the
majority of U.S. assets are for commercial or civilian uses, the U.S. military increasingly dominates the direction taken by space policy in the
United States. Satellites are critical to military operations, as demonstrated in every successful U.S. military campaign from the Gulf War in
1990–91, to Bosnia, Afghanistan, and the twenty-two-day march to Bagh-

dad in 2002. They are also very vulnerable to attack; hence the need for protection.

The approach currently being taken by the United States to address the vulnerability of its satellites relies on developing technology to (1) protect our satellites and (2) deny other countries the ability to use space in ways the United States deems threatening. Use of the word "deny" stems from multiple Air Force documents, including the 2003 *Transformation Flight Plan*[2] and 2004 *Air Force Doctrine Document 2–2.1*,[3] as well as the earlier 2002 *Joint Doctrine for Space Operations, Joint Publication 3–14*,[4] prepared under the direction of the Chairman of the Joint Chiefs of Staff. It means "to stop" by whatever means necessary, including destruction of other countries' assets. The United States wants to dominate space in terms of assets, investments, and—through technology—control. It is basically the same approach that President Ronald Reagan wanted to take with his Strategic Defense Initiative program (SDI, or "Star Wars" as the program was dubbed) to shield America from the nuclear threat. Reagan wanted scientists to build a nuclear umbrella to protect Americans. The problem was that without breaking the U.S. treasury, with still no guarantee of success, scientists were unable to achieve technically what they were being asked to do. Nevertheless, remnants of the program continue today as missile defense, with over 8,000 people employed full-time or as contractors by the Missile Defense Agency (MDA); President George W. Bush requested $10.8 billion for missile defense in the fiscal year 2009 budget alone.[5]

Now, scientists are again being tasked potentially to defy the laws of physics to develop ways to protect satellites. The issue is not whether satellites should be protected. Clearly, they must. The fundamental question addressed in this book is whether protecting satellites with technology is a viable means to an end. If the answer to that question is "no," then the technology approach becomes moot. Whether protecting satellites with technology is a viable approach is a question rarely asked, and when it is—usually not at the behest of those advocating technology programs[6]—if the answer is not supportive of proposed technology programs, the results are ignored by assurances that "anything is possible." Hannah Arendt discussed the belief that "anything is possible" in the context of hubris and ideology being used to justify actions of governments in *The Origins of Totalitarianism*. In the present context, hubris and ideology again come into play. Further, if the answer to the viability question is "no," and yet efforts in that direction are still pursued, the unintended consequences, in terms of reactions from other countries, will be highly counterproductive to U.S. security. Other countries will feel extremely threatened by U.S. actions and feeling threatened can result in so-called security dilemmas where countries then take actions counter to their own interests.[7] In such a security dilemma, the United States would likely feel compelled to counter the actions of others, and so on, and a spiral of escalating, dangerous activity is set into motion. How to counter feelings of threat will be a key question all space-faring nations must consider in the future.

Why might countries feel threatened in space by the United States? There is considerable disparity between U.S. space efforts and those of other countries. The budget for the National Aeronautics and Space Administration (NASA) in 2006 was over $16 billion, compared with Europe's civil space budget of $3.52 billion, Japan's $1.46 billion, India's $820 million and China's $1.5 billion.[8] The gap is even wider when considering military-space budgets, where U.S. expenditures account for nearly 95 percent of global military-space expenditures. Unclassified U.S. defense-related spending on space was over $44 billion in 2006.[9] By comparison, for example, the ratio between military-space spending in the United States and Europe is about fifteen to one.[10] Overall, the U.S. government accounts for over 80 percent of global space expenditures.[11] However, while the expenses of other countries in space are less than that of the United States, their interest in space is not.

Nearly 400 of the 800 active satellites in space are non-U.S. owned: "As of August 2007, around fifty countries, international consortia, and nongovernmental organizations (NGOs) have at least one satellite in space, mostly for reasons that have more to do with economic performance and earth monitoring than with military applications."[12] As already stated, most U.S. satellites are nonmilitary as well. Satellites are considered key enablers for a globalized world, connecting people and countries on a round-the-clock basis. Space assets are information providers and conveyers, and information is a prerequisite for building a knowledge-based society, considered the successor to industrial-based societies. Space, in the view of many countries, is a "global commons" to be shared by all.

But whereas the rest of the world considers space primarily from a "globalized world" perspective, where overlapping economic and commercial interests dictate emphasis on win-win scenarios (all parties benefiting), the United States still considers space from a Cold War, zero-sum political perspective: one country's advances must be at the expense of someone else. One would hope that in a globalized world where connectivity and interdependence are increasingly the norm, the United States would recall Montaigne's declaration, "The statement that one man's boon is the other man's damage is valid with regard to robbery, war, and booty."[13] At least regarding space, however, Montaigne's premise seems not to be recognized.

The first U.S. antimissile effort was undertaken after the launch of

Sputnik in 1958. Called Project Defender, multiple technologies were explored, but the scientists who had been assembled—among the best and brightest in the country—quickly found it much harder than anticipated to develop a shield that did not "leak" and subsequently their plans became ever more grandiose and expensive, including one design for an orbiting battle station carrying no fewer than 3,000 nuclear weapons.[14] Consequently, during the Cold War, "strategic restraint" was the guiding principle for U.S. (and Soviet) space policy; building legal and policy frameworks in support of deterrence and deliberately avoiding military expansion and adventurism in space. The 1967 Outer Space Treaty (OST),[15] signed and ratified by ninety-eight countries,[16] was the cornerstone of those efforts.

Two events changed the direction of history. First, the number of space-faring nations grew, as did the range of their activities and technical capabilities. The value of space assets as information tools was recognized by all countries and none felt they could afford to be shut out. Space went from being a two-player game with both players starting from the same point and nearly equally matched, to a multiplayer game with one leading player and many others along various points of a spectrum of capabilities. But rules to clarify the game, through elaboration of OST principles, failed to keep up. Part of the reason for that lay with the second event: the election of Ronald Reagan as President of the United States. With the Reagan administration and SDI, a program Reagan never vetted through the National Security Council but instead commenced based on advice solicited from a highly selective group of individuals known primarily for their personal loyalty to him, the United States began veering from its previous policy path. And while SDI was the flagship of Reagan-era space policy, it was complemented by other separate, or only loosely linked, military-space programs including anti-satellite weapons (ASATs), military shuttle missions, national security interference with the space station program, and the emergence of tactical applications of space systems. Suddenly, the significance of space for warfighting began to weigh more heavily on space policy than using space as a stabilizing force supporting deterrence and as a development and economic tool. When George W. Bush's administration considered space primarily as a warfighting medium—the fourth battlespace, it became embedded policy. Those who support that view and feel it essential that space be controlled as the ultimate "high ground" are sometimes referred to as "space hegemonists."[17] Given the negative global response to what many countries considered unilateralist and hegemonist U.S. actions in Iraq, a similar U.S. approach to space will undoubtedly meet with resistance.

One group of space-faring nations, those akin to liberal international-

ists, seeks rules and the establishment of a legal regime that would promote stability and encourage private investment, yet the United States
specifically rejects such approaches and instead seeks military domination of the heavens—something other countries are unlikely to accept.
Challenges to the U.S. view are often critiqued by space hegemonists as
favoring economics (and by nefarious extension, greed) over national
security, when in fact the argument actually is that changes in the international environment—specifically, globalization—change the equation
to one where cooperation in some areas and competition in others is
not only possible, but required for security.

Space hegemonists tend to argue that their position is right, and
therefore, all others must be wrong. They rely on persuasion, which
depends more on eliciting an emotional response than a rational one.[18]
A favorite tactic of the space hegemonists, for example, is proclaiming
the inevitability of military conflict in space. If one accepts that presumption, and it is only a presumption, then there is an obligation to prepare
for conflict with a full range of weapons, immediately, to seize the "high
ground." Acceptance of the inevitability presumption and the space
weapons it demands—over consideration of less expensive, less vulnerable, and less challenging terrestrial options for the same military missions—is expected on trust. By contrast, hegemonists require challenges
to the inevitability presumption to be proven.

Those with commercial perspectives are seeking to make investments
in space, to expand the potential services that can be provided and
opportunities to be mined. Entrepreneurship is a private enterprise,
though, not a function of government. Private capital investors go to
areas of high profit potential and manageable risk, often defined in
terms of stability and a predictable environment. One of the fundamentals of stability and predictability is rules. The United States, however, is
focusing on increasing its military presence in space and resisting any
boundaries on its actions. Professor Everett Dolman from the Air Force
School of Advanced Air and Space Studies has argued that the United
States should seize military control of Low Earth Orbit (LEO) to stop an
arms race in space and thereby safeguard the peaceful use of space for
all nations.[19] The implication of course is that the United States will
determine all rules and can use space for whatever purposes it feels necessary, though the same would not necessarily be true for other countries. These countries, however, are unlikely to see a U.S. seizure of LEO
as benevolent or in their best interests.

The disparity between U.S. assets and investments and those of other
countries does not provide the United States with an unchallengeable
ability to impose its will around the world, or even in space, as one might
imagine—or as the United States might wish. In fact, the disparity of

investment might well instead put the United States in a more vulnerable position because other countries will detect a challenge to their sovereignty and therefore their security—something all governments are charged with providing—and respond more assertively and aggressively than they might have otherwise. Disproportionate power will not go unchallenged without assurances to those with less influence that they have no reason to fear. Force does not equal assurance. Since 2000, the United States has removed or revised policies built up since the Eisenhower administration intended to reassure other countries that the United States supported the peaceful use of space for all countries and restrain the development and use of military power in space. Instead the government has tacitly moved into the weaponization of space against both terrestrial and space-based targets, causing considerable consternation in many countries.

Assuring countries about the benign intentions of a country with disproportionate power is necessary for multiple reasons. A country like the United States that has superior capabilities in observation, navigation, and communication enjoys considerable advantages in military conflicts, as proven since the 1990–91 Gulf War. Add to that the apparent U.S. quest for antisatellite weapons, space-based missile defense interceptors, and space-based global strike capabilities against terrestrial targets, and the United States "would have the ability to observe potentially hostile activities as they occur, to enable rapid counterstrikes, and to be able to deny similar capability to other countries. If those aspirations were ever to be achieved, they would enable highly intrusive forms of coercion that could be undertaken without the burdens of occupation."[20] Any country with those capabilities would become, in effect, unassailable and able to impose its will virtually without question. While from a U.S. perspective that would provide the ultimate security umbrella, other countries view the prospect with considerable trepidation. Fearing their sovereignty at risk, they will seek to develop space assets to thwart that scenario. That action, however, could trigger further escalation of U.S. military efforts to dominate space.

Disproportionate power can also lead countries to embark on indigenous programs to avoid dependence on the United States for what they see as critical space services. Europe developed the Ariane launcher and Japan the H-2 launcher so as not to rely on the United States for launch services. France and Israel recently developed and launched their own reconnaissance satellites to avoid relying on the United States for imagery. Europe is still struggling to develop its own navigation satellite system, Galileo, because regardless of assurances given by the U.S. government that services will not be denied, Europe does not want to rely on the U.S. military-owned GPS system. China is talking about developing its own global navigation satellite system as well. The more other countries develop indigenous space systems, the more elusive domination becomes.

The American public is almost completely unaware of the changes in U.S. policy, by design, or of U.S. actions. "How many Americans know," a May 2008 editorial in the *Boston Globe* asked, "that the nation refusing to discuss a treaty aimed at preventing an arms race in outer space is their own? Indeed," it went on, "the United States, in various Pentagon documents published during the Bush administration, is explicit in aiming to put weapons in space—lasers, directed energy, kinetic-kill vehicles."[21] Even those constituencies traditionally concerned with space activities, including those interested in space exploration and the aerospace industry, appear not to fully understand the details of the new policies or their implications. Further, neither the economic nor technical feasibility of achieving the goal of space dominance has been realistically assessed "by Congress, a balanced independent commission, or any other expert-level group that represents the broad array of interests at stake."[22] Rather, policy changes have been driven by nontechnical advocates at think tanks and military schools, and implemented through organizations driven by the parameters of organizational and bureaucratic behavior, specifically, short-term gain and self-perpetuation.

The key questions to be addressed in this book concern space dominance. Is it a viable policy option? If space dominance is not possible, then why is it being pursued? What alternatives exist to maximize protection of space assets? To begin to address these questions, the threat must first be understood.

Why the Quest for Dominance?

Unfortunately, the threat to our space security is real and growing. The threat can take many forms. A report by the U.S. Space Commission staff identifies at least eleven distinct categories of antisatellite attack: from ground segment attack or sabotage to kinetic kill to nuclear ASATs, particle beam weapons, and electronic attack. The space threat posed by China is multifaceted. The "painting" in September of a U.S. satellite by a ground-based laser shows that the Chinese program includes a broad range of capabilities, from kinetic kill to directed energy. The January 11 test also shows China's ability to hit targets in Low-Earth Orbit, where most American reconnaissance assets are deployed. But reports suggest that the Chinese also seek the ability to attack satellites in Medium- and High-Earth Orbit, such as GPS. Other nations also may have ASAT capabilities.[23]

In this January 2007 statement, while Senator Jon Kyl (R-Arizona) does not attribute the threat to American space assets as emanating only from China, he clearly sees the threat as primarily from China.

What is the threat? Generally speaking, successful space missions require an exchange of commands and engineering data between a satellite and ground controllers, and the processing and transmission of data from the satellite to the users. There are four basic elements involved in a network to make all that happen: the satellites in orbit; the Earth-based antennas and receivers, called ground stations; the command authority which controls both the satellite and all other elements in the network; and relay satellites, or additional satellites that link the primary satellite to the ground stations. Information moves among these network elements through various links: uplinks (ground station to primary satellite), downlinks (primary satellite to ground station), forward links (ground station to primary satellite through a relay satellite), return links (primary satellite to ground station through a relay satellite), and crosslinks (between primary and relay satellites).[24] While the focus of most antisatellite discussions is on blowing up or destroying satellites, nothing so dramatic need be done.

Interference with any part of the network or linkages can successfully negate the value of the space asset. Destroying a ground station is obviously technically much easier than blowing up a satellite and is an accepted military tactic. Ground stations were among the first targets hit by the United States in both Kosovo and Iraq.[25] Space-weapons advocates argue that blowing up a satellite is less provocative than hitting a ground station because collateral damage does not involve killing anybody or even violate sovereign territory; it just destroys property, like shooting down a drone. Equally as likely, however, is the very real potential that destroying a satellite will escalate hostilities because the satellite owner will feel blinded or robbed of a key capability, and therefore will retaliate before they incur unacceptable risk or are further weakened. Whether attacking a satellite may be viewed as an act of war is ambiguous. Barry Watts compares satellites to ships to illustrate the point.

Sinking a nation's ship on the high seas, whether a military or commercial vessel, has long been viewed as an act of war. Article VIII of the 1967 Outer Space Treaty states that any party "on whose registry an object launched into outer space is carried shall retain jurisdiction and control over such object, and over any personnel thereof, while in outer space or on a celestial body." In 1996, the United States declared as national policy that the space systems of any nation are "national property with the right of passage through and operations in space without interference." Nevertheless, damaging or destroying satellites does not seem to have quite the same status as damaging or sinking a nation's ships and killing its crew. Satellites may have owners and operators, but, in contrast to sailors, they do not have mothers. Granted, the destruction of a KH-11 or comparable satellite at a key juncture in a crisis with a major regional power would be taken very seriously by American leaders. Whether this act would inevitably lead to war, however, is far from clear.[26]

One thing is clear: ambiguity can be dangerous.

The range of methods possible for interfering with space missions is varied, and some analysts feel that too much emphasis is being placed on dealing with unlikely extremes.[27] Nevertheless, it is the job of the military to consider all risks, including ASATs. The real challenge is determining an appropriate response.

An antisatellite weapon interferes with or destroys the space-based portion of the communication network previously described, thereby impeding the owner's ability to receive or transmit information. The basic types of ASATs currently considered most viable are isotropic (nondirectional) nuclear weapons (INW), kinetic-energy weapons (KEW), and directed-energy weapons (DEW) using, for example, lasers or high-powered radio frequencies.[28] INW weapons are detonated in space, within range of the target satellite, radiating energy to destroy the target. Kinetic-kill ASATs destroy their target by the force of an impact, either from a ground-, air-, or sea-based missile, or another satellite that slams into the target. Lasers (on the ground, in the air, or space-based) can have two effects: on the optical sensor of a satellite and on the body of the satellite. At relatively low power, the light from the laser swamps the light from the ground so that the sensor cannot see anything on the ground. This is called "dazzling" and is reversible. At higher power, the laser may permanently damage part of the sensor. This is typically called "blinding," though only a small part of the sensor is affected, so the satellite is not actually blind. At much higher power, a laser might cause the satellite itself to malfunction either by overheating or by physical damage. It is important to note, however, that lasers are also used to illuminate, or "paint" satellites for non-nefarious tracking purposes and can inadvertently dazzle the sensors. Other types of ASATs are possible as well, but these are the categories of those most feasible in the near future. Early U.S. ASAT programs were INW focused. The far-reaching destruction from the electromagnetic pulse created by INW weapons, however, turned the United States away from that approach. Nevertheless, any country capable of launching a nuclear weapon on a missile has a potential ASAT capability.

For the United States to be dominant in space, it would have to be able to render other countries' ability to use ASATs ineffective. It would have to be able to successfully defend against all offensive measures. U.S. satellites would have to be, if not technically invulnerable, extraordinarily resilient in the face of attempts to disrupt their essential capabilities. In January 2007, the Chinese demonstrated to the United States just how difficult that might be.

At 5:28 P.M. EST on 11 January 2007, in a test designed to evaluate their antisatellite missile capability, the People's Liberation Army of the People's Republic of China successfully destroyed one of their defunct weather satellites, the Feng-Yun 1C.[29] The method used to destroy the satellite was a direct-ascent, kinetic-kill vehicle using an optical tracking system—technically similar to the missile defense system being developed by the United States (though U.S. missile defense kill vehicles use infrared sensors, not optical).[30] Traveling at nearly 18,000 mph, the vehicle slammed into the six-foot long satellite, instantly obliterating it into an estimated 35,000 individual particles of one centimeter or larger in size.[31] The debris field quickly dispersed along the satellite's original orbital path, with all of these individual particles traveling at over 16,000 mph on paths that cross the paths of many other spacecraft in low Earth orbit.

Space shuttle missions and the International Space Station (ISS) have been potentially put at risk from the debris created by this test. According to the United States Air Force Space Command (AFSPC), roughly 400 active satellites in low Earth orbit are now at increased risk of collision with debris from the resulting cloud.[32] Because debris falls out of orbit gradually, the increased risk of collision to satellites at significantly lower altitudes is minimal. The real issue is the increased risk to the many satellites near the collision altitude. The neighborhood will be cluttered for some time to come as well. While some early estimates stated that as much as 85 percent of the debris cloud would be in orbit in one hundred years,[33] a subsequent report by NASA experts states that less than 10 percent of the debris will be in orbit in one hundred years and more than half will be out of orbit in a couple of decades.[34] That is still a problem.

The current state of U.S. space surveillance capability, our "eyes" in space, makes a bad situation even worse. While the United States has the world's most robust space surveillance system, its capabilities are nevertheless limited. Though smaller objects can potentially be detected, objects in space are routinely tracked from Earth only if they are ten centimeters or larger. To put that in perspective, the United States Air Force is currently tracking about 2,000 ten-centimeter or larger particles from Feng-Yun 1C. That leaves an estimated 35,000 particles less than ten centimeters that are not being tracked, capable of causing catastrophic damage to orbiting spacecraft.[35] According to Theresa Hitchens, director of the Center for Defense Information, "This incident highlights the irresponsible nature of the Chinese test, as well as more generally the threat from any future testing or use of debris-creating ASATs. And it makes it all the more urgent that responsible space-faring nations get together to ban such testing and use."[36]

Aside from the debris concern, of course, is the very nature of an anti-satellite missile capability. When China's Foreign Ministry finally issued an official statement on 23 January 2007, twelve days after the test, it said that the ASAT test "was not directed at any country and does not constitute a threat to any country."[37] Furthermore, Foreign Ministry spokesman Liu Jianchou reiterated China's opposition to the weaponization of space or a space arms race.[38] At a press conference he further claimed that China had formally notified the United States, Japan, and other countries about the test in advance.[39] Liu went on to state, "There's no need to feel threatened about this" and argued that "China will not participate in any kind of arms race in outer space." [40] China will likely continue to develop hit-to-kill ASAT technology, the same basic technology the United States is developing for missile defense, as well as develop laser technology for potential ASAT use. In the aftermath of the unprecedented amount of hazardous debris created by the test, Chinese reassurances rang hollow to U.S. military leaders. China's possession of ASAT capabilities and their likely further development raises obvious questions of China's long-term intent for their use. And intent is the key issue.

Determinations regarding capabilities are relatively easy as technical analyses; determinations of intent are far more subjective. While some analysts cite the 2006 "blinding" of a U.S. satellite by the Chinese as further evidence of nefarious Chinese intent in space,[41] General James Cartwright, then head of U.S. Strategic Command, said in reference to that "dazzling" of the U.S. satellite that there were no clear indications that China had intentionally disrupted U.S. satellite capabilities,[42] and no blinding had actually occurred. As already stated though, satellites can also be tracked by "painting" a satellite with a laser beam, which can inadvertently "dazzle" the satellite, and China is known to have satellite laser ranging capabilities.[43] Charges that the Soviets had earlier attempted to blind U.S. satellites were dispelled by Donald Rumsfeld during his first time as Defense Secretary. Even then the United States had been using lasers to illuminate and track Soviet satellites for years.[44] Moreover, while not routine, some countries let other countries "see" their lasers as a demonstration of capabilities. Indeed, it is interesting to note the parallels between press coverage of the two incidents across decades, both evidencing a certain amount of political motivation and journalists with minimal experience with space topics preparing sensationalist stories. The bottom line is that not only does uncertainty of intent plague countries in their threat assessments, but intent itself depends on who is doing it and how it is presented to the public. The Chinese "blinding" incident is often speciously cited as part of a pattern from which Chinese nefarious intent can be discerned.

The inherently dual-use nature of space technology, meaning that it simultaneously has value to both civil and military communities, further complicates determinations of intent. The motivations behind and purposes of the Chinese space manned space program are, for example, questioned. China has reaped all the same benefits from its manned program, including international prestige, jobs, ascent of the technology learning curve, and a keen interest in science and engineering education programs, as the United States reaped from the Apollo program. But manned spaceflight is not the easiest, cheapest, or fastest way to advance technology, making it an unlikely stalking horse for Chinese military space purposes. After the Shenzhou 7 manned mission in October 2008, conservative analysts raised concerns about whether a soccer-ball sized microsatellite released as part of the mission had military value as a antisatellite weapon, because of its maneuverability.[45] A technical analysis, however, showed otherwise. "Chinese development of a minisatellite that can maneuver around a larger satellite has raised some questions about its potential military uses. However, our analysis of the BX-1's guidance mechanism appears to indicate that it could not maneuver at close range around another country's satellite since it does not have the ability to determine the distance to the other satellite to high accuracy."[46] So, while maneuverability in general is an enabling technology for ASATs, clearly in this case technical analysis could remove ambiguity and hence demonstrates the value of such technical analyses whenever possible.

There were two previous Chinese direct-ascent tests that did not result in an intercept, results believed to be intentional. Notably, the United States was aware of these tests. Launchers used to conduct the tests sat on the launch pad in China visible to overhead imaging, alerting the United States, and unclassified assets were used to track the fly-by missions. However, the United States chose to remain silent until after the successful test.[47] An interesting legal question could be raised as to whether, under the "do no harm" principle of the Outer Space Treaty, the United States had an obligation to warn the international community of the possibility of an impact test, given the known potential for damage to the space "global commons" from the debris which would be, and was, created. Speculation as to why the United States chose not to say anything or try to stop the tests through a diplomatic demarche include deciding it was more valuable to gather intelligence on Chinese capabilities and fear of appearing foolish if a public demarche was stated by the United States and ignored by China.[48] Most likely, both were factors. In any event, not objecting apparently sent an unintended message to the Chinese, since they would have known that the United States was able to observe and monitor their launches, that resulted in their severe miscalculation regarding international, and in particular, U.S., response to the January 2007 direct hit. More cynically, the successful Chinese test has done more to spur political support for U.S. space dominance efforts than the U.S. military could have ever done on their own. Thus, advocates for space weaponization could have perceived that allowing the Chinese ASAT test to proceed unfettered was in the best interests of their cause in the long run.

Throwing Stones in a Glass House

China's twelve-day delay in issuing an official statement following the destruction of the satellite produced wide speculation regarding the calculus behind the Chinese decision to test their ASAT capability and a multitude of works have been produced in that regard. Some of the more hard-line analyses have taken the position that the Chinese test was merely a predictable culmination of a well-laid-out blueprint for space domination.[49] Others have taken a broader perspective, stating that "Discussions about space security are cluttered with commentators and advocates fretting too much about the potential implications of 'militarizing' and 'weaponizing' space. But it is too late: space is already militarized and weaponized."[50] The implication there seems to be that restraint on part of the United States is unnecessary. It has also been suggested that "the key messages are that the United States could not expect to dominate space alone and that intervention on behalf of Taiwan would be increasingly risky and costly."[51] Perhaps as well, China was primarily sending a message to other Asian nations.[52]

A different view from Union of Concerned Scientists researcher Gregory Kulacki, who helps facilitate dialogue between American and Chinese space communities, and Jeffrey Lewis, director of the New America Foundation's Nuclear Strategy Initiative, is that the Chinese ASAT test was not a direct response to a perceived American threat. Rather, it was the culmination of a long-standing Chinese interest in general military-space capabilities dating back to the 1970s, with work starting in earnest in the 1980s toward achieving an ASAT capability. (In the 1980s, the United States was testing ASATs.) Due to funding constraints, Chinese development was slow, and the timing of the test was primarily the result of when the technology matured. Under this scenario, based on discussions with Chinese involved with the program development, "the ASAT test story has mainly been a technocratic one, involving the failure of the bureaucracy to effectively predict the response of the international community to the ASAT test. The test is therefore viewed in certain communities in China as a policy failure."[53] This view is supported by the fact the ASAT tested was part of a General Armaments Department program, the Chinese bureaucracy responsible for development, procurement, and supply and maintenance of hardware, not policy decisions. Regardless of Chinese motivation, international reaction was swift and concerned. Among the countries issuing formal protests, inquiries, and statements were the United Kingdom, Japan, India, Russia, Australia, Canada, and Taiwan. All countries essentially protested the test as irresponsible and not in line with China's declared policy of peaceful use of space. At least one country, India, took the opportunity to justify its own intent to assess the need for and pursue as necessary its own antisatellite capabilities. India declared its intent to explore such development, thereby raising the risks of an eventual Asian space arms race.[54] So far, India's actions have focused primarily on setting up a national space command to increase their space situational awareness, and taking a wait-and-see approach to space weaponization. Because other nations have fewer space assets, those assets can become critical, potentially even decisive in regional military conflicts, thus making them especially attractive targets.

The Bush administration was quick to express concern over the Chinese ASAT test. On 18 January, National Security Council spokesman Gordon Johndroe stated, "The U.S. believes China's development and testing of such weapons is inconsistent with the spirit and cooperation that both countries aspire to in the civil space area. We and other countries have expressed our concern regarding this action to the Chinese."[55] Expressing the official U.S. government position on the test in early February, a State Department official said, "We still await a complete explanation from China as to how this ASAT test squares with its professed desire to seek only peaceful uses of space."[56] Of note, however, the United States has, so far, officially tread carefully and has not specifically renounced the use of antisatellite weapons that generate debris. Doing so could potentially conflict with the 2006 National Space Policy and with U.S. military doctrine for offensive counterspace operations (a euphemism for ASATs). The United States finds itself on the horns of a tough policy dilemma, unable to claim the moral high ground in this political and military face-off due to its own space policies and professed military doctrine.

In one successful antisatellite test, the Chinese essentially put the U.S. military, particularly the United States Air Force, on notice that dominating space might be a lot harder than generally presumed and purported in U.S. policy and military doctrine. The military reaction has been predictably both alarmist and cautious, and in line with stated defense policies and doctrines.

There are four military-space missions defined in the United States: space support (infrastructure, such as launch capability and satellite maintenance); force enhancement (support to the warfighters, such as weather, communications, and precision-guided munitions); space control (the ability to use space when needed and deny its use to the adversary, increasingly defined to include space-to-space weapons); and force application (combat operations in, through, and from space).[57] The line between space control and force application is often blurred. The first two are unquestionably essential to maintain U.S. space superiority. Other countries, however, question whether the United States actually is satisfied with space superiority, being first among many, or whether through the second two missions the United States actually aims toward space dominance, whereby other countries could potentially be shut out of the space arena. It is the wide range of highly sophisticated, many as-yet-not-invented technical capabilities needed to fully carry out those missions, especially space control (including defenses against any offensive weapon an adversary could develop), which makes feasibility questionable.

Military strategists know there are three key elements of any plan that must be in balance to achieve success: there must be a clearly identified goal, an approach identified to reach the goal, and appropriate means provided to carry out the approach. Operation Iraqi Freedom provides a useful (though imperfect) analogy. While the desire of the United States to quickly stabilize and democratize Iraq was a good idea, it simply did not prove feasible given the troops and resources allocated. The means were not available. Instead, stability will come only with time, and democratization is still highly tenuous. There was a strategy-means mismatch that predetermined failure. Space control is even more likely to be elusive, and a money pit. The goal requires perpetual defensive superiority, to be achieved through difficult if not impossible technical approaches, within limited means. Force application, including space-to-Earth weapons, will unquestionably provoke responses from other countries that will induce even further cries for space control from space hegemonists, and a vicious arms race—largely the United States against itself since defense is much harder than offense—will ensue.

In April 2007, Air Force Chief of Staff General T. Michael Mosely called the Chinese ASAT test a "strategically dislocating event" because China had demonstrated the capability to kill satellites in low Earth orbit. He later added, "This is no different than when the Russians put Sputnik up."[58] He also implied that to extend the capability to medium Earth orbit (MEO) or geosynchronous Earth orbit (GEO) is nothing more than an energy and physics problem: "If you can hit something at 500-plus miles in orbit then you can certainly hit something out beyond 20,000 miles. It's just a physics problem."[59] At least preliminary technical analysis seems to support that the weapons system used against the defunct weather satellite was harder to hit than more strategically important satellites such as communications and early warning satellites in geostationary orbits.[60] Additionally, it is now clear that the closing speed of the Chinese interceptor, key in judging the sophistication of the technology, was approximately eight kilometers per second.[61] That puts China much closer to being on par with U.S. ASAT technology capabilities than had been thought.

General Mosely's reaction to the Chinese ASAT test is not surprising. The United States had just had its aspirations for space dominance challenged and was very worried about it. An organization charged with both offensive and defensive counterspace operations as defined in Air Force doctrine could hardly be expected to react in any other way. What the Chinese did, through deliberate design or by accident, was to challenge U.S. space superiority, and certainly its ability to be dominant. Subsequently a process of political and military assessment was put into motion in the United States to gauge the threat and respond accordingly with detailed contingency planning, changes to strategy and doctrine, and development and acquisition of new offensive and defensive capabilities. In that sense, it truly was a "strategically dislocating event" for the service that operates and is charged with the protection and assurance of the lion's share of U.S. space-based defense assets. Air Force Secretary Michael Wynne, speaking in Washington on 19 September 2007, said, "We were not surprised, we were shocked."[62] Given that the Air Force had watched the two previous fly-by events and anticipated the January 2007 event, their shock is surprising. Perhaps it was the degree of Chinese technical ability that Wynne was referring to.

Comments from other military officers and security officials, however, acknowledge the rationality of China's actions from a strategic and operational perspective, and downplay concerns such as General Mosely voiced. The day after Mosely made his remarks, then U.S. Strategic Command Commander General James Cartwright and National Reconnaissance Office (NRO) Director Donald Kerr cautioned against reading too much into the 2007 Chinese ASAT test in separate remarks at a conference in Colorado Springs.

Marine General Cartwright, heading a command responsible for space and strategic weapons asked: "Was this event a watershed? Not in my mind. This is not the defining moment in U.S.-China relations." He went on to point out that China's use of a mobile launcher to hit an aging weather satellite was not dissimilar to ASAT tests conducted by the United States and Soviet Union in the 1970s and 1980s. "Let's give the Chinese credit for trying to move forward and bring these attributes to their nation," he said, adding that the 11 January test was a wakeup call for the United States to improve its intelligence and response capabilities. NRO Director Donald Kerr was similarly circumspect.[63] Admiral William Fallon, then in charge of the Pacific Command, speaking in March 2007 about the Chinese ASAT test, stated that China, as a sovereign nation, would sometimes take military measures that others will not like. "A nation is going to do what they think they need to do."[64]

On 31 May 2007, the Department of Defense released its annual report to Congress entitled, "Military Power of the People's Republic of China 2007." This report, widely read and akin to the old Cold War–era "Soviet Military Power" annual assessment, is mandated by the National Defense Authorization Act for Fiscal Year 2000 (Public Law 106–65). In this document, the Chinese ASAT test is mentioned prominently in several places. Regarding China's space and counterspace capabilities, the document states, "China's space activities and capabilities, including antisatellite programs, have significant implications for anti-access/area denial in Taiwan Strait contingencies and beyond. China further views the development of space and counterspace capabilities as bolstering national prestige and, like nuclear weapons, demonstrating the attributes of a world power."[65] References to Taiwan highlight the crux of tension between the United States and China. It would be unacceptable to China if Taiwan, which mainland China considers part of China as much as the United States considers Manhattan Island part of the United States, would declare its independence. China would, without hesitation, do whatever it had to, to keep an independent Taiwan from becoming a reality. The U.S. position has been that differences between Taiwan and mainland China should be resolved by the people on both sides of the Strait themselves, and peacefully. If Beijing were to use force against Taiwan, the United States might well be drawn into the conflict. Taken in this context, it should come as little surprise that China would pursue capabilities it sees as useful to deter Taiwan from precipitating disastrous actions, and to give the United States pause against interference. Further, space power may be seen as the logical progression of military capabilities following acquisition of nuclear weapons, intercontinental ballistic missiles, and long-range strike capabilities using submarines and air power. The Soviet Union had these capabilities, and exercised them, much as the United States did during the Cold War. It is not unexpected that China, as a rising power, would do the same. The military understands that if you develop a capability, sooner or later you have to test it or it is of no value to you. Whether Chinese ASAT capabilities degrade the ability of the United States to defend Taiwan is really the underlying issue.

Geoffrey Forden holds a doctorate in physics, is a Massachusetts Institute of Technology (MIT) research associate, and is a former UN weapons inspector and strategic weapons analyst at the Congressional Budget Office. He has both impeccable technical training and a national security background, so he cannot be accused of being soft on defense. In 2008, he wrote a three-part series for *WIRED* entitled "How China Loses the Coming Space War," examining the possibilities of an all-out Chinese attack on American satellites and how that would affect U.S. war-fighting capabilities. Theoretically at least, the answers to that question should help the United States assess the threat of China's ASAT capability.

There is at least one way to answer these questions: "war-gaming" a massive Chinese attack on U.S. satellite, where China is only limited by the laws of physics and the known properties of their ASAT, and see how much damage could be done. Such an exercise reveals what the U.S. could do, and what it could not do, to minimize the consequences. The results of my calculations are reported here. They assume that China launches a massive attack and that everything works as planned; every ASAT launches, the U.S. does not respond until after the attacks are launched even though it will have overwhelming evidence ahead of time, and every ASAT hits its target. Thus, this is a worst case scenario for the United States. In the end, we'll show, the U.S. would still have sufficient space assets to fight a major conventional war with China, even after such an attack. America's military capabilities would be reduced, for a few hours at a time. But they would not be crippled.[66]

The day after Forden's article appeared on-line, Bill Gertz, columnist for the *Washington Times,* ran a story with a very different perspective. Gertz says, "By some estimates"—noticeably undocumented—"China could produce enough space weapons to knock out all low-Earth orbit satellites by 2010." He did, however, quote Air Force Brigadier General Ted Kresge, director of air, space, and information operations at the Air Force Space Command, specifically noting that Kresge is an F-15 fighter pilot (as though that gives him credibility about space operations when in fact even the 2000 Space Commission report pointed out pilots running space command as a problem, as discussed later in this chapter). Kresge was quoted as saying, "We have embraced the notion that we now operate in a contested domain."[67] Space is in fact a domain the United States cannot technically "control."

An anticipated argument against Forden's analysis might be that it focused primarily on the Chinese direct-ascent ASAT they tested in 2007, when in fact their program is more comprehensive, and war-gaming only that capability underestimates the threat. However, even estimating what could be involved with a broader attack would be speculation, and would assume capabilities not tested. The reliability of any untested technology must be assumed to be very low.

We live in an era where communications, cum spin, cum propaganda are increasingly important. "Message" can be everything. Particularly revealing about how the Chinese ASAT test has been "spun" in the United States to further the quest for space domination is a comment by Air Force Secretary Wynne in September 2007. Talking about the sense of urgency within the Air Force to replace and protect U.S. satellites, Wynne said, "And now, of course, *with China saying there is no sanctuary* [in space], everyone is starting to pile on about maybe you ought to protect them, maybe you ought not to be so big" (emphasis added).[68] The message implies that the Chinese ASAT test crossed a previously sacred boundary, compelling the United States to take actions it would not consider otherwise, when in fact neither was the case.

The United States has been developing and in possession of antisatellite technology for over forty-five years. Furthermore, other dual-use "defensive" systems being developed by the United States, such as the Airborne Laser and National Missile Defense systems, can be applied to the offensive antisatellite task (as well as terrestrial force application). China and the rest of the world are keenly aware of this. In fact, it is a much easier physics problem to target and destroy a single orbiting satellite in a fixed path than it is to engage a ballistic missile accompanied by countermeasures, such as decoys.[69] Also, it is unlikely other countries have forgotten that the most spectacular ASAT test in history was executed in the Cold War and involved the detonation of a 1.4 megaton nuclear warhead 250 miles above the Pacific Ocean. This event, known as Starfish Prime, took place on 9 July 1962. The resulting electromagnetic pulse knocked out over 300 streetlights on the island of Oahu in Hawaii while producing an eerie artificial glow in the sky for twenty minutes.[70] The test destroyed seven satellites in seven months, nearly one-tenth of the seventy-two satellites in orbit in 1962,[71] and created an artificial radiation belt lasting until the early 1970s.[72]

In the case of the Chinese test, originally it was thought that Chinese officials were provided low-estimate, inaccurate data regarding debris that would be generated by the test by determined bullies of the People's Liberation Army, as a way to explain why the Chinese officials had allowed it to proceed. Lewis and Kulacki posit that Chinese General Armaments Department engineers and scientists were the ones advocating the tests to the politicians and it is "likely that Chinese officials were advised not on the relative increase in the amount of debris created, but instead on the absolute increase in the risk of damage to another satellite, which is about 1 percent. To an engineer that number doesn't seem all that high."[73] Under that scenario, which appears increasingly likely, the Chinese ASAT test was less akin to the placing of the Soviet SS-20s in Europe by the chest-thumping Soviet military over the objections of the Foreign Ministry, as originally thought, and more akin to NASA engineers not initially understanding the importance of delaying the Shuttle landing on 4 July 1986 so that President Ronald Reagan could attend the landing. Engineers think differently than politicians and military officials. Any further tests by the Chinese, however, could not be attributed to bureaucratic politics, or technical or political miscalculations on their part, but would have to be assumed as deliberate and intentionally provocative.

While rhetoric about the Chinese ASAT test has been mixed, the United States has not explicitly altered its public position that it does not have a space-weapons program. Tacitly, however, the Chinese test clearly provided an impetus for a more aggressive approach on the part of the United States. The media reported in October 2007 on a July 2007 classified memo from President Bush to various government agencies, including the Defense Department and the State Department, to form a cohesive government-wide approach to future ASAT launches, and "a funding plan to procure needed technologies." Further, "thanks to the Chinese, says Major General William Shelton, 14th Air Force commander, it has become 'more palatable' to openly discuss the issues of space situational awareness and the more politically sensitive areas of offensive and defensive space operations."[74] Dominating space had been an agenda pushed primarily by Air Force Space Command and, to not unfairly target just the Air Force, their cohorts at MDA, the Defense Advanced Research Projects Agency (DARPA), Army Space and Missile Defense Command, and to a lesser extent, the NRO.[75] The Chinese, however, managed to broaden support for that unattainable plan.

The Culture of Support for Space Dominance

If making a course correction to our current policy is to be possible, understanding the impetus for supporting the space dominance quest, including missile defense and ASATs for space control and space-to-Earth weapons for force application purposes, is critical. There are four pillars of support for the quest: one philosophical/theoretical; one based on historical military strategy analogies; one a function of bureaucratic politics; and one—not surprisingly—based on money. All are significant forces and all are bolstered by references to missile defense and space weapons in popular culture, past and present, which make plans for both appear feasible to the American public. What may appear through popular culture as technically feasible to the public, however, is not necessarily considered desirable, as will be discussed in Chapter 4.

The influence of popular culture in shaping "facts" should not be underestimated. The American public falls into four basic groups: the masses, or the uninformed Joe-bag-of-donuts crowd; the informed public (at least on some issues) which makes the effort not just to watch news shows, but read; experts, technical and nontechnical; and decision makers. Lines between fact and fiction quickly blur for the masses when they see or are told something enough by the political elite or the media.[76] This is especially true during periods when religious convictions prevail over science, as has recently been the case for both politicians and the public. Dinosaurs cavorting with children at the Creationism Museum in Kentucky[77] evidence the willingness of individuals to mold facts to accommodate beliefs. In fact, contempt for science seen to contravene conviction is common. Susan Jacoby, author of *The Age of American Unreason*,[78] argues that "anti-intellectualism (the attitude that 'too much learning can be a dangerous thing) and antirationalism ('the idea that there is no such things as evidence or fact, just opinion') have fused in a particularly insidious way." Not only are Americans generally ignorant about science, they think science is not important.[79]

Scientists launched an effort in 2007 to try and get presidential candidates to state their views on science. The response was lukewarm at best, though most candidates eventually released statements on their science policy. A May 2007 televised debate, however, featured three early Republican candidates—Mike Huckabee, Tom Tancredo, and Sam Brownback—indicating that they did not believe in evolution, and in December 2007, Mitt Romney and Mike Huckabee sparred over whether Romney believes Satan and Jesus Christ are brothers, apparently an obscure doctrine of the Mormon faith.[80] Lawrence M. Krauss, a physics professor at Case Western Reserve University and author of *The Physics of Star Trek*,[81] argued that while the public may not care if a candidate believes in evolution, the candidate's position should matter because so much science drives policy, and bad science leads to bad policy. According to Krauss, not believing in evolution is akin to not believing in the laws of gravity.[82]

Space weapons have been a favorite theme of science fiction writers, television shows, and movies since before the Cold War, and more recently of video game designers. From Jerry Purnelle writing about "Rods from God" in the 1950s, *Battlestar Galactica: Stargate SG-1*, multiple generations of *Star Trek* on television, and James Bond trying to save the world from *GoldenEye* in 1995, space weapons have been a theme of the future. More recently, the Halo video game series features United Nations Space Command using ships armed with magnetic coil guns which launch extremely large projectiles at high speed. Perhaps the most famous space weapon, a moon-sized space station called the Death Star in the blockbuster *Star Wars* movies, had the power to destroy a planet. All this exposure, to the delight of space hegemonists, makes their inevitability an easy sell to the public.

The feasibility of creating technology to protect the United States from attack also has a long pedigree. A classic Cold War propaganda film called *Rocket Attack USA,* released in 1961, was intended to rally public support for a national missile defense system. The plot has the Soviets gaining all the information they need from Sputnik to be able to build a nuclear-tipped missile against the United States—ready to be used unless the American military and science community can save America in time. Dan Ackroyd and Chevy Chase bumbled their way through the 1985 film *Spies Like Us* as two government employees who think they are trying to stop nuclear war but are actually being duped by military and government missile defense advocates determined to show their program's importance—only it does not work. The 2002 James Bond video game *Nightfire* has the villain trying to take over the world by hijacking a space defense platform and launching its arsenal of nuclear weapons against major NATO bases in an attempt to wipe out global security. Lucky for mankind, the villain is killed in a space station by Bond. The point is that the idea of a national missile defense system is not foreign to much of the public. The difficulties in actually implementing such a system, however, are largely not known nor considered.

It is also important to note that terminology and multiple programs confuse the issue of missile defense for the public. Theater Missile Defense (TMD) to protect troops, military installations, and small population centers, has been politically acceptable even when the Anti-Ballistic Missile (ABM) Treaty was in effect, and the technology is difficult but possible. National Missile Defense (NMD), intended to protect the entire United States from being successfully attacked by missiles carrying weapons of mass destruction, is far more technically difficult, if not impossible. Through the Clinton administration the programs were separated, with funding and research emphasis on TMD. With the George W. Bush administration though, the funding emphasis shifted to NMD, and the nomenclature changed to Ballistic Missile Defense (BMD), to include both, thereby blurring the lines of distinction between the two efforts.

In an interesting pre-9/11 Pew Research Center opinion poll,[83] individuals were asked whether they heard about certain reasons for opposing the creation of a national missile defense system. Sixty-five percent of the respondents said they had not heard that technological immaturity was a valid reason to oppose creation of such a system. Further, 54 percent said that they did not think the current unavailability of key technologies was an important reason to oppose the creation of a national defense system. That number likely reflects the confidence of the American people in the competence of the American scientific community. Ironically though, they are often unwilling to accept expert advice if it is inconvenient for them or challenges their beliefs.

The Philosophical/Theoretical Impetus

The theoretical proponents behind a doctrinal change from stabilizing deterrence to space dominance are primarily at military schools and

think tanks. The broadest factor affecting the push for unrealistic policies such as space dominance is capabilities-based planning (CBP). In
the 2001 Quadrennial Defense Review (QDR) Report a "paradigm shift
in force planning" was announced. The QDR, one of the most important Pentagon planning documents, stated that "the new defense strategy is built around the concept of shifting to a 'capabilities-based'
approach to defense,"[84] as opposed to the threat-based planning that
had guided the Department of Defense (DoD) in the past. Many analysts, and certainly Defense Secretary Donald Rumsfeld, felt that "with
the collapse of strategic clarity, it was natural for defense planners to
turn back to reliable principles of analysis and resource allocation."[85]
Subsequently, the 2005 National Defense Strategy and 2006 QDR have
reaffirmed this approach, resulting in major changes in processes and
organizations throughout DoD to implement capabilities-based planning.

The four principles around which CBP is built are relatively simple:[86]
(1) broaden the range of missions for which forces should be prepared,
(2) make the joint (military services working together cooperatively
rather than independently) perspective predominant in all planning
and programming activities, (3) use risk as a strategic measure of effectiveness, (4) shift the requirements generation process away from a plat-
form/systems centric focus. In theory, you get more military capabilities
more efficiently and effectively from this process, providing more military options to the commander in chief. In reality, however, the process
deems zero risk as acceptable, so the military needs to be prepared for
everything, everywhere, anytime—an ideal but not realistic goal. Having
access to every capability is desirable, but not all are technically or eco-
nomically feasible.

The philosophical impetus is prevalent among policymakers, based
largely on what they "want" rather than "feasibility." Understandably,
and admirably, politicians—people—believe in protecting their charges.
It is the "moral imperative" argument that dates back not only to the
Reagan years in the United States, but has lineage back to U.S-Soviet
relations in the 1960s. John Newhouse, in his 1989 book *War and Peace
in the Nuclear Age*, writes about the Soviet perspective. "Dean Rusk recalls
Johnson dealing with Kosygin 'in a go for broke' fashion. He was saying,
in effect, 'Just set a day and I'll have McNamara there in Moscow.' Kosygin's problem was that he didn't have . . . [any] authority to discuss limiting arms, least of all ABMs. He replied, in effect: 'How can you expect
me to tell the Russian people they can't defend themselves against your
rockets?' "[87] Later, Soviet leaders were as interested in missile defense as
President Reagan but, not surprisingly, simply could not make it work.
Part of what scared the Soviets about SDI was the fear that U.S. scientists

and engineers had made technology breakthroughs where they had failed.

Analysts at the conservative Heritage Foundation think tank spoke about SDI as a moral imperative in 1983.[88] A 1984 *Foreign Policy* article entitled "The Star Wars Debate: Nuclear Policy and the Defensive Transition" by Keith Payne and Colin Gray extended the premise.

A defensive transition—particularly one including the global coverage that space-based systems or components could provide—would reduce the risk of a global climatic catastrophe by intercepting nuclear weapons after they are launched. Given the fact that nuclear deterrence can never provide the certainty of stability, and given the reported possibility of climatic disaster resulting even from the limited use of nuclear weapons, transition to a defense dominant strategic policy should be seen as a moral imperative. At the very least, given the perils of the arms competition in offensive systems, the United States is obligated to seek to alleviate those perils through defense. Success in this venture is not guaranteed, but there would seem to be no excuse for the United States not making the attempt.[89]

Reagan himself raised missile defense to being a "moral imperative" at the 1985 Geneva Summit with the Soviets. Since then, the "moral imperative" argument has consistently been the rationale for national missile defense by conservative Republicans.

The beauty of elevating missile defense to a moral imperative is that questions of technical feasibility are muted if there is even the slightest chance it could work. Imagine a scientist being drilled by a pro-missile defense Senator at a Congressional hearing. Senator: "Dr. Naysayer, can you tell me with 100 percent certainty that given enough time and enough money we cannot make missile defense—to protect the American people against a catastrophic nuclear attack—work?" Dr. Naysayer: "Based on my expert opinion, it is not likely." Senator: "Dr. Naysayer, I repeat, can you tell me with 100 percent certainty that given enough time and enough money we cannot make this crucial missile defense technology work?" Dr. Naysayer: "No. I cannot, indeed, guarantee it could not work." New fact: Scientist says missile defense is technically possible.

Historical Military Strategy Analogies

It is not coincidence that Pearl Harbor imagery is regularly evoked in connection with potential attacks on U.S. space assets. Pearl Harbor, and now 9/11, are mental triggers that remind us that the United States, for all its might, remains vulnerable. The lesson learned from both is to be prepared for the unexpected. According to at least some analysts, the way to be prepared is to seize the high ground first. Everett Dolman

states: "Once a state has established weapons in space capable of shooting down rockets and launch vehicles in boost, no other state can put
weapons there. Total domination of space is effected. Fears of an arms
race in space are eliminated."[90]

The idea of seizing the high ground has a historical legacy. One argument—that had the United States taken a stronger military stand earlier
against both Germany and Japan, their military buildups could have
been thwarted and war potentially averted or at least thousands of American and Allied lives saved—is raised to justify the United States acting
now to secure space. But this is where considerations about the physical
environment come strongly into play.

When an army takes the high ground on Earth, they have an advantage. They can see others before others see them, and protect themselves behind castle walls, or even a rock. That is not the case in space.

In the "high ground" of space, you're a thin-skinned sitting duck with a bull's
eye painted on your side. Anybody has a chance to shoot at you whenever they
feel like it. . . . On earth, from high ground you can strike anywhere around you
while those below are limited in reaching you. In space, the attacks that you
might make, the trajectories that your vehicles might follow, follow paths that
are predictable in advance, predictable in both space and time. Ground attacks,
meanwhile, on a point in space can be almost random; they are highly visible in
time and space and are unpredictable. On earth, on the high ground, you have
weapons that are more effective when you aim downward, but the "high
ground" in space is the easier target, being unprotected. Attacking uphill
involves difficulty and delay on the ground but in space, uphill and downhill
attacks take about the same amount of time and your "high ground" is very
much harder to resupply and rearm. Lastly, on earth, high ground allows a permanent control over some strategic road or territory, a choke point that inter-
dicts all hostile traffic around it. In space, the so-called high ground is a shifting
Maginot line that is easily avoided, outwaited, and circumvented.[91]

If technology could offer the United States a way to "control" space,
then pursing that course would make sense. But it does not. Politicians
do not want to hear that because they want to believe otherwise. In other
cases, supporters do not want to hear it because it goes against all the
rules of survival in bureaucracies. Underestimating the power of bureaucratic politics is everyone's peril.

Bureaucratic Politics

Issues concerning the organizational politics of Air Force Space Command become exacerbated within the context of capabilities-based planning. The United States Air Force is the "executive agent" for space,
meaning that it owns and operates the bulk of U.S. military-space assets.
The mission of the Air Force is to deliver sovereign options for the

defense of the United States of America and its global interests to fly and fight in air, space, and cyberspace. However, because space is a capability utilized by all branches of the military and the security community (as well as the civil and commercial communities), it is impossible to centralize responsibility for space assets and planning in the same way it can be done for ships or tanks. Therefore, "management" issues quickly become ones where ownership or protection of territory, or what the military calls "rice bowls," becomes involved. Issues between the services were theoretically dealt with by DoD naming the Air Force the "executive agent" for space in 2003.[92] Within the Air Force, however, whether space is a real priority remains an issue, and the issue is largely cultural.

The Air Force was split off from the Army in 1947 to assure airpower received the time, attention, and money it needed and deserved. More recent debates have focused on whether a "Space Corps" should be split off from the Air Force for the same reasons. Even words indicate the problem. Often through its vision or mission statements, the Air Force has called itself an Air Force, an Air and Space Force, a Space and Air Force,[93] an Aerospace Force,[94] and now, an Air, Space, and Cyberspace Force.[95]

Because of the inherent emphasis on flying in the Air Force, its organizational culture is characterized by more of an occupational as opposed to an institutional orientation. According to George Mastroianni in an article comparing cultures and leadership in the Army and Air Force, "The institutional orientation is conceptualized as rooted in a calling to serve higher ideals represented by a shared vision of an organization, rather than in self-interest. The individual with an occupational orientation, on the other hand, approaches his or her work as a job, to be retained or abandoned based largely (though perhaps not solely) on a calculus of self-interest."[96] While making it clear that he is not suggesting that Air Force officers are "somehow less patriotic, less loyal, or more mercenary than Army or Navy officers," Mastroianni states "it cannot be denied that the occupational and institutional dimensions of service culture are simply different across the three services."[97] Within the Air Force, Mastroianni suggests "leaders are constantly struggling to symbolically sustain and justify the independent service identity of the Air Force and to create and protect a unique Air Force culture. . . . This mainly manifests itself in the focus on technology in the Air Force." Further, he says there is "an absolutist and anti-intellectual strain in Air Force culture that resonates with a view of the world as simple and clear."[98] The cultural proclivities of the Air Force are evidenced in a number of ways.

Perhaps more than the other military services, the Air Force is an advocacy organization. Its direct contribution to any fight is airpower—as opposed to providing space and cyberspace support to *all* warfighters—so understandably the Air Force leaders are airpower advocates. Pilots are the warfighters at the "tip of the spear," who all others support, and hence all others become secondary. Even among pilots, there is a pecking order, with fighter pilots first and bomber pilots close behind. Fighter pilots have long ruled the Air Force. With an aging air fleet where planes are sometimes older than the pilots flying them, when budget choices are between a new airplane and a new satellite, the airplane usually wins. In choices between types of airplanes, fighters and bombers have traditionally won out over tankers and transports, the latter currently needed in Iraq. Even the visuals in one of the Air Force videos released in 2008 and run as a television commercial seems to imply you need an F-22 to fight hackers.[99]

When in April 2008 Secretary of Defense Robert Gates chided the Air Force for what he referred to as its tepid response to pleas for support of the ground wars in Iraq and Afghanistan, the Air Force Association responded harshly, defending the Air Force's contributions to the ground wars. But as one news analysis put it, "the last thing Air Force leaders want to hear is a push away from glamorous, white-scarf mission in high-tech fighters to take up, instead, the greasy wrenches and winches to put eyes over Iraq and Afghanistan and ferry troops and gear, food and fuel to the fight."[100]

Within the Air Force, AFSPC champions space causes. They start, though, at a cultural disadvantage. Pilots wear cool jackets, fly planes, and fight enemy pilots. Space warriors fly a desk and battle microscopic particles blown in on the solar wind that could damage satellites. That is not very sexy or dangerous. Beyond fighting the mundane, they must also fight against potential snickering. "Planetary defense," guarding against potentially catastrophic collisions with "near earth objects" such as asteroids and dramatized by movies such as *Armageddon* and *Deep Impact,* means defending against rocks. The Air Force has avoided taking responsibility for that mission, for reasons that include what has been referred to as "the giggle factor."[101] So AFSPC has, of necessity, undertaken to show that they are relevant and more like other warfighters.

A 2006 study in *Air & Space Power Journal* entitled "Air Force Space Command: A Transformational Case Study"[102] discusses how AFSPC has successfully "transformed" to a force able to guarantee future U.S. space superiority by adopting business methods for successful transformations. Drawing from John P. Kotter's best-selling book *Leading Change* the first step is to "Establish a Sense of Urgency," defined as "Some internal or external stimuli, either recently introduced or predicted to occur soon, create a threatening change in the operational environment."[103] AFSPC needs to be needed to survive in its own bureaucracy.

What you end up with in AFSPC is—and not nefariously, just inherently—an organization constantly needing to be seen as responding to a concrete, urgent military problem. Challenges to U.S. space superiority, real or perceived, immediate or potential, probable or possible, stated or overstated, all become concrete, urgent problems. Billets with titles such as "Director of Space Forces," originally created during Operation Iraqi Freedom, encourage that attitude and approach.

Air Force Space Command officers have reasons to be zealots on their own behalf,[104] especially as they rise in the ranks. The Report of the Commission to Assess United States National Security Space Management and Organization (known as the Space Commission) issued a report in 2000 finding that among 150 personnel serving in key operational space leadership positions, fewer than 20 percent of the flag officers possessed a space background (two and one-half years background was the norm). Among commanding officers at space wings, groups, and squadrons, only one-third had space backgrounds.[105] Many, if not most, were pilots, and usually fighter pilots. That same year, at the Air War College, the Air Force's premier professional military education institution, only 7.4 percent of its core curriculum and 4 percent of its electives focused on space, with most other classes focusing on airpower, a clear indication of priority.[106] Reexamining the Air War College curricula through their on-line catalog in 2007 showed fifty-eight electives listed, with only one directly relating to space. Discussions within the Air Force in 2006 about potentially downgrading Air Force Space Command from a four-star to a three-star billet are indicative of even less organizational clout.[107] Since U.S. Space Command merged with Strategic Command in 2002, AFSPC has had to fight not to be seen as a subsidiary of that group.[108] Budget numbers perhaps speak loudest of all. Only roughly 10 percent of the annual Air Force budget is devoted to space, and recapitalization needs post-Iraq will almost certainly mean that space funding will not get a budget boost over planes. All this being the case, it is understandable that within an organization historically committed to promoting air power, Air Force Space Command must aggressively promote its own value.

AFSPC has four strategic priorities, one of which was to develop, field, and sustain dominant space capabilities on time and on cost.[109] Nowhere does it say anything about evaluating the need. Theoretically, considerations of need are supposed to be done in the Operational Requirements process and approved by the Defense Acquisition Board, all above the AFSPC level, and sometimes that happens. "A former civilian Air Force Chief Scientist—whose job placed him on the senior uniformed Air Staff at the Pentagon—once remarked that one of his jobs consisted of serving as a reality check for goofy proposals from Air Force Space Command, like using lasers to blow up tanks."[110]

The general question, however, is whether that process overall employs the appropriate mix of expertise required to evaluate major space programs, and the answer seems to be a resounding "no." The number of "goofy" proposals seems to overwhelm the system. Within Air Force Space Command, a 2005 study concluded that of the more than 2000 "space" billets in AFSPC, only thirteen carry AF specialty codes requiring an advanced technical degree.[111] As a result, officers with little technical background or depth of knowledge about "space" are placed in space billets for two or three years, with "success" (and promotion) often judged by what technology programs they get approved for development. Individuals who get programs approved will not be around to see if they reach fruition and, realistically, nobody will be promoted based on their willingness to say "We don't need this." With stress on warfighting as an intraservice cultural imperative, it is no wonder that the Air Force would be simultaneously pleased by a visible threat they can point to and dismayed by a clear indication that space dominance is not possible.

More broadly, at places like the Air Force Space and Missile Systems Center in Los Angeles, charged to "develop, demonstrate, acquire, field, and sustain the world's best space and missile capabilities for the joint warfighter,"[112] even those with technical backgrounds often have low levels of experience, especially in systems engineering. Also, schedule slips and cost overruns are increasingly blamed on lack of experienced acquisition people (which does not necessarily equate to technical people). The lack of promising career paths—technical specialists and bean-counters are not promoted, warfighters are—is, understandably, a hindrance for getting good, committed people into both career fields. It is worth noting that a number of high-quality space-related programs have been created at the Air Force Academy, and yet a relatively low number of cadets, especially top cadets, pursue space as a career field.

The space community within the Air Force is keen to bolster its own organizational position, and the Chinese ASAT test will likely serve them well. Air Force Space Command has sent officers to the United States Air Force Weapons School at Nellis Air Force Base since 1996, making up approximately 10 percent of the class. Officers who complete the course are awarded a "W," for "weapons," to their specialty codes. General Kevin Chilton, as commander of the Air Force Space Command, said "I want a 'W' in every squadron on my watch. I want our people to aspire, compete, and come back and run a weapons and tactics shop."[113]

Political support for making General Chilton's goal a priority will likely be enhanced consequent to the Chinese test.

Bureaucratic politics are by their nature rarely rational. So the bad news is that there is little rational basis for discussion of threats and needs within the organization that is charged with developing, fielding, and sustaining space capabilities for the U.S. military. The good news is that space weapons are neither an Air Force nor an Air Force Space Command organizational priority, so there is no coherent senior-level plan and that will seriously inhibit attempts to "dominate" space. Rhetoric, however, can be damaging in and of itself, because others feel compelled to respond.

Follow the Money

According to the supportive Heritage Foundation, the original cost of the Strategic Defense Initiative was overestimated at $1 trillion, underestimated at $40 billion, but assumed to fall in the range of $115–120 billion spread over ten years.[114] The Congressional Budget Office stated in 1984 that: "The Administration plans substantial growth in SDI spending over the next two years; from $991 million in 1984 to $3.79 billion in 1986. Press reports suggest continued though slower growth through 1989. While such rapid growth is not atypical of newly started research and development (R&D) programs, the SDI will consume an increasing share of DoD R&D resources, growing from about 4 percent in 1984 to about 16 percent by 1989."[115] They also admitted difficulty, however, in trying to decipher what was to be included in SDI program costs, and what not—with administration inclusions seeming to err on the conservative side. While the SDI program has been largely transformed between Ronald Reagan and George W. Bush, missile defense has persevered. Between 1986 and 2006, over $90 billion was spent on trying to develop a system to keep missiles carrying nuclear weapons from being able to hit the United States. The annual missile defense budget is larger than that of the Bureau of Customs and Border Protection within the Department of Homeland Security, and that of the Coast Guard.

Unlike the Apollo program and its successors, missile defense is not a jobs program spread among all fifty states, which might make the exorbitant costs understandable from a political perspective. Quite the contrary, missile defense work has been highly concentrated geographically. Approximately 90 percent of the contracts issued between 1998 and 2004 went to firms in just four states: California, Alabama, Colorado, and Virginia.[116] Firms such as Boeing, Lockheed Martin, Raytheon, Northrop Grumman, and General Dynamics compete for contracts that have numerous advantages: "huge contracts over extended periods of time; ongoing upgrades to the systems once they are deployed; minimal accountability and oversight because of changes in Pentagon policies."[117] Understandably, players are eagerly vying for a piece of the program and urging its continuation.

Curiously perhaps—given the technical bent of the issues—missile defense has drawn some unlikely star power to promote the cause. Former San Francisco professional football player Riki Ellison is president and founder of the Missile Defense Advocacy Alliance, an organization to rally public support for missile defense—with the help of $500,000 in funding largely provided by contractors. Jeff "Skunk" Baxter, former guitarist for the Doobie Brothers, became a paid consultant for defense contractors after he wrote a paper on mobile missile defenses some years back that caught the eye of conservative lawmakers.[118] Their role as advocates again illustrates the emphasis on persuasion over argumentation of facts and technical premises.

Just how far institutions and companies have been willing to go in order to keep the money stream flowing has been questioned. There have been, for example, allegations of test-data manipulation by the companies and organizations that benefit from program continuance. Former Reagan administration Navy science advisor and MIT physics professor Ted Postol brought considerable wrath onto himself after he sent letters to Congress and the White House regarding a 1997 missile defense test and consequent study by Lincoln Laboratory (a federally financed MIT research institute), alleging a cover-up of serious problems with missile defense technology. Postol's allegations stemmed from the case of a senior engineer at TRW, Nina Schwartz, who accused her employer of faking missile test results on a prototype antimissile sensor intended to distinguish enemy warheads from decoys. The argument was that if the sensor could not accomplish this task, the credibility of the entire system was questionable. TRW, not surprisingly, denied the charges. A 1998 report by federal investigators cleared the company of wrongdoing. Coincidentally, the report was conducted under the direction of Lincoln Labs, which received in excess of $700 million in federal work in 2003. Eventually, the General Accounting Office issued two reports in 2002 concerning the 1997 missile defense test.[119] Although the reports stopped short of casting blame on any one party, they did find that the 1997 test had failed, rather than turning in an "excellent" performance, as the contractors had claimed.

Missile defense is only one program on the wish list of space control and force application advocates. The list is long and potentially creates what the military calls a "self-licking ice cream cone"—a stream of money which perpetuates more need for more money. A confluence of factors—including the potential for an uninterrupted money stream, a "moral imperative," strategic questions without the benefit of past experience to learn from, and bureaucratic politics—all lead to space weapons having a promising future unless a course change is quickly made.

The Illusion of Dominating Space

In his March 1983 "Star Wars" speech Ronald Reagan said: "What if free people could live secure in the knowledge that their security did not rest upon the threat of instant U.S. retaliation to deter a Soviet attack, that we could intercept and destroy strategic ballistic missiles before they reached our own soil or that of our allies?" He then called upon "the scientific community in our country, those who gave us nuclear weapons, to turn their great talents to the cause of mankind and world peace, to give us the means of rendering these nuclear weapons impotent and obsolete."[120] The notion that the United States could erect an umbrella of impenetrable antimissile defenses over itself and its allies, thus rendering an attacker's weapons impotent, was alluring. No longer would "crisis stability" between the superpowers rely on a policy with an acronym MAD (mutually assured destruction) that appropriately characterized what was, in effect, a suicide pact. But the technology required to protect the United States from nuclear attack proved as elusive as the technology which will now be required of the United States to dominate space.

Dominating space will require the "ability to prevent the successful insertion into Earth orbit of any unauthorized object or the unauthorized use of any space asset while assuring orbital access and subsequent operation for those that are authorized."[121]

One can argue—and some analysts already are—that technically, anything is possible given enough time and resources. Scientists, especially those not on the receiving end of a continuous stream of research dollars, may disagree. Even assuming technical possibility, however, resources are, unfortunately, limited. Therefore, it is not feasible that the United States will be able to dominate space. Yet a quest to try is quietly building momentum and will result in negative consequences that will place U.S. space assets more at risk than otherwise. There is still time for the United States to change course, but not much time.

The trajectory of U.S. space policy was consistent from Eisenhower through Kennedy, both of whom recognized the inherent limitations and dangers of viewing space as just another battle environment. The direction began to change with the Reagan administration under which, intentionally or not, technical and economic feasibility were dropped from policy considerations. While Bill Clinton slowed their speed somewhat, space hegemonists have employed stealth, deception, and persistence in their unrealistic quest to have America dominate space. With the George W. Bush administration, directives advocating space weapons previously supported only by groups such as Air Force Space Command now have become embedded in national policy, and programs have been created to execute those policies. Understanding the full evolution of U.S. space policy, then, is the focus of Chapter 2.

Chapter Two
The Evolution of U.S. Space Policy

> If the U.S. is to avoid a "space Pearl Harbor," it needs to take seriously the possibility of an attack on U.S. space systems.
> —Rumsfeld Space Commission, 2001

"Sovereignty" is the principle around which international relations has been built since the 1648 Peace of Westphalia. According to international law, sovereignty is the legitimate exercise of power by a state: de jure sovereignty is the legal right to do so; de facto sovereignty is the ability in fact to do so. Ideally, de jure and de facto circumstances coexist, though in times of turmoil or revolution that is not always the case. The sovereignty of Taiwan, for example, is a highly contentious issue. Traditionally, sovereignty has implied a doctrine of noninterference in the affairs of any state by any other state. While that doctrine has increasingly been challenged, first because of humanitarian crises and then concerns over attacks with weapons of mass destruction,[1] it remains a mainstay of how states relate to each other. For example, states have sovereign rights in their territorial waters and airspace, meaning they have exclusive control of that area. Space, however, presents unique problems with regard to sovereignty.

Since the advent of spaceflight and particularly during the Cold War, it has been recognized that the nature of the space environment makes it impractical if not impossible to apply the premises of sovereign jurisdiction regulating the use of territorial waters or airspace at orbital altitudes. Therefore, both the Soviet Union and the United States instead endorsed the principle that sovereignty cannot be extended to space. Both countries took the approach that it was in their interests to use space to stabilize *deterrence*, the guiding strategic doctrine of the day, and to support arms control toward that goal. That meant that in order to protect their own interests, both had to accept the use of space by each other, and eventually other countries. This acceptance reflected a largely tacit acknowledgment that the physical environment of space was so different, and limiting, that there was little choice but to treat it differently in terms of expectations of sovereign rights.

In fact, the United States led the way in the early days of spaceflight promoting both informal and formal rules advocating uses of space considered advantageous to the United States and to minimize potential issues. That action reflected the judgment that space could not be physically controlled by the military in the same way as other "battlespaces." If space could not be controlled physically, then other accommodations had to be made.

The Cold War Years: Eisenhower to Carter

The Cold War years are generally characterized as oscillating periods of cautious congeniality between the United States and the Soviet Union, interspersed with periods of bullying, chest thumping and harsh rhetoric, the latter kept within boundaries largely by the existence of hair-trigger nuclear weapons.[2] Trust and confidence were largely in short supply. Part of the problem for the United States was that the Iron Curtain made dealing with the secretive, closed Soviet state very difficult. During the Eisenhower administration, it was a priority of the United States to "see" into the Soviet Union. President Eisenhower proposed an Open Skies Treaty in 1955 to allow the United States and the Soviet Union each to fly surveillance over the other country to facilitate confidence building. The Soviets immediately rejected the idea. Satellites, however, provided a potentially desirable alternative because while airplane overflight was clearly considered an intrusion on a nation's sovereignty, spaceflight was not so clearly defined. Therefore, the United States deliberately pursued a course of action toward establishing a legal precedent that space was a different environment. Some U.S. government lawyers even encouraged allowing the Soviets to launch a satellite first, and the United States not object to their overflight, so that it was the Soviets that set the legal precedent. In fact, with the launch of Sputnik in October 1957, Open Skies became the de facto policy for spacecraft. Officially, in some instances the Soviets still objected to satellite overflight as an infringement on their national sovereignty. In others, they did not. Subsequent to the 1960 shootdown of the American U-2 spy plane, for example, Charles de Gaulle raised the issue of cameras in Sputnik as it orbited over France. Khrushchev replied that he objected to airplane overflights, but not satellite-based surveillance.[3]

While the Eisenhower administration achieved its goals of being able to look into the Soviet Union, the price paid domestically was far higher than expected. "Sputnik shock" among the American public was far more substantial than anticipated and reached near panic levels. Consequently, Eisenhower faced considerable political fury from Democrats, who were taking advantage of the public alarm to make the Republican administration look bad. Eisenhower and his team knew they must forcefully respond. The introduction to the 1958 "Preliminary U.S. Policy on Outer Space" stated: "The USSR has surpassed the United States and the Free World in scientific and technological accomplishments in outer space, which have captured the imagination and admiration of the world. The USSR, if it maintains its present superiority in the exploitation of outer space, will be able to use that superiority as a means of undermining the prestige and leadership of the United States and of threatening U.S. security."[4] Eisenhower subsequently approved a U.S. policy response that included creation of the civilian-run NASA as the face of the U.S. space program, as opposed to the military-run Soviet program. In terms of space security, the policy focused on cooperative rather than competitive efforts to counter the psychological and political impacts of perceived Soviet space superiority by using space primarily for reconnaissance and verification purposes.

Four objectives were identified in the 1958 Preliminary Policy intended to guide evolving space policy toward cooperation rather than competition. The first supported development of U.S. capabilities to achieve scientific, military, and political purposes and to demonstrate U.S. leadership. The second directed increased international cooperation. The third focused on achieving agreements to assure the orderly development of national and international programs for the peaceful uses of space. And finally, the fourth was to use space to assist in "opening up" the Soviet bloc through intelligence and scientific cooperation.[5]

Politically, during the Cold War, "space" was a warfighting tool as much as any tank, plane, or gun. There was a battle being fought between the East and West blocs for the hearts and minds of the non-aligned countries, with space being used as a demonstration of which bloc was the most technically advanced and therefore the best bet for alignment. Within the United States, the launch of Sputnik and the subsequent presumption (made by a largely technically illiterate press and a willing-to-believe public) that if the Russians could launch into space they must have an arsenal of missiles they could launch at the United States, created the so-called missile gap. That perceived gap—demonstrating the power of erroneous perceptions—provided fertile ground for partisan political accusations that the Republican administration was responsible for allowing the United States to fall behind in East-West competition. Democratic Senator Lyndon Johnson led the charge, referring to the launch of Sputnik as a grave threat to national security and a challenge even greater than Pearl Harbor, generating fears of warfare conducted from space. Specifically, the notion that the Soviets could orbit nuclear weapons to rain down on the United States at will was widely perpetuated.

Initially, the Western bloc powers made a series of proposals to bar the use of outer space for military purposes. Addressing the United Nations General Assembly on 22 September 1960, President Eisenhower proposed that the principles of the Antarctic Treaty, negotiated during the International Geophysical Year 1957–58 and the first arms-control agreement signed during the Cold War, be applied to outer space and celestial bodies. The first article of the Antarctic Treaty states that the area covered by the treaty would be used for peaceful purposes only; military activity, such as weapons testing, is prohibited, though military personnel and equipment may be used for scientific research or any other peaceful purpose. The Soviets initially refused, wanting to link any agreements on space to other disarmament issues. Meanwhile, the missile gap was a myth (in fact, there was a gap—in favor of the United States) and Wernher von Braun's rocket team in Huntsville, Alabama, actually provided the United States with space launch capabilities nearly comparable to those of the Soviets. Perceptions, however, were dictated by the beep generated by Sputnik, and parlayed as a factor into the election of Senator John Kennedy as President in 1960. When the Kennedy administration entered office, with Johnson as Vice President, the administration quickly decided to pursue arms-control agreements to assure the scenarios about weapons in and from space that they had used so successfully to generate public fear would not actually come to pass. A 1963 agreement between the United States and the Soviet Union that banned weapons of mass destruction (WMD) in space was among the first arms-control efforts between the superpowers. That agreement was the basis for the 1967 OST,[6] known as the Magna Carta of space, developed by the Johnson administration.

Lyndon Johnson was well versed on space activity from his post-Sputnik days in the Senate. He had been among those most adamant that the Soviets not claim space, thereby supporting freedom-of-use as one of the basic principles of the treaty. As a Senator, Johnson said: "We of the United States do not acknowledge that there are landlords of outer space who can presume to bargain with the nations of the Earth on the price of access to this domain."[7] In the OST, freedom of use is stated in Article I, and strengthened in Article II. Article IV contains the substance of the arms-control provisions of the OST. Specifically, it includes provisions prohibiting the orbiting of nuclear or any other weapon of mass destruction around the Earth, on the Moon or any other celestial body, and limits the use of the Moon and other celestial bodies exclusively to peaceful purposes and expressly prohibits their use for establishing military bases, installation, or fortifications; testing weapons of any kind; or conducting military maneuvers. The military use of space, however, was not prohibited. In fact, both the United States and the Soviet Union saw space as offering key capabilities toward helping to stabilize deterrence, through arms-control verification, early warning, and crisis management.

Additionally, the OST does not specifically prohibit the placement of conventional weapons in space, having nuclear warheads carried through space on ballistic missiles or deploying antisatellite weapons. Those activities also, however, fall under the purview of Article III, requiring that all space activities be conducted in accordance with international law, including the United Nations Charter. Presumably, that limits the legitimate use of force in or from space to self-defense and operations authorized by the Security Council.

Several key legal-cum-policy questions relating to the Outer Space Treaty remain unresolved today. First and foremost, what does "peaceful use" mean? The topic was discussed during the Thirteenth UN General Assembly in 1958. While nearly all states considered "peaceful" as nonmilitary,[8] thereby attempting to create space as a sanctuary from military activity, neither of the two superpowers agreed, as they already had military space programs underway, and they were the only space-faring nations at the time. Consequently, "nonaggressive" became the default definition.[9] Initially, the United States position was that nonaggressive meant that it would develop, deploy, and utilize passive space systems only, toward stabilizing deterrence. With the Reagan administration, however, the question of defining "nonaggressive" was reopened. The administration and the military argued that nonaggressive includes "defensive"—which leads to another discussion on what defensive operations include, a discussion particularly vexing in that almost all space technology that has a defensive use can also be used for offensive operations.

Clearly, in the formative years of spaceflight both the United States and the Soviet Union believed space was best used as a tool for stabilization, and saw clear disadvantages in trying to use space as a warfighting medium. Multiple agreements were actually signed toward that end. The 1963 Limited Test Ban Treaty limited nuclear explosions to underground, thereby prohibiting tests of nuclear-tipped antisatellite missiles. With the 1971 Agreement on Measures to Reduce the Risk of Outbreak of Nuclear War, the superpowers agreed to immediately consult with each other in the event of interference with communication or early warning satellites. Antisatellite weapons posed a special case.

The ability to target and destroy an object traveling in or through space at hypersonic speed—with only minutes between missile launch and intercept—has been likened to a bullet hitting a bullet. It is technically difficult at best; operationally impossible according to some scientists and engineers. The difference between being technically possible and operationally possible is important. Something may be possible under textbook laboratory conditions, but not in real world, multivariable-dependent, and time-dependent operational conditions. There are far more variables and time-related complications with missile defense than antisatellite weapons.

If the object to be intercepted is a missile traveling through space to a terrestrial target, then the interceptor sent to stop it is performing "missile defense." If the object to be intercepted is a satellite in orbit around the earth, then the interceptor sent to destroy it is an antisatellite weapon. The systems, however, are largely the same, though the latter is technically easier than the former, because satellites in orbit travel in known paths and are bright objects against a dark sky. Neither of these weapon systems is prohibited by the Outer Space Treaty. Nevertheless, recognition that deployment of a missile-defense system by one superpower would inherently compel the other to respond, likely by either increasing its offensive weapons to preserve deterrence—remember, stability was the goal—or by developing capabilities to thwart the missile-defense system, or both. Consequently, in 1972 the United States and the Soviet Union signed the ABM Treaty, allowing for only very limited missile-defense systems and specifically prohibiting space-based ABM systems or components. Additionally, it implicitly banned interference with "national technical means of verification"—those satellites used for monitoring compliance with ABM prohibitions.

An ASAT treaty, however, was never signed. Both the United States and the Soviet Union had ASAT programs, but both kept them at relatively low levels, pursuing a policy of contingent restraint:[10] restraint by one was thereby contingent upon restraint by the other. Negotiations were held during the Carter administration to try to ban ASATs, but collapsed when the Soviet Union invaded Afghanistan, and never resumed. Interestingly, even during those negotiations, part of the problem lay with trying to determine exactly what constituted an ASAT. The Soviets had the Space Shuttle on their list of U.S. antisatellite technology because, at least in theory, it could pluck satellites out of the sky with its robotic arm.

The Cold War: The Reagan Years

Elected in November 1980, Ronald Reagan came into office and escalated the Cold War by reversing a number of Carter's policies deemed "soft" on defense generally, and the Soviet Union specifically. The administration revived the B-1 bomber program that had been cancelled by the Carter White House and initiated the MX "Peacekeeper" missile. In response to Soviet deployment of the SS-20 missiles in Eastern Europe, Reagan oversaw NATO's deployment of the Pershing II missiles in West Germany. In June 1982, the United States announced its intention to test a new-generation ASAT weapon, the Air-Launched Miniature Vehicle (ALMV), also called the Miniature Homing Vehicle for the heat-seeking missile it carried. The two-stage missile would be launched from a high-altitude F-15 aircraft, ascend directly to a target satellite in LEO and attempt to destroy or disrupt the satellite by the force of impact. Meanwhile, Reagan's flagship space program, the Strategic Defense Initiative (SDI), was just getting under way.

Much has been written about Ronald Reagan's motivations for initiating the Strategic Defense Initiative.[11] Pulitzer Prize-winning historian and journalist Frances Fitzgerald's *Way Out There in the Blue* suggests that Reagan sold SDI to the public to prove himself a visionary and a leader at a time when his poll numbers were down. According to Fitzgerald, before the March 1983 SDI "Star Wars" speech "Reagan's approval rating had declined to 41 percent—an all time low for an elected president in his second year of office. . . . A Lou Harris poll released in January found that 66 percent of Americans believed that Reagan was doing an unsatisfactory job in arms control and 57 percent were worried that he might involve the U.S. in a nuclear war. The President was well aware of this sentiment, for he spoke to friends about the problem of his 'hawkish image,' and he told an outside adviser that something was wrong with his policy toward the Soviet Union, though he did not know where the fault lay."[12] After the speech, Fitzgerald states that Reagan wrote in his diary: "'The reports are in on last night's speech. The biggest return—phone calls, wires, etc., on any speech so far and running heavily in my favor . . .' On 25 March he wrote: 'A poll taken before the speech shows I've gained on job approval with regard to the economy, but the drum beat of antidefense propaganda has reduced my ratings on foreign affairs. I'd be interested to see how that holds for a poll after the speech.' This is all Reagan's diary tells us about the speech, but on 26 March Michael Deaver told Ambassador Dobrynin at a reception that he saw the initiative as a campaign issue because it held out hope to the American voters that the nuclear threat would be neutralized, thus blunting Democratic attacks on Reagan as a warmonger."[13]

Others say the idea went back to his love of science fiction movies, the influence of the Citizens' Advisory Council on National Space Policy (a group including a number of science fiction writers),[14] or even his own role in the 1940 film *Murder in the Air*, a low-budget film featuring

Reagan as Secret Service agent Brass Bancroft. In the movie, "Brass" foils a plot by an evil spy trying to steal the "inertia projector"—technology capable of shooting down planes at long distance before they could bomb the United States. Urban myth also has it that after touring the North American Aerospace Defense Command (NORAD) with physicist Edward Teller (or after visiting Lawrence Livermore Labs to see Teller, depending on the story version), Reagan realized the United States had no protection against incoming nuclear missiles and set about to fix that.

Supporters argue SDI was exactly what Reagan said it was in his March 1983 speech: a response to what he found to be an intolerable Mutually Assured Destruction doctrine that required the world live in a state of nuclear terror. In later years, Reagan himself wrote that SDI was part of his dream for "a world free of nuclear weapons and for the eight years I was president I never let my dream of a nuclear-free world fade from my mind."[15] Clearly, Reagan abhorred nuclear weapons. Whether he really believed that a technology system could be developed to protect the United States is a different and harder question. Actions taken during the Reagan era to develop such a system, however, have become embedded into U.S. security planning today.

Sitting before a television camera in the Oval Office, Reagan began his speech by noting that his predecessors had appeared there before to describe the threat posed by Soviet power and proposed steps to address that threat. "But since the advent of nuclear weapons," he continued,

those steps have been increasingly directed toward deterrence of aggression through the promise of retaliation. This approach to stability through offensive threat has worked. We and our allies have succeeded in preventing nuclear war for more than three decades. In recent months, however, my advisers, including in particular the Joint Chiefs of Staff, have underscored the necessity to break out of a future that relies solely on offensive retaliation for our security. Over the course of these discussions, I've become more and more deeply convinced that the human spirit must be capable of rising above dealing with other nations and human beings by threatening their existence. Feeling this way, I believe we must thoroughly examine every opportunity for reducing tensions and for introducing greater stability into the strategic calculus on both sides. One of the most important contributions we can make is, of course, to lower the level of all arms, and particularly nuclear arms. We're engaged right now in several negotiations with the Soviet Union to bring about a mutual reduction of weapons. I will report to you a week from tomorrow my thoughts on that score. But let me just say, I'm totally committed to this course. If the Soviet Union will join with us in our effort to achieve major arms reduction, we will have succeeded in stabilizing the nuclear balance. Nevertheless, it will still be necessary to rely on the specter of retaliation, on mutual threat. And that's a sad commentary on the human condition. Wouldn't it be better to save lives than to avenge them? Are we not capable of demonstrating our peaceful intentions by applying all our abilities and our ingenuity to achieving a truly lasting stability? I think we are. Indeed, we must. After careful consultation with my advisers, including the Joint Chiefs of Staff, I believe there is a way. Let me share with you a vision of the future which offers hope. It is that we embark on a program to counter the awesome Soviet missile threat with measures that are defensive. Let us turn to the very strengths in technology that spawned our great industrial base and that have given us the quality of life we enjoy today. What if free people could live secure in the knowledge that their security did not rest upon the threat of instant U.S. retaliation to deter a Soviet attack, that we could intercept and destroy strategic ballistic missiles before they reached our own soil or that of our allies? I know this is a formidable, technical task, one that may not be accomplished before the end of this century. Yet, current technology has attained a level of sophistication where it's reasonable for us to begin this effort. It will take years, probably decades of effort on many fronts. There will be failures and setbacks, just as there will be successes and breakthroughs. And as we proceed, we must remain constant in preserving the nuclear deterrent and maintaining a solid capability for flexible response. But isn't it worth every investment necessary to free the world from the threat of nuclear war? We know it is. In the meantime, we will continue to pursue real reductions in nuclear arms, negotiating from a position of strength that can be ensured only by modernizing our strategic forces. At the same time, we must take steps to reduce the risk of a conventional military conflict escalating to nuclear war by improving our nonnuclear capabilities.

America does possess—now—the technologies to attain very significant improvements in the effectiveness of our conventional, nonnuclear forces. Proceeding boldly with these new technologies, we can significantly reduce any incentive that the Soviet Union may have to threaten attack against the United States or its allies. As we pursue our goal of defensive technologies, we recognize that our allies rely upon our strategic offensive power to deter attacks against them. Their vital interests and ours are inextricably linked. Their safety and ours are one. And no change in technology can or will alter that reality. We must and shall continue to honor our commitments. I clearly recognize that defensive systems have limitations and raise certain problems and ambiguities. If paired with offensive systems, they can be viewed as fostering an aggressive policy, and no one wants that. But with these considerations firmly in mind, I call upon the scientific community in our country, those who gave us nuclear weapons, to turn their great talents now to the cause of mankind and world peace, to give us the means of rendering these nuclear weapons impotent and obsolete. Tonight, consistent with our obligations of the ABM treaty and recognizing the need for closer consultation with our allies, I'm taking an important first step. I am directing a comprehensive and intensive effort to define a long-term research and development program to begin to achieve our ultimate goal of eliminating the threat posed by strategic nuclear missiles. This could pave the way for arms-control measures to eliminate the weapons themselves. We seek neither military superiority nor political advantage. Our only purpose—one all people share—is to search for ways to reduce the danger of nuclear war. My fellow Americans, tonight we're launching an effort which holds the promise of changing the course of human history. There will be risks, and results take time. But I believe we can do it. As we cross this threshold, I ask for your prayers and your support. Thank you, good night, and God bless.

It is curious to note that the word "space" is never used in the speech. It is unclear whether that was intentional or not, but Reagan did deny that SDI was a space-weapons program in the 1984 election campaign. Reagan refused to get nailed down on the issue in an exchange with Mondale during the second presidential debate.

Reagan: Now, if you're willing to join us in getting rid of all the nuclear weapons in the world, then, we'll give you this one so that we would both know that no one can cheat—that we've both got something that if anyone tries to cheat—but when you keep star-warring it—I never suggested where the weapons should be or what kind. I'm not a scientist. I said, and the Joint Chiefs of Staff agreed with me, that it was time for us to turn our research ability to seeing if we could not find this kind of a defensive weapon. And suddenly somebody says, oh, it's got to be up there—Star Wars—and so forth. I don't know what it would be, but if we can come up with one, I think the world will be better off.

Moderator: Mr. Mondale, your rebuttal?

Mondale: Well, that's what a President's supposed to know—where those weapons are going to be. If they're space weapons, I assume they'll be in space.[16]

Reagan did say in his March 1983 speech that he had consulted with advisors before deciding to develop SDI, but those who might have been willing to vocalize dissenting opinions were not necessarily asked, and even among those who tacitly went along with the idea, more than a few really did not believe in the technical feasibility of the program. National Security Advisor William Clark, Defense Secretary Caspar Weinberger, Counselor Edwin Meese, CIA Director William Casey, and U.N. Ambassador Jeane Kirkpatrick have been described as "steadfast" in their support of SDI.[17] Others, however, such as George Shultz, Colin Powell, and Robert (Bud) McFarlane regarded it largely as a "pipe dream"[18] but potentially useful as a bargaining chip with the Soviets.[19] Richard Perle's initial reaction, while Reagan's assistant secretary of defense, was said to consider the whole high-tech space venture as "the product of millions of American teenagers putting quarters into video machines."[20] The military was certainly split; always eager to sign on to a new idea if it means additional defense dollars would be sent their way but unwilling to give up any traditional platforms (e.g., planes, ships, tanks) to pay for it. Not surprisingly, though perhaps cynically, among the scientific community there seemed to be a high correlation between federal money being received and optimism toward an eventually successful outcome.

TABLE 1. Public Attitudes Toward Star Wars During the Reagan Administration

The Reagan administration is now working on this program known as Star Wars. It will attempt to build a new defensive system in outer space that could shoot down nuclear missiles fired at the U.S. Since the program is currently only a research project, it is impossible to predict how complete a defense it will provide. I'm going to read a list of four possible Star Wars systems. For each one, tell me if you would strongly support, support, oppose, or strongly oppose building each type of system.

September 1985	Strongly Support	Support	Oppose	Strongly Oppose	Not Sure
A system that was perfect and could successfully defend against all incoming nuclear weapons.	58	28	5	4	4
A system that could protect our missile sites and some population centers but could not guarantee the safety of many of our major cities.	12	32	34	16	6
A system designed only to protect U.S. missiles, key military bases, and Washington, D.C., but not other areas.	5	16	39	34	5
A system that could provide a complete defense against long-range nuclear missiles but cannot defend against missiles fired from submarines or bombers.	8	32	34	17	10

Source: Thomas W. Graham and Bernard M. Kramer, "The Polls: ABM and Star Wars," *Public Opinion Quarterly* 50 (Spring 1986): 132.

Although Reagan later denied that he expected SDI to provide an impenetrable shield against nuclear attack,[21] that he did was the widely held impression after the speech. Opinions vary on the importance of maintaining the impression of SDI as providing a 100 percent effective safeguard against nuclear attacks for public support. A 1985 poll found that 85 percent of the U.S. public favored development of a missile defense "even if it can't protect everyone."[22] When broken down more specifically, however, public support for SDI dropped considerably as the realities of its capabilities, or lack thereof, were considered (see Table 1). At least initially, administration officials allowed if not encouraged the "umbrella" impression to be perpetuated, if only by silence on the reality.

Paul Nitze, the Reagan administration's most experienced and respected arms-control advisor, gave a speech in 1985 that undermined the program, saying that "a Star Wars system would have to meet two criteria to be effective. First, it has to be 'survivable,' or able to withstand a preemptive attack. Otherwise, 'the defenses would themselves be tempting targets for a first strike.' Second, it has to be 'cost-effective at the margin.' Translation: It must be cheaper to add new defenses than new offensive systems. If it were cheaper to build new offensive weapons, it would just set off a new and dangerous round in the arms race as each side looked for ways to overwhelm the other's defenses. 'If the new technologies cannot meet these standards,' Nitze told the World Affairs Council of Philadelphia, 'we are not about to deploy them.'"[23] Obviously, the rest of the administration did not share Nitze's view, or were not willing to state those views publicly.

Also in 1985, the administration was trying to gain NATO support for the program, and found very little. A 1985 BBC report discussing Norway's decision against joining onto the SDI program stated: "Washington promises to protect Western Europe with a space umbrella in the event of nuclear war, but no reasonable military specialist has ever asserted that it is possible to give a 100 percent guarantee of the interception of all ballistic missiles."[24] The *Globe and Mail* (Canada) ran an article in 1985 as well, discussing strains in the NATO alliance caused by SDI. "If the Soviets can't match the Americans—if they think the United States will develop a leak-proof umbrella—the danger of a preemptive strike grows."[25] A speech given at a 1985 conference in Munich on behalf of Defense Secretary Caspar Weinberger (bad weather prevented his reaching Munich in time to deliver it himself) offered what the *Economist* called a "radically altered" line on what the United States expected SDI to do. "This speech put forward the argument that such a defense could be less than perfect and still, by making a preemptive attacker less confident of near-complete success, help to stabilize the nuclear balance. The emphasis Mr. Weinberger laid on protecting American forces was apparently expected to appeal to Europeans more than President Reagan's original 'Star Wars' speech of March 1983, which held out a vision—unrealistic in the views of many scientists—of an impermeable umbrella protecting American cities."[26]

A 1986 U.S.-European conference report evidences that Europeans were unsure what SDI was supposed to do. The report stated: "Part of the disagreement over the appropriate objectives for the SDI program stemmed from what many conference participants saw as conflicting U.S. statements. For instance, the conditions that some participants placed on individual points of agreement reflected a belief that the goals of the SDI was to create a 'perfect defense'—that is, the protection of military assets and populations with impenetrable defenses. This was widely viewed as an enormously challenging, if not impossible, technological task. Participants who envisioned a less demanding role for strategic defenses—defense for military forces only—were less inclined to attach conditions to their agreement with the points noted above. In short, divergent (and sometimes unstated) perceptions of the objectives of SDI produced conflicting assessments of the technological feasibility and strategic desirability of the program."[27] Nevertheless in the United States, the "umbrella" impression held a while longer.

In 1987, in a speech to the American Defense Institute, Edward Teller stated that SDI would not be able to provide a leak-proof umbrella against nuclear missiles. Newspaper reports subsequently noted that: "The Administration has been gradually backing away from its initial claim that SDI would provide a leak-proof umbrella to any missile attack. Teller's comments give new authority to this change. He said that SDI would enhance the ability of the American ICBM force to survive an initial Soviet missile attack, and thus deter the start of a nuclear war."[28] The realities of technological limitations largely had become apparent within the science community, even if those scientists in the funding pipeline were certainly willing to keep trying as long as the money continued, and those in some military and political communities would never come around.

Lt. General James Abrahamson, USAF, had been named to oversee the program in 1984, through the newly established Strategic Defense Initiative Organization (SDIO). Originally, SDI was conceived as including cutting-edge ground and space-based technology systems, including electromagnetic rail guns, nuclear-explosion-powered X-ray lasers, particle beam weapons, and kinetic kill systems, few of which were more than concepts at the time. One of the concepts that garnered particular attention was an interceptor concept called Brilliant Pebbles. "'Brilliant' technologies refer to the use of powerful, miniaturized computers and miniaturized sensors to give the capabilities previously possessed only by large, expensive satellites to much smaller, inexpensive satellites."[29]

Whatever SDI technically did or did not accomplish, clearly both Ronald Reagan and Mikhail Gorbachev were driven by it in ways far beyond its technical potential. Even if Gorbachev did not believe it would work, politically he had to push Soviet scientists to try to technically maintain the perception of superpower parity, which exposed the Soviet house-of-cards economy to more strain than it could bear. Additionally, while SDI did not and likely could not provide an umbrella of protection against nuclear attack for the United States, it did push scientific and technological areas such as computational analysis and miniaturization to previously unrealized levels.

Meanwhile, the ALMV ASAT system was tested twice in 1984. Both of those first tests involved firing interceptors but deliberately not hitting targets. The only test where a satellite was actually hit was performed on 13 October 1985, destroying an aging U.S. satellite and creating considerable space debris. Nevertheless, the Air Force aggressively continued to pursue the program, even scheduling a number of tests for the following year. In December 1985 though, the Democratic-controlled House and the Republican-led Senate included a ban on testing the ALMV on a target in space in its budget authorization bill. This action was taken the day after the Air Force had sent two target satellites into orbit for another round of tests. The Air Force tested again in 1986, but did not engage a target.

The test ban was renewed in 1986 and the Soviets continued to observe a voluntary moratorium on ASAT testing, both sides still observing contingent restraint. The White House and Congress negotiated a compromise on arms-control provisions in the authorization bill in 1987 that extended the ASAT testing ban, but allowed the ban to be lifted if the Soviets resumed ASAT testing. As political opposition to pursuing an ASAT system appeared unyielding, the Air Force finally dropped development of the ALMV system.[30] Besides, SDI was a high presidential priority by then.

Beyond physics and cost, the ABM Treaty stood in the way of SDI implementation. Therefore, abolishment or circumvention of the ABM became a quest for Reagan administration lawyers. Basically, Reagan's lawyers reinterpreted the ABM Treaty,[31] claiming that technologies not in existence at the time of the treaty signing were not covered, and that as a research program, SDI generally was not covered by the treaty. The debate featured Judge Abraham Sofaer, legal counsel to the State Department and willing reinterpreter of what was intended when the treaty was written on one side, and Senator Sam Nunn (D-Georgia), no slouch on either national defense or constitutional law, on the other, with Nunn as the champion of the "traditional" interpretation of the ABM Treaty. The new, "broad" view of the treaty allowed space-based and mobile ABM systems and components based on such exotic technologies as lasers and particle beams to be developed and tested but not deployed. The "traditional" interpretation of the treaty was narrower, saying that development and testing, but not deployment, of ABM systems based on such physical principles are allowed only for fixed, land-based systems and components. Tortured logic though it was, Sofaer's view supported presidential policy and held until SDI officially collapsed under the weight of its own cost and technical infeasibility. Even then, however, the program did not really collapse, as much of it was repackaged and announced in George H. W. Bush's 1991 State of the Union address as an intended theater missile-defense program called Global Protection Against Limited Strikes (GPALS).

The Post–Cold War Years: Bush 41 and Clinton

By the time he was preparing to leave SDIO in 1989, Abrahamson stated that an entire space-based missile-defense system based on the Brilliant Pebbles concept could be deployed in five years, for a cost of no more than $25 billion. President George H. W. Bush announced in an address to a joint session of Congress that he would "vigorously pursue" the Strategic Defense Initiative.[32] Brilliant Pebbles would consist of thousands of interceptors each capable of independent operations against whatever came within its field of vision.

What SDI technology could and could not do, however, was becoming increasingly acknowledged. Bush's first nominee for Secretary of Defense, John Tower, stated in January 1989 that "I don't believe that we can devise a [BMD] umbrella that can protect the entire American population from nuclear incineration. I think that's unrealistic."[33] Tower was never confirmed as Defense Secretary. Dick Cheney, however, stepped in as Defense Secretary instead, continuing to echo Tower's sentiments about missile defense not providing an umbrella against nuclear weapons, stating that he felt the whole concept had been "oversold."[34] Vice President Dan Quayle went so far as to label Reagan's implied promise as "political jargon."[35]

SDI, it now seemed, would protect "hard targets," like missile silos, rather than provide an umbrella over "soft targets," like cities and people. Nevertheless, in December 1989, Secretary of Defense Cheney asked Ambassador Henry Cooper to carry out a review of the SDI program for President George H. W. Bush. In March 1990, Cooper submitted his report endorsing Brilliant Pebbles and outlined concepts that would become the GPALS system. President Bush appointed Cooper as the first civilian director of SDIO in July 1990. In August, Iraq invaded Kuwait.

Besides general skepticism over "the nuclear umbrella" concept, support for TMD was gaining traction as well, because of the anticipated war effort. The 1991 fiscal year (FY 1991) Appropriations Conference Committee Report called for the Secretary of Defense to establish a centrally managed TMD program, and to accelerate R&D on theater and tactical ballistic missile-defense systems. SDIO was given responsibility for TMD in November 1990, and on 17 January 1991, U.S.-led coalition forces commenced military operations against Iraqi forces.

The next day, 18 January 1991, press reports stated that for the first time in history, a Patriot missile hit and destroyed a Scud missile headed for a U.S. air base in Saudi Arabia. A reporter for the *Los Angeles Times* wrote: "The age of 'Star Wars' had arrived."[36] Soon after the end of the Gulf War, questions were raised about whether or not this first "kill" actually occurred. This was part of a general public debate about the operational effectiveness of the entire Patriot system that began soon after hostilities ended and continued for about two years (discussed further in Chapter 3).

In his 1991 State of the Union address, President Bush announced a change in the mission of the SDI program from defense against a large-scale ballistic missile attack to "providing protection against limited ballistic missile strikes—whatever their source."[37] The new GPALS program would include some 1,000 space-based "Brilliant Pebbles" interceptors, 750 to 1,000 long-range ground-based interceptors at six sites, space-based and mobile sensors, and transportable theater ballistic missile defenses.

Besides the alleged success of Patriot missiles shooting down Scuds in the Gulf War, the value of space assets was becoming appreciated in other ways as well. Fearing that a direct frontal assault on heavily dug-in Iraqi defenders could lead to thousands of allied casualties, Coalition Commander General Norman Schwarzkopf launched a flanking maneuver later compared to a Hail Mary play, the last-ditch football maneuver. Schwarzkopf's tactical commanders questioned whether more than 150,000 soldiers could be moved, with all their armor, artillery, and sixty days of ammunition and supplies, over a desert with only rough roads. If his subordinates doubted it could be done, Schwarzkopf believed Saddam Hussein's generals would also doubt that such a move could be executed and, lacking reconnaissance to indicate it was actually under way, would leave a big, open Iraqi flank largely undefended. Schwarzkopf was right. He was able to pull off the Hail Mary largely because Iraq had no space reconnaissance assets and Iraq assumed that the allies could not navigate through the desert. With GPS though, a largely unknown technology outside of the military at the time, that assumption proved wrong. The idea that the United States must control space began to gain ground.

President George H. W. Bush continued to push theater missile defense. The Missile Defense Act of 1991 specifically stated that DoD would "aggressively pursue the development of advanced theater missile-defense systems, with the objective of downselecting and deploying such systems by the mid-1990s." A Memorandum of Agreement was concluded between Ambassador Henry Cooper at SDIO and the secretaries of the military services that established the organizational structures and procedures for handling the acquisition of the GPALS system, as DoD moved forward with deployment of missile defenses in accordance with instructions contained in the Missile Defense Act of 1991.[38] DoD was to develop a cost-effective, operationally effective and ABM compliant anti-missile system to protect the United States against limited ballistic missile attacks, including accidental, unauthorized, or Third World attacks. The idea that some country or some lunatic would shoot a nuclear missile at the United States indicated the beginning of a shift away from deterrence theory, which relies on rational state-actors. Increasingly, whether other international actors would be rational or at least operate with the same logic as the United States was being questioned, thereby questioning the logic of deterrence itself.

During the presidential campaign in 1992, it became evident that George H. W. Bush and Bill Clinton had very different views on pursuing space control. Clinton came out against a space-based missile-defense system, but supported theater missile defense, the Anti-Ballistic Missile Treaty, and the option of a limited missile-defense system within that framework. With Clinton's victory, the direction of U.S. space policy began to change quickly. Cooper resigned from SDIO. Secretary of Defense Les Aspin renamed SDIO the Ballistic Missile Defense Organization and refocused it on TMD. The rationale continued along the same lines as Aspin had begun earlier in Congress, that the United States no longer faced a massive Soviet threat such as SDI was intended to thwart, but more potentially theater ballistic missiles in the hands of Third World dictators. Almost immediately as well, the Clinton administration returned to the "traditional" interpretation of the ABM Treaty.

Regardless of what Clinton wanted though, advocates were not about to let their long-held quest for national missile defense die. Three hundred and fifty Republican candidates for the House of Representatives had signed pledges to develop and deploy an ABM system in their Contract with America election platform. Only by a narrow margin in 1995 did the House defeat the portion of the Contract that would require a national missile defense "as soon as practical." When Henry Cooper left SDIO, he took up residence at the pro-missile defense group High Frontier, began advising the Center for Security Policy, and became a Fellow at the Heritage Foundation—all hard-line conservative think tanks advocating deployment of missile-defense programs.

Meanwhile, in 1995 two significant events took place. The 1995 National Intelligence Estimate (NIE 95–19) declared that "No country, other than the major declared nuclear power, will develop or otherwise acquire a ballistic missile in the next fifteen years that could threaten the contiguous forty-eight states or Canada." Also, the United States and Russia agreed on a framework for determining a line separating allowable TMD activities, and prohibited ABM activities. These two activities paved the way for the Clinton administration to announce a reorientation of the missile-defense program in 1996, toward TMD and away from NMD. These activities did not stop the zealots.

The Defend America Act—declaring it U.S. policy to deploy a limited missile defense by 2003—was introduced in both houses of Congress in March 1996. It did not come to a vote only because of the estimated cost of deployment. In recognition of the fervor behind the support, however, and to fend off even more zealous programs, Clinton agreed to a "3 + 3" NMD plan which allowed for three years for development and, if then warranted, three more years to deploy a system. In response, the Pentagon changed the purpose of the "national" missile-defense plan from a "technology" readiness program to a "deployment" readiness program.

There was no clear-cut threat to justify the rush. A congressionally chartered panel chaired by former CIA Director and future Defense Secretary Robert Gates issued a report in December 1996 that concurred with the 1995 NIE. Nevertheless, Senate Majority Leader Trent Lott and twenty-five cosponsors, all Republicans, introduced the "National Missile Defense Act of 1997" requiring the United States to deploy a national missile-defense system by the end of 2003.

Also in 1996, the Air Force offered its first Space Operations Doctrine. That doctrine reiterated and defined the four military space missions referenced in Chapter 1: space support, force enhancement, space control, and force application. While Air Force Space Command had been created in 1982, during the Cold War, space operations had focused primarily on missile warning, and national command and control capabilities, both of which require space support capabilities. "Space [force] support is carried out by terrestrial elements of military space forces to sustain, surge, and reconstitute elements of a military space system or capability. These activities deploy, sustain, or augment on-orbit spacecraft, direct missions, and support other government or civil organizations. Space support involves spacelift and satellite operations."[39] The benefits of force enhancement capabilities became increasingly recognized after the Gulf War. Force enhancement refers to "operations conducted from space with the objective of enabling or supporting terrestrial forces"[40] such as navigation, communications, and reconnaissance. Only after the Gulf War—when the vulnerabilities of space assets were considered—did space control and force applications gain attention. Force application "consists of attacks against terrestrial targets carried out by military weapons systems in space."[41] Air Force Space Operations Doctrine goes on to specifically say: "Currently, there are no force application assets operating in space, but technology and national policy could change so that force application missions can be performed from platforms operating in space."[42] Space control is stated as "the means by which we gain and maintain space superiority to assure friendly forces can use the space environment while denying its use to the enemy."[43] Defining space security very quickly became an important part of evolving U.S. space policy.[44]

The lineage of current Air Force—and tacitly U.S.—positions on space control and increasingly force application includes such documents as *Vision for 2020*, published in 1997 by U.S. Space Command, which stated, "The emerging synergy of space superiority with land, sea, and air superiority will lead to Full Spectrum Dominance."[45] Given the dominance of U.S. investment and number of U.S. military assets in space, clearly the United States enjoys a position of space superiority, being preeminent among other countries. Dominance, however, carries a connotation of control that other countries are wary of under any circumstances given the potential impacts on their sovereignty, but especially given recent U.S. proclivities toward unilateralism, primacy, and preemption. In 1997–99 under the Clinton administration, however, the views—and mission and programs wish lists—expressed in Air Force doctrine were not considered mainstream.

Meanwhile, the 1995 National Intelligence Estimate kept getting in the way of plans for a national missile-defense system. A threat had to be found to justify the system. So in August 1997, CIA Director George Tenet informed Secretary of Defense William Cohen that, in accordance with the FY 1997 National Defense Authorization Act, he was appointing nine individuals to serve on the Commission to Assess the Ballistic Missile Threat to the United States, which became known as the Rumsfeld Commission after its chair, former Defense Secretary Donald Rumsfeld. He was joined by Barry Blechman, General George Lee Butler, USAF (retired), Dr. Richard Garwin, William Schneider, Jr., former Senator Malcolm Wallop, General Lawrence Welch, USAF (retired), Dr. Paul Wolfowitz, and former CIA Director James Woolsey. Steve Cambone served as staff director for the group. The members were to complete their work within six months, making a substantively in-depth study difficult if not impossible.

As well as serving on the Rumsfeld Commission, General Larry Welch also chaired a panel to conduct annual reviews on missile-defense programs underway. In the first of those reviews, issued in February 1998, the Welch panel criticized overly ambitious timelines in what amounted to a "rush to failure" in various BMD programs. These findings were not well received.

Not to be swayed though, when the Rumsfeld Commission report was released, missile defense was vindicated because an increased threat was identified, even though responses to missile threats were not included in the commission's charter. As commission member Richard Garwin, a renowned Republican physicist known for his fierce independence and one of the three commission members picked by Democrats, stated: "The charge was cooked. We were not asked what were the most likely ways in which the United States might be attacked and how they compared to the ICBM. We were only asked to study the long-range missile threat. Nor did they ask us what to do about it. If they asked us about that, we would never have reached agreement in six months."[46] Methodology also played a key part in shaping the findings of threat assessments in the Rumsfeld Commission Report.[47] The Rumsfeld Commission made three major changes in the assessment methodology from previous assessments, which resulted in dramatic shifts in the findings not only in the Rumsfeld Commission Report itself, but in subsequent NIE reports since commission methodology became the standard when Rumsfeld became Secretary of Defense.[48]

First, the commission employed what has been referred to as a hypothesis-based threat assessment, or the "could" standard. "Could" is highly ambiguous, subjective terminology with a range of meanings from "remotely possible" to "will." While it is the responsibility of security analysts to consider all threat possibilities, it is also their responsibility to make best determinations of where limited defense dollars should go for defense based on probability. Otherwise, in the words of Frederick the Great, "He who attempts to defend too much defends nothing."[49] The Rumsfeld Commission focused on whether countries "could" do something, not whether it was likely, or even more likely than something else.

The second change involved substantially reducing the range of missiles considered serious threats by shifting from threats to the forty-eight continental states to threats to any part of the land mass of the fifty states. An Intermediate Range Ballistic Missile was considered to have a range of 2,400–5,500 kilometers in the 1987 Intermediate Nuclear Forces Treaty between the Soviet Union and the United States; an Intercontinental Ballistic Missile, a range of over 5,500 kilometers. The distance between China and Seattle is over 6,000 kilometers and the distance between North Korea and Seattle over 5,000 kilometers, thereby requiring ICBMs to attack the United States. However, the distance from Seattle to the western-most tip of the Aleutian Island chain in Alaska is some 5,000 kilometers. By expanding the parameters of what constituted a capability of hitting the United States, an intermediate-range ballistic missile could now be considered essentially the same as an intercontinental-range missile for counting purposes in the Rumsfeld Commission Report.

Third, whereas in the past, the timeline from when a country could *deploy* a long-range missile (now required to be capable of a much shorter range due to the second change instituted) was standard in assessments of how quickly a country could develop a missile, now when it could first *test* a long-range missile became the important metric. Essentially, that shift in metrics represented a difference of about five years (what previous estimates said was the difference between first test and likely deployment).

Consequently, a much higher—nearly histrionic—threat to the United States was found in the Rumsfeld Commission Report and the 1999 National Intelligence Estimate than in past reports. According to analyst Joseph Cirincione in testimony before Congress in 2000: "These three changes account for almost all of the differences between the 1999 NIE and earlier estimates. Thus, the new estimate, rather than representing some new, dramatic development in the ballistic missile threat, represents a lowering of the standards for judging the threat. This NIE may lead some observers to conclude that there has been a significant technological leap forward in Third World missile systems, when, in fact there has been only incremental development in programs well known to analysts for years."[50] Clearly, these new threat assessments were intended to provide rationale for National Missile Defense, and not just Theater Missile Defense.

Whatever resistance remained in the intelligence community against the new threat assessment methodology was quashed with the 31 August 1998 launch of the North Korean Taepo Dong-1 missile. The North Korean launcher tried, but failed to place a small satellite into orbit. While incapable of striking any part of the United States with a large payload, such as a nuclear warhead, it potentially might be able to strike the westernmost parts of Alaska and Hawaii with a very small payload. In theory, its successors could have a longer range, capable of striking parts of Alaska and Hawaii with a heavier payload.

That launch, along with the new threat assessments, cinched the justification of National Missile Defense programs for some, and revived "moral imperative" arguments for others. Among the first to use the "moral imperative" language again in the 1990s was Family Research Council President Gary Bauer in a 1998 Heritage Foundation lecture even before the Taepo Dong launch: "The evidence is overwhelming that ballistic missiles pose a very real threat to the United States and that the technology to defend America exists and is affordable. Incredibly, however, the country remains unprotected. Reversing this intolerable situation is a moral imperative as powerful as the defense of the unborn and the fostering of the family."[51] After the launch, references to the moral imperative are found in speeches by such individuals as Heritage Foundation President Edwin Feulner,[52] House Republican leader Dick Armey of Texas,[53] and Donald Rumsfeld.[54] Representative Armey said,

"It's a moral imperative to you and me, senator, if we can use all our American genius and technology to give our children something better than the duck-and-cover we had when we were in school" in the event of a Soviet missile attack.[55] Donald Rumsfeld stated: "No U.S. president can responsibly say that his defense policy is calculated and designed to leave the American people undefended against threats that are known to exist . . . It is not so much a technical question as a matter of a president's constitutional responsibility. Indeed, it is in many respects . . . a moral issue."[56] By establishing National Missile Defense as a moral imperative, questions regarding cost and technical feasibility become irrelevant and could be quashed.

In the spring and summer of 1999—in reaction to the North Korean launch—Congress passed a series of measures committing to deploy a national missile defense "as soon as technically possible," which by then was being stated as 2005. Democrats dropped their opposition both to avoid being cast as soft on the North Korean threat and in return for a renewed commitment to arms control. Indeed, dropping their opposition or even failing to raise opposition rather than fighting a tough battle against public perception, even when in the right, too often has been the response of Democrats. Nevertheless, when Clinton signed the National Missile Defense Act of 1999 in July, he listed four criteria that would be used before a decision to deploy would be made: threat, cost, technological status of the NMD program, and adherence to a renegotiated Anti-Ballistic Missile Treaty. Meanwhile in September, the Welch panel took a second look at the NMD timelines, and again concluded that the program was "high risk." The panel recommended that the President again consider the feasibility of the system rather than whether it was "ready to deploy," but a new NIE again supported missile-defense advocates, stating that within fifteen years the United States would likely face ICBM threats from Russia, China, and North Korea, probably from Iran and possibly from Iraq.

By 2000, NMD was being pushed hard by Congressional Republicans, with Clinton merely trying to slow down the fast-moving and still-gaining-speed NMD train. In February 2000, Philip Coyle, Director of the Pentagon's Office of Operational Test and Evaluation, testified before Congress saying, "Undue pressure has been placed on the [NMD] program by artificial goals for deployment in 2005." The third Welch panel report was issued, still stating that timetables for deployment are "high risk" and pointing out that the flight tests undertaken so far represented only "a limited part of the required operating envelope."[57] That comment is part of an overall—and ongoing—controversy and debate on the utility and results of missile-defense tests conducted.[58] Ultimately, in

September 2000, President Clinton decided to not authorize work toward deployment of NMD.

In January 2001 the results of another commission, the Commission to Assess United States National Security Space Management, again chaired by Donald Rumsfeld, were released. While the short history of space policy is littered with studies and reports from blue-ribbon panels, this one carried particular weight given that Rumsfeld resigned as commission chair two weeks before the panel ended its work to become Secretary of Defense. As such, not only does the report reflect Rumsfeld's thinking on space, but its philosophical underpinnings became those of the Defense Department regarding space.

Not only did the report call for bureaucratic reorganizations to give space security more focus, but it also sought to establish an organizational structure to keep space security a high-profile national priority. More attention was to be paid as well to the establishment of a cadre of space professionals, and the report recommended that the military needed to stop the practice of assigning only combat "operators"—pilots—to top space posts. "Military leaders with little or no previous experience or expertise in space technology or operations often lead space organizations," the report said. The commission laid the foundation for an eventual move toward the creation of a U.S. Space Corps, though it stopped short of actually recommending creation in the short term.

Equally if not more important to the organizational suggestions made were the philosophical underpinnings that came to guide DoD's approach to space. Most infamously, the report warned of a potential "space Pearl Harbor" that the United States must protect against. The report argued that space would "inevitably" become a battlefield because air, land, and sea all had gone that route earlier. Under that presumption, the United States would be remiss not to prepare for such, which explains why the report recommended that the option for deploying space weapons be maintained. "In the coming period," the report stated, "the U.S. will conduct operations to, from, in and through space in support of its national interests both on the earth and in space." Further, the report indicated that new arms-control efforts to curb potential space warfare were perhaps not in the best interests of retaining ultimately flexibility for the United States. Overall, the report offered a blueprint that the George W. Bush administration eagerly followed.

George W. Bush: Full Speed Ahead

Enter the second Bush administration. Even as a candidate at the Republican National Convention, Bush had made his position clear:

"My administration will deploy missile defenses to guard against attack and blackmail. Now is the time, not to defend outdated treaties, but to defend the American people."[59] As president, Bush followed through on his pledge to develop and deploy a national missile-defense system, even when public opinion and threat assessments did not support a perceived prioritization.[60] In a pre-9/11 poll, when asked "What's the greater threat to the United States at this point: The possibility of a missile attack by an unfriendly nation or a terrorist group bringing weapons of mass destruction into the U.S.?" a full 77 percent of the respondents answered "terrorist bringing weapons into the U.S." Ten percent said "possibility of a missile attack" while the remainder said "about the same" or "don't know." The phrasing of questions influenced the findings of polls taken on support for missile defense as well. A 1998 Republican National Committee poll question read: "Recent reports say the Chinese have thirteen long range missiles targeted at the west coast of America. Knowing this, would you favor or oppose an effective National Missile Defense system capable of defending U.S. territory against limited ballistic attack?" Fifty-five percent strongly favor, 21 percent somewhat favor, 9 percent somewhat oppose, 10 percent strongly oppose.[61] With the question phrased as it was, the surprise was that anyone opposed missile defense. Generally, before 9/11, even when cost was not considered, and the public still largely uninformed on the topic, Americans were largely split regarding support for missile defense.[62]

In terms of threat assessments, the 2001 unclassified summary of the National Intelligence Estimate, *Foreign Missile Developments and the Ballistic Missile Threat Through 2015,* stated, "In fact, U.S. territory is more likely to be attacked with these materials from nonmissile delivery means—most likely from terrorists—than by missiles, primarily because nonmissile delivery means are less costly, easier to acquire, and more reliable and accurate. They also can be used without attribution."[63] Within a short time, however, terrorism would be used as further justification for missile defense. Specifically, after 9/11, the tactic of linking terrorist threats to missile defense—a link without foundation—came into play for pollsters looking for support.[64]

With 9/11, the Bush administration got, and took, carte blanche from the American public and press to forward policies and programs that had been slow or hard sells previously. Further, diplomacy became a lost art, pushed to the wayside by hubris masquerading as need. Whereas the Anti-Ballistic Missile Treaty had been under renegotiation with the Russians prior to 9/11, on 13 June 2002, six months after giving the required notice of intent, the United States simply abrogated the treaty. Though the organizational name behind the efforts has changed, from the Strategic Defense Initiative Organization, to the Ballistic Missile

Defense Organization, to the Missile Defense Agency in 2002, Star Wars lives on. As the administration prepared to install the first interceptors in Alaska in 2004, a group of forty-nine retired generals and admirals sent a letter to President Bush calling for a financial shift in spending toward fighting terrorism rather than missile defense, as "the militarily responsible course of action."[65] That advice was ignored.

A plethora of documents, most but not all from the Air Force, provide the military genesis of current policy. The *Joint Doctrine for Space Operations*, published by the Office of the Joint Chiefs of Staff in August 2002, states, "The United States must be able to protect its space assets and deny the use of space assets by its adversaries."[66] The 2003 Air Force *Transformation Flight Plan* included plans for orbiting weapons that would send giant metal rods crashing to Earth, officially called Hypervelocity Rod Bundles, though dubbed "Rods from God."[67] While the technology is still largely conceptual, the document makes it clear that development and potentially deployment has advocates. That document, however, only talked about hardware. The 2004 *Air Force Doctrine Document 2–2.1, Counterspace Operations*[68] adds another component part to the trend of developing space as the fourth battlespace: the component that states when and how such hardware would be used.[69] Space superiority is defined in that document as, "The degree of dominance in space of one force over another that permits the conduct of operations by the former and its related land, sea, air, space, and special operations forces at a given time and place without prohibitive interference by the opposing force."[70] While the *Counterspace Operations* doctrine document says the United States seeks "space superiority," an advantage over other countries by some potentially minimum amount, the language makes it not unreasonable to conclude that "space dominance"—the unchallengeable ability to control the space environment—is the ultimate U.S. goal.

The new National Space Policy (NSP) released by the Bush administration in 2006 did nothing to assuage concerns about the United States seeking space dominance.[71] Released on a Friday afternoon during a sleepy news cycle before the three-day Columbus Day weekend, the White House Office of Science and Technology Policy produced the long-awaited new policy, a sweeping document providing overarching guidance for America's multiple space programs. Initially, there was little reaction, which was almost certainly the point of burying the story on a slow weekend. In fact, the document was actually signed by President Bush on 31 August, but then apparently held for a few weeks and then released with as little fanfare as possible, thus continuing a previously established administration approach regarding the direction of U.S.

space policy of maintaining a low profile to avoid too much scrutiny and controversy.

On first reading, the new National Space Policy looks much like the Clinton administration's policy enunciated in 1996. Supporters of the Bush policy in fact state that it is little different, except that the language is perhaps a bit less diplomatic. Upon closer examination, however (and more importantly, in the context of actions since 9/11), the changes are dramatic. They are also ambiguous and sometimes inconsistent with already existing policies and programs, and reveal a kind of incoherence and disingenuousness—and militancy—about American space policy in the twenty-first century.

The NSP was actually the fifth space policy document to emerge from the Bush White House. Previous space policy documents from the Bush administration concerned remote sensing; position, navigation, and timing; space transportation; and the Vision for Space Exploration.[72] The new document states that the United States will be guided by several principles in its space policy, some dating back to the Eisenhower administration that clearly indicate the United States is committed to the peaceful uses of space. The publicly released version of the new policy does not endorse space weapons. What it does is make it clear that the United States will not accept a situation whereby other countries can deny America access to space.

A content analysis of the document elucidates differences and similarities from the previous Clinton document.[73] For example, international cooperation and arms control are greatly deemphasized in this new policy. It specifically states, for example, that the United States will accept no limits on what it can do to protect its assets, which basically rejects arms-control efforts and continues the trend initiated by the Rumsfeld Space Commission.

First and foremost, the Bush administration policy enunciates a U.S. space program that is focused on security. A simple indicator: previous NSPs began by elucidating civil space objectives, but in the Bush policy national security objectives come first. Further, whereas the 1996 policy outlined five goals for the U.S. space program and mentioned national security for two of them, the new policy outlines six goals for the U.S. space program and mentions national security in four of them. The opening paragraph of the publicly released version of the policy makes no mention of the administration's earlier space policies, nor were they referenced, so most readers would naturally get the impression that the NSP, allegedly a "comprehensive document," was extraordinarily heavy on security. While the emphasis on security makes obvious sense given U.S. dependence on space assets, the blunt and even confrontational language of the new policy puts the United States at odds with the priorities of the other space-faring nations, for which space assets are primarily considered as essential tools of globalization.

Other areas emphasized or not emphasized in many cases reflect changes in the environment and programmatic priority changes since 1996. The need for space professionals is addressed, citing this need as among the most critical for the future.[74] Space launch is given far less attention in the 2006 policy than in the 1996 policy, likely because the government Evolved Expendable Launch Vehicle program had reached fruition between policies. Frequency spectrum, orbit management, and interference protection—all technical aspects of operating an increasing number of satellites in an increasingly crowded environment around Earth—were included in 2006, whereas they were not addressed in 1996, because the problems and awareness of potential problems in the future had become more acute. Bush's Vision for Space Exploration was mentioned, but not emphasized even though it had been deemed the centerpiece for NASA activities for the foreseeable future. This might well be because it had warranted a policy statement all its own earlier. Ironically, the NSP does state that the Vision is not all NASA should do, though the NASA budget apparently does not provide even enough to accomplish Vision goals. There is no mention of the Space Shuttle or the International Space Station, likely because those programs have fallen from grace in favor of the Vision. Space science, Earth science, and Earth observation are given cursory nods at best. And curiously, a section on space nuclear power is included. It likely refers to specialized equipment used in smallsats and microsats, which are of considerable potential military value.

The NSP is not out of character for the Bush administration. That's good news for some, not-so-good for others. Hence, interpretation of the policy depends on the lens you view it through. From an international perspective, in light of recent U.S. actions abroad, specifically Iraq, it is understandable that administration vows to "take those actions necessary to protect its space capabilities, respond to interference and deny, if necessary, adversaries the use of space capabilities hostile to U.S. interest" are not viewed as an assertion of defense, but a promise of aggression.

Within the United States, if you are among those who see missile defense as a moral imperative and technical success, see technology as the answer for protecting U.S. space assets, see the Chinese ASAT test in 2007 as crossing a space-weapons Rubicon, and continue to cite (long-discredited) claims that the Chinese have a parasite satellite,[75] then this policy is a reasonable response to a clear (and immediate) threat. If you are among those who see the United States as increasingly moving toward the weaponization of space without any clear rationale beyond the presumption of the inevitability that space will become the fourth battlespace, and see technological limits to protecting hardware in space, then this policy merely continues reckless movement in the direction of weaponization, complementing *Air Force Document 2.2–1, Counterspace Operations.*

Less than a week after the new U.S. National Space Policy was released, on 11 October 2006, Robert Luaces, Alternate Representative of the United States to the United Nations General Assembly First Committee, made a statement on the NSP. He talked about the United States recognizing the critical importance of space access and use for its economy and for national security, and encouraged all countries to be committed to that right. He also stated that while America intended to protect its space assets, that did not necessarily mean the use of force.[76] While clearly intending to convince other countries of benign U.S. intentions, actions sometimes speak louder.

The Missile Defense Agency in its FY 2007 budget documentation, cited plans to ask for $45 million in FY 2008 to begin research on a testbed for Space-Based Interceptors (SBI). Presented as purely defensive, that characterization is based on intent rather than technological capability, and clearly, "intent" can change. SBI would add to the inventory of space technology research and development programs with potential for use as weapons, including several microsat programs and other "geewhiz" ones. While Congress has not been supportive of the Space-Based Test Bed through budget allocations,[77] the 2007 Chinese ASAT test provided an opportunity to try to change that.

Other countries, Russia and China in particular, are also interested in many of the same technologies as the United States, especially ground-based laser ASATs, co-orbital microsats, air-launched direct-ascent ASATs, and missile defenses. Even while questioning the technology, defense planners everywhere must act prudently and assume that some of it will be effective in some capacity. Russian President Vladimir Putin voiced strong concerns about plans for ten U.S. missile-defense interceptors to be placed in Poland, and in fact Russia threatened to retarget its missiles toward Europe as a consequence. Negotiations between Poland and the United States for placing those interceptors in Poland hinged largely on money and aid that Poland would receive from the United States—with the Poles driving a "hard bargain" for their support,[78] not any ideological commitment to missile defense.

In the case of the Polish interceptors, the United States has argued that those missiles are intended to counter a missile threat from Iran and would be incapable of taking out Russian missiles. Ironically, a number of prominent U.S. physicists—who do not believe the system will ultimately be effective as a missile defense—have argued that if past government claims about the effectiveness of missile defense are correct, then those Polish missiles will indeed be technically capable of targeting Russian missiles. The physicists claim that presentations by Lt. General Henry "Trey" Obering, director of MDA in Europe (to reassure both Europeans and Russians that U.S. interceptors were of no threat to Russia) were misleading and inconsistent on key points.[79] The scientists making the claims would seem to have the background and be in positions to know what they were talking about: Ted Postol from MIT and former scientific advisor to the chief of naval operations; George Lewis, associate director of the Peace Studies Program at Cornell University; Pavel Podvig from Stanford University's Center for International Security and Cooperation; Richard Garwin, the National Science Award winner who served on the Rumsfeld Commission to assess the ballistic missile threat to the United States in the 1990s; David Wright from the Union of Concerned Scientists; and Phillip Coyle, former assistant secretary of defense during the Clinton administration, in charge of testing U.S. weapons systems. The Missile Defense Agency responded to the criticism saying that the technical assertions made were based on theory, not real world operating premises, and Heritage Foundation analyst Baker Spring, who holds a nontechnical master's degree in national security studies from Georgetown University, said, "I don't think it changes the basic assertion of the administration that this does not pose a threat to Russia."[80] Technical issues aside, others believe the proposed U.S. missile-defense system in Europe "creates much havoc and provides no security in return."[81]

Threat assessments on other countries' capabilities and intents in these areas are widely varied, with exaggerations common and possible because the technological difficulties involved are not commonly understood, are dismissed, or because "intent" is impossible to discern. While the United States adamantly rejects arms control as a limitation on what it could do, arms control would also constrain others from doing things that hold our important assets at risk. While hawks cry "they all cheat!"—there are confines on testing that are verifiable and which limit the development of capabilities. Further, attacks on satellites should be strongly stigmatized, in the same way the use of chemical or biological weapons is stigmatized, with assurances of severe retribution sanctioned by the international community. If the United States proceeds with development of threatening technologies, at staggering costs, others can and will do the same[82]—only in a cheaper, easier, defensive mode rather than trying to become invincible.

Hence, the real danger of the NSP could well be perpetuation of the false belief that space assets can be defended. As already stated—and as the Chinese demonstrated in January 2007 in reality—it is impractical if not impossible from a technical perspective to defend space assets. The only way to protect assets is to outlaw attacks and the technologies that enable attacks, and to try to implement a regime under which attacks can be verified.

In a period when the importance of strategic communications is increasingly recognized in the fight against terrorism, that same importance must be recognized as extending to other policy areas as well. While the more blatant language about space weapons and U.S. intentions to dominate space that many feared would appear in the new NSP is missing, its echo remains. Because space is inherently not the purview of any one country, and increasingly globalized, setting unattainable goals with thinly veiled threats as the implied means for carrying them out is not in the best interests of the United States. The United States would be better served by convincing others that it is not in their interests—economic, societal, or political—to interfere with space assets and by using the rule of law to our benefit—establishing Codes of Conduct for space which would identify nefarious actors and prescribe sanctioned action against them.

Theresa Hitchens's observation in her congressional testimony of 23 May 2007 captures the current situation. She states, "If nothing else, U.S. declaratory policy gives Beijing an excuse to pursue a similar course. China's actions—despite its public dedication to the nonweaponization of space—make it abundantly clear that U.S. space dominance strategy will not go unchallenged."[83] The Chinese ASAT test in January 2007, on the other hand, makes it equally clear that other countries will not hand the United States a veto over their space activities.

Some U.S. lawmakers have considered the Chinese test as an opportunity to point out the threat posed to U.S. space assets and the need for more action on the part of the United States to counter that threat. Republican Senator Jon Kyl from Arizona is among those legislators. Senator Kyl referred to the Chinese ASAT test as a "wake-up call" for lawmakers and made six recommendations for a proposed U.S. response to China:[84]

Implement the proposals of the 2001 Space Commission.
Hold hearings to assure that the Chinese ASAT technology was not based on U.S. technology, shared or stolen.
Assure that the U.S. military has access to operationally responsive space—meaning, the ability to launch and activate quickly militarily useful satellites.
Provide immediate funding for the "Space-Based Test Bed," to include both kinetic and directed-energy components to destroy missiles in their boost phase.

Increase the budget for "space control" programs.
Make "space security" via military means a conservative priority again.

Other politicians have spoken out as well, potentially providing impetus for more weaponization activity. Consequent to the Chinese test, congressman Terry Everett (R-Alabama) argued for a comprehensive space protection strategy. He says: "As an advocate of vigilant defensive space policy, the Chinese antisatellite test is worrisome to me and warrants a clear and considered U.S. response. America must develop a comprehensive space protection strategy, rethink its national security space architecture, and reexamine its policies on space protection and the use of space."[85] Again turning primarily to technology and the military for answers, many of the elements of Everett's strategy have broad-based appeal. He advocates, for example, enhancement of Space Situational Awareness (SSA) capabilities. Besides space debris, with more countries having more assets in space, SSA becomes increasingly important to monitor activities of all sorts, nefarious, unintended, or otherwise. Increased attention to SSA has drawn support from military leaders such as General Kevin Chilton. Speaking at the Twenty-Third National Space Symposium at Colorado Springs in 2007, Chilton said, "Before you can start to address any of these threats and the sustainment of any of these capabilities, a commander in this domain must have the same tools that a commander in every other domain has and needs. Whether it's on land, sea, or air. You need situational awareness."[86] But even with broad spectrum support, rationality and funding are not guaranteed. Even after considerable attention was focused on the need for increased SSA after the Chinese ASAT test, only about $100 million was added to the SSA budget, a paltry amount by Pentagon standards.

Everett also argues for reexamining our national space architecture, including acquisition programs that lead to cost overruns and schedule delays, and developing operationally responsive space (ORS) capabilities in order to reconstitute assets quickly when needed.[87] While inertia and vested interests have always inhibited the former and resources the latter, it is difficult to argue with the logic of either. The Pentagon established an ORS office at Kirtland Air Force Base in New Mexico but it has been consistently underfunded. Further, in 2008 the Pentagon announced it was slashing the already spartan ORS budget to build a next-generation missile warning system. Space system versatility and redundancy are given lip service, but the funding needed to actually develop the capabilities is sacrificed for more near-term programs.[88]

More problematic is Everett's tendency regarding "weapons in space" not to acknowledge that what is defensive dual-use technology from one perspective is often seen as offensive from another. Not acknowledging that reality perpetuates the myth the United States can address its space security issues exclusively through military and technology "fixes" and disregards the clear fact that U.S. policies generate counterproductive responses from other countries.

Finally, it is important to note that whereas the U.S. government has rejected arms control as an approach to enhancing U.S. space security, even members of the military have on occasion spoken out in favor of "rules of the road," which many analysts consider an important first step in moving away from technological solutions to space security problems. General Cartwright has likened "rules of the road"—sometimes also referred to as Codes of Conduct—for space to highway safety laws, allowing parties to sort out incidents according to conduct. "It's not a . . . pointing-a-finger thing," Cartwright said. "But it is an understanding of responsibility and making sure that we have some measure [of behavior]. You expect me to stay on the right-hand side of the road when you approach me and that type of thing."[89] A free-for-all is clearly not in anyone's interest, least of all the United States, with the largest number of space assets potentially at risk. But a free-for-all is where we are headed if a course correction is not made soon.

After the Reagan–Bush Legacy

The United States turned a corner regarding space during the Reagan administration, away from recognition of the physical limitations imposed by the space environment requiring it to be treated differently than the air, land, and sea, and away from using space for stability-reinforcement purposes. Instead, the United States began to treat space as the fourth battlespace and technology as the panacea to all the problems arising from the vulnerabilities inherent in placing valuable assets in an environment out of terrestrial control. Though the inertia built toward treating space as a battlespace and technology as the answer to all problems during the Reagan administration slowed somewhat through the Clinton years, it was reinvigorated when George W. Bush came into office. It is a path doomed to fail. Technology will not be the panacea and pursuing such a course will not only be obscenely expensive with no guarantee of success, it will be counterproductive to U.S. interests because it *will* generate responses from other countries that will neither be to the liking of the United States nor in its best interests. Clearly, other countries have their own agendas (and not always purely benign) in space. The United States, however, is still the leader in space others do not necessarily follow, but certainly key their activities from, to at least some extent. Generating more and more technology is currently the focus of U.S. activity. Therefore, a consideration of the limits of technology—as far as can be discerned—is in order.

Chapter Three
Space Weapons
Fact and Fiction

> Two aliens out in space were looking down on our planet. The first alien said, "It seems the dominant life-forms on Earth have developed satellite-based weapons." The second alien asked, "Are they an emerging intelligence?" "I don't think so," the first responded. "They have the weapons aimed at themselves."

What do the movies *Mission Impossible 2, Enemy of the State, The Peacemaker, Shadow Conspiracy, Patriot Games, The Bourne Identity,* and *Eagle Eye* all have in common? What they all share is their fictionalized use of satellites to further their plots and keep moviegoers interested. Though space policy analyst and writer Dwayne Day set the record straight about how much of what is seen on the movie screen is fictionalized in a 2000 *Washington Post* article,[1] the public likely will be more influenced by images on the big screen born from imagination than factual information either stumbled on or actually sought out. Day states, "In . . . *Mission Impossible 2,* the good guys command a spy satellite to locate a bad guy on the ground. Peering over a computer screen, they watch a terrorist and his former girlfriend kiss on a boat dock in Sydney while the satellite hovers overhead like the Goodyear blimp. The people who build and operate spy satellites would love to be able to do that. But they can not. Such satellites exist only in the movies, where the laws of physics do not apply and satellite technology owes more to *Star Trek* than Silicon Valley." The laws of physics—pesky and inconvenient as they are—must be considered in any evaluation of the feasibility of the American domination of space. Actually, the 2002 movie version of Tom Clancy's book *The Sum of All Fears* was the first and one of the few movies to use and properly portray high-resolution satellite imagery. And even in that movie, imagery was at times doctored to meet the director's needs.[2]

Karl Mueller at the RAND Corporation has suggested the need to acknowledge four "truths" about space weapons that are often overlooked:[3]

Space weapons are inherently political because their utility and impact will depend on how other countries react to them, and the resources required to build them, more than science and engineering;
Military and technical details matter and should not be ignored or oversimplified when discussing space weapons;
Capabilities should be presented realistically, along with costs; and
Debates about space weapons include a great deal of educated guessing and speculation, not certainty.

The first two points are not contradictory though they may look so at first glance. Space weapons are political even if they exist only on a drawing board, because they will generate a reaction whether or not the scientific knowledge or technical ability exists to get them off the drawing board—and at a price that does not result in national sticker shock. Whether or not that scientific knowledge or technical ability exists is important too, because if it does not, funding may be misspent, and negative reactions from other countries may be needlessly generated. While it is beyond the purview of this book to present or analyze technical details of particular programs, the point is that there are those who can, and do, and they are largely being ignored or refuted by armchair pundits, as are those who scrutinize potential costs.

Understandably, beyond the image of an apple falling from a tree and hence Newton's Law of Gravity, the general public does not understand nor care to understand the laws of physics in much depth, especially orbital mechanics. Nor have many members of Congress studied much about physics. But, as pointed out in *The Physics of Space Security*,[4] written by three physicists, consideration of certain facts is critical.

Serious public discussion of military space plans has not yet occurred in the United States, though important questions of policy, planning and budgeting loom: What missions are best carried out from space? What are the likely costs and available alternatives to various space-weapons proposals? How susceptible are satellites to interference? How easily can they be disabled or destroyed? What measures can be taken to reduce their vulnerability? The answers to these questions depend on physical laws and technical facts that are not widely understood outside a rather narrow slice of the science and engineering community.[5]

Quite simply, though space is often compared to the other battle-spaces—air, land, and sea—it is fundamentally different, making most comparisons moot. Proponents of space dominance argue that the United States should seek dominance on land, at sea, and in the air, and doing so in space should be no different. But achieving space dominance is profoundly different from the other areas, in an obvious way that space warriors either do not recognize or choose to ignore. It does not require arguments about specific system architectures to demonstrate this either. To illustrate, a comparison with the Air Force, which wants to dominate the airspace over a theater of operations, is useful. At any given moment, does the Air Force dominate the airspace over Argentina? Or South Africa? Or most other countries? No. Could it attain dominance of the airspace in those locations? Yes, given the time to deploy. But it would only sustain that dominance for as long as needed to support an operation. So their dominance would have limited geographic scope and limited duration. Space dominance, on the other hand, if it is to be effective in the ways its proponents hope (for example, in the ways air dominance is effective in a theater of operations), must be unlimited in scope and duration. It must cover the entire globe, all the time. And hegemonists wonder why this makes foreigners nervous? It sounds like an orbital Iron Curtain.

The challenges of operating on and under water, in the air, or across landmasses are significant and there is no intent to downplay those challenges. Silver bullets are always alluring, on Earth as well as above it. But what is desirable and what is possible are not always the same. In Iraq, directed-energy weapons intended to zap roadside bombs with lasers, microwaves, or electrical bolts—"Darth Vader stuff" as Rear Admiral Arch Macy called them—has proved to be an illusive dream. "The physics get in the way," Macy admits.[6] The physics of space are equally if not considerably more difficult. The challenges of operating in space require that the laws of physics not be ignored, regardless of how much some might like to, and consequently "it is very doubtful that dominance in space can be achieved at feasible cost for basic physical reasons."[7]

Further, it is important to note that in evaluating proposed military systems, physical constraints impact the feasibility of technology development, and consequently cost as well, and unless cost is no object, it must be a consideration of feasibility. While it can and is often argued that technology development changes the parameters of the possible —witness the advancements made in flight generally, regarding both airplanes and spacecraft—and security classifications obscure identification of cutting edge technological accomplishments, physics imposes fundamental limits on space operations that will not change over time. Contrary to the impression given in *Enemy of the State*, a satellite in low orbit of the type they were talking about simply could not hover over a single point on Earth to continually observe Will Smith.

The Physics of Space Security authors point out that new military space systems are intended to carry out four general missions:[8]

Defending U.S. satellites and ensuring U.S. freedom to operate in space.
Denying adversaries the ability to use space assets.
Intercepting ballistic missiles using space-based interceptors.
Attacking targets on the ground or in the air using space-based weapons.

These missions relate to space control and force application rather than space support and force enhancement. A look at some of the constraints related to these missions is in order.

Location, Location, Location

It's all about real estate. Space assets clearly offer advantages not available on Earth. Satellites can see over larger areas than airplanes, offering wide-scale simultaneous observation of the Earth's surface, as well as the ability to communicate between and broadcast to large areas. But as in every real estate market, some spatial neighborhoods are more desirable than others, for particular reasons. For our purposes, four orbits are especially important to consider.

The neighborhood closest to Earth is called low Earth orbit (LEO). It extends roughly from an altitude of 160 kilometers to 2,000 kilometers above the Earth's surface. If the universe were analogous to an urban area, and Earth was one house in one neighborhood, venturing into LEO barely represents leaving the driveway. The Space Shuttle flies in LEO as does the International Space Station. Because LEO is the closest to the Earth, it is also used for many imaging satellites where high resolution is important. The closest view affords the best picture.

Medium Earth orbit (MEO) begins at an altitude of about 10,000 kilometers. MEO is an especially harsh space environment because the Van Allen radiation belts—swirls of radioactive particles potentially damaging to solar cells, integrated circuits, sensors, and humans—are located there. Satellites located in MEO must have built-in protection against the severe environment. MEO is home to the GPS satellites.

Geostationary orbit (GEO) is at an altitude of approximately 35,800 kilometers. GEO is a unique orbit, in that a satellite in GEO rotates at a speed so it remains over a specific spot on the Earth's surface. The satellite is not hovering—it is moving in orbit—but it is moving at a speed that keeps pace with a specific spot below on Earth. The distance from Earth is also such that three equally spaced satellites in GEO can provide almost full Earth coverage, especially important for providing or relaying communications transmissions. Because satellites in GEO remain over one spot, ground antennas critical to signal reception do not have to move. Consequently, most of the large communication satellites are in GEO.

LEO, MEO, and GEO are all orbits around the equator or in a plane that passes through the center of the Earth. If a satellite is traveling in LEO, MEO, or GEO, it will "see" or be able to reach only certain parts of the Earth, within what is called its "footprint." Also, satellites in LEO move relative to the Earth's surface. That is, they circle the Earth approximately every ninety minutes. Therefore, they "see" a particular point on the Earth for only a very short time when overhead, and when returning on its next rotation, the Earth will have moved as well, so they do not "see" the same points each time they pass overhead. This means that there will be coverage "gaps," sometimes for significant (days) periods of time. To alleviate those gaps, constellations of satellites (with mobile communications systems, for example) are often used. Consequently, satellites in some orbits have an inherent problem with absenteeism, meaning that if a satellite is required to be at a specific location at a specific time, multiple satellites are required.

Polar orbits, just as they sound, travel around the Earth's poles. Satellites in polar orbits provide full Earth coverage but again, any particular point on Earth will only be revisited periodically. The National Oceanic and Atmospheric Administration operates two polar satellites known as Polar Operational Environmental Satellites to complement their satellites in GEO.

Space real estate, in any orbit, has inherently high costs. Satellites are expensive, as are launches.

Any object resting on the earth's surface and therefore moving with the earth's own rotational and orbital velocity must acquire nearly eight kilometers per second additional velocity to achieve an orbit around the earth. The cost of imparting that additional velocity has remained constant for several decades despite continuous efforts to reduce it. Once placed in a given orbit, all objects of whatever mass will remain at constant velocity indefinitely, but any change in velocity and therefore in the initial orbit will require an expenditure of energy that does depend on mass. The heavier the object the more expensive it is to launch in the first place and to maneuver out of its initial orbit. Some maneuvers, moreover, are more difficult than others. A proportionate change in altitude—distance to the earth's surface—requires less energy to accomplish for a given mass than a comparably proportionate change in inclination—the angle at which an orbit intersects the earth's equator. Since the energy required for maneuver must be provided by the object itself and adds to its initial launch weight, satellites have been designed to accomplish their purposes with as little weight and orbital maneuver as possible.[9]

That means it takes a lot of rocket fuel to reach space; a significant part of the calculus for how much fuel depends on weight; once in a particular orbit, all objects in that orbit, regardless of weight, travel at the same speed; and maneuvering a satellite once it is in orbit requires the satellite itself to carry fuel, which adds weight and increases the initial launch cost.

In terms of weight and fuel, the weight of satellites carried to LEO on modern rockets is only 2–4 percent of the total rocket weight at the time of launch. "Roughly forty-five tons of propellant are required for every ton of payload placed in orbit."[10] The newest version of the Space Shuttle external tank, for example, which carries the fuel required for liftoff and was specially designed to be as light as possible, weighs 1.680 million pounds at liftoff, and uses all of the fuel contained in the tanks within about eight and a half minutes. How does that translate into cost? A fairly conservative rule of thumb is that it costs between $7,000–$10,000 per pound to launch a satellite into space. Where you want to go and how much your satellite weighs will largely determine the basic cost of what you want to do. Not surprisingly, there is a push to miniaturize satellites and satellite components to conserve weight, but with that miniaturization often comes decreased capability.

Maneuvering in orbit is also an issue. Sending a satellite into space is like buying a car that cannot have the gas tank refilled. You can drive the car until the gas runs out, but after the tank is empty the best you can hope for is to coast for a while longer before you stop. Remember that once a satellite is in orbit, it continues to move in that orbit at a consistent speed unless something changes its speed and/or direction. Satellites have small engines on board to allow them to make those changes. The fuel carried on board the satellites for those motors is like the fuel in a one-tank-of-gas car: once it's gone, it's gone. Maneuvering a satellite—as movies would have audiences believe is done at the drop of a hat—takes fuel and once the fuel is gone the satellite cannot be maneuvered again. Therefore, satellites are not moved willy-nilly. While it seems intuitively obvious that satellites would be sent to orbit with as much fuel as possible, there are practical limits to those amounts since fuel adds weight to the total mass to be launched.

All the space real estate premises, positive and negative, must also be considered within the reality that satellites are also inherently vulnerable. They are bright objects traveling in consistent, predictable, observable orbits against a dark sky, subject to disruption, damage, or destruction from natural (radiation, objects traveling in space) and man-made measures. There is no place for them to hide. "Billion dollar assets with advanced equipment can be disabled by much less sophisticated means—a fact that provides very high leverage to disadvantaged antagonists. Disruption is much easier to accomplish in space than constructive use."[11]

Once a spacecraft is placed in orbit it is, for all intents and purposes, self-reliant. While designed so that people on the ground control the hardware, if there is a problem, they are limited to whatever they can do from Earth. "Repairing, refueling, or updating satellites in orbit is difficult and costly, so it is rarely done."[12] Because the hardware becomes inaccessible once it is launched, the reliability of space-based systems inherently decreases with time. While it is relatively easy to determine if a communication satellite is operating properly because it is routinely used, the reliability of a space-based weapon—on operational standby for extended periods of time but unavailable for either routine or emergency maintenance—would be questionable. While redundancy might seem the answer to this dilemma, figuring that at least one of a constellation of three or four spacecraft would be likely to function in times of crisis, it would take time to move assets to the location needed, potentially losing the time critical to successfully accomplish the mission. The conclusion of a 2007 study by the Center for Strategic and Budgetary Assessments was that ground-based systems were almost always both more cost effective and reliable than space-based weapons, regardless of whether they were being used to attack missiles, enemy satellites, or targets on land.[13]

These real estate issues become clear in two examples relevant to determining whether space dominance is feasible. Consider first a space-based system intended to attack targets on the ground with either kinetic or explosive weapons. To reach Earth quickly, and speed must be considered an important element for military missions, such a system would be located in LEO. If in LEO, because of absenteeism issues, a constellation of satellites would be required. In fact, to be able to attack any point on Earth within thirty minutes would require a constellation of nearly 100 satellites—with commensurate costs. Testing that system would be difficult if not impossible under realistic conditions, and then it would have to sit basically idle until needed, trusting that it will work when called upon. The same arguments hold true for space-based missile defense, intended to intercept long-range missiles during their boost phase. The boost phase of a rocket, when the rocket motor (to get it to orbit) is still burning, lasts only minutes. While it may be impossible to place interceptors close enough to the launch site to reach them from Earth during that short boost phase, a system based in LEO could afford global coverage. The problem is that if a country can launch a missile, even a short-range missile, it also has the capability to reach a target in LEO, making the system extremely vulnerable. Destroying one or more of the space-based interceptors creates a hole through which a long-range missile could be launched. The vulnerability of this kind of a space-based interceptor system also means that it would be virtually impossible for one nation to deny another nation access to space. Certainly having to first destroy an interceptor before launching a payload into orbit raises the risk and cost of launch in all kinds of ways, but if a country were willing to assume the risk and cost, it technically could do so. These kinds of considerations are too often ignored.

Plans to defend vital U.S. space assets and "control" the space domain through technology, including potentially denying others access to that domain, are fraught with peril. Therefore, it is worth considering some of the programs those plans currently include.

Silver Bullet or White Elephant?

Missile-defense programs are generally divided into three categories, boost phase, mid-course phase, and terminal phase, corresponding to the different phases of the ballistic missile flight regime being targeted for destruction. Additionally, the initial portion of the mid-course phase, after the missile's booster burns out but before the warhead is deployed, is sometimes considered separately, as the ascent or early ascent phase.[14] Each phase offers different advantages and disadvantages to a missile-defense system; therefore a layered defense should theoretically improve overall defense effectiveness. Currently, attempts to provide the United States with a missile-defense system focus on ground-based, mid-course missile-defense programs, and is therefore officially called the ground-based, mid-course missile-defense (GMD) system. Besides mid-course programs, there are also programs to destroy missiles in their boost, ascent, and terminal phases, though these programs are being less aggressively pursued at this time.

Missile defense is either the nation's most important moral imperative or it is an unworkable solution to a problem that does not exist, depending on your perspective. On that spectrum of opinions, there is not much middle ground either. If you believe that (1) the risk of a country firing a nuclear-tipped missile at the United States is high enough that (2) the United States should be willing to spend whatever amount of national treasure (likely hundreds of billions of dollars) is necessary to develop technology that many top physicists do not believe will work, then (3) it is the nation's most important moral imperative. If you believe that (1) countries realize that firing a missile at the United States would lead to devastating consequences, (2) that terrorism is the bigger threat (and it is highly unlikely terrorists could acquire missiles with such capabilities), and (3) that ultimately the technology will not work as a defensive capability, then (4) the program is a profitable boondoggle for contractors and science labs, and primarily serves as rhetoric for politicians seeking to show that they (as opposed to those who do not support the program) care about protecting U.S. citizens.

According to the White House in 2003:

We are pursuing an evolutionary approach to the development and deployment of missile defenses to improve our defenses over time. The United States will not have a final, fixed missile-defense architecture. Rather, we will deploy an initial set of capabilities that will evolve to meet the changing threat and to take advantage of technological developments. The composition of missile defenses, to include the number and location of systems deployed, will change over time.

In August 2002, the Administration proposed an evolutionary way ahead for the deployment of missile defenses. The capabilities planned for operational use in 2004 and 2005 will include ground-based interceptors, sea-based interceptors, additional Patriot (PAC-3) units, and sensors based on land, at sea, and in space. In addition, the United States will work with allies to upgrade key early warning radars as part of our capabilities.

Under our approach, these capabilities may be improved through additional measures such as:

Deployment of additional ground- and sea-based interceptors, and Patriot (PAC-3) units; Initial deployment of the THAAD [Theater High Altitude Area Defense] and Airborne Laser systems; Development of a family of boost-phase and mid-course hit-to-kill interceptors based on sea-, air-, and ground-based platforms; Enhanced sensor capabilities; and Development and testing of space-based defenses.

The Defense Department will begin to implement this approach and will move forward with plans to deploy a set of initial missile-defense capabilities beginning in 2004.[15]

With no final architecture anticipated, cost estimates are elusive at best. As mentioned in Chapter 1, the range of estimates has been between $40 billion—which has already been surpassed by a factor of more than two—to $1 trillion. The administration request of $9.3 billion for missile defense in FY 2007 was the largest single research and development program in the FY 2007 Pentagon budget, most of it focused on GMD systems. Congress funded it at an even higher rate, $9.4 billion.[16] According to the Congressional Budget Office, annual costs for missile defense could rise to $19 billion in a few years. Further, the Government Accountability Office (GAO) issued a report in February 2008 stating that the previous year, "MDA [Missile Defense Agency] fielded fewer assets, increased costs by about $1 billion and conducted fewer tests. Even with the cost increase, MDA deferred work to keep costs from increasing further, as some contractors overran their fiscal year 2007 budgets."[17] And all this even though it was already the largest research and development program in the Department of Defense. GAO's particular concern was that "MDA has been given unprecedented funding and decision-making flexibility. While this flexibility has expedited BMDS fielding, it has also made MDA less accountable and transparent in its decisions than other major programs, making oversight more challenging."[18] In other words, spending is rampant and there is little accountability.

If the system could protect the United States from a nuclear attack, $1 trillion would be a bargain price. But it can not. If the system worked perfectly, it could stop one or a very few warheads launched by ICBMs from reaching the United States. Many technical experts, who should and do know, do not believe the system will work perfectly. Further, it would have no capability against such alternative attacks as cruise missiles or WMD brought into the country through likely cheaper, easier, and more "plausibly deniable" methods, such as a suitcase bomb. And, while risks certainly remain, "the number of long-range missiles fielded by China and Russia has decreased 71 percent since 1987. The number of medium-range ballistic missiles pointed at U.S. allies in Europe and Asia has fallen 80 percent."[19] Nevertheless, support for missile defense endures. As George Orwell once reminded us, "One does not dispose of a belief by showing that it's irrational."[20]

Hitting a bullet with a bullet, as missile defense has been described, is hard—harder than hitting a satellite in a known, predictable orbit. Even theater missile defense, less technically challenging, has experienced significant technical difficulties. During the Gulf War in 1991, Patriot missiles were heralded as successfully defending against Iraqi Scud missiles. Yet, MIT's Ted Postol and George Lewis challenged that assertion, stating that contrary to Pentagon claims, Patriot missiles had shot down few if any Iraqi Scud missiles. The authors were originally ridiculed for their contentions, but Clinton administration Secretary of Defense William Cohen eventually admitted that the Patriot had not worked.[21] In fact, retrospective assessment questions whether there was even one successful hit.[22]

National missile defense requires multiple connected systems to work flawlessly within a period of minutes. Once a missile is launched, the rocket plume must be detected and the impact point established, requiring sophisticated space and ground tracking systems and computational analysis capabilities. The interceptor must then be fired and its flight path refined while it is in its short flight, as sophisticated tracking systems continue to follow the target. Ideally, the interceptor reaches and destroys the target in midcourse. Obviously, it is impossible to test these multiple systems in operational conditions, making reliability tenuous. A review of tests to date, however, indicates that even in highly choreographed tests, the results have been mixed at best.

The Clinton administration had committed to national missile defense only if it proved technically feasible. The first tests conducted, while Clinton was in office, were perhaps understandably highly scripted.

Tests were designed for the interceptor to zero in on the brightest thing in the sky, so the target was illuminated. But even under these conditions, things did not go as intended. Of the three ground-based interceptor tests conducted between 1999 and 2000, only one could be counted as a success, and that success was more luck than skill. Initially, the kill vehicle was unable to find the mock warhead, and instead began to home in on a bright balloon decoy (evidencing the importance of a satellite being a bright object against a dark sky). Luckily, the balloon and the warhead were close enough that the warhead appeared in the field of vision of the kill vehicle, which then found its target. The Pentagon's director of operational testing and evaluation subsequently stated that there was no basis to classify the test as either a success or failure, because it was unclear whether the kill vehicle could have found the warhead were it not for the fortuitous position of the decoy balloon.[23]

When the Bush administration took office, paced development and deployment of missile defense based on successful testing was jettisoned. In 2002, operational deployment of interceptors in Alaska and California was ordered to take place by September 2004 even though only preliminary developmental tests of system components, rather than the system as a whole, had been conducted. Test failures were no longer an option. Before a December 2001 test, the media reported, "The head of the U.S. missile-defense program said a planned test Saturday night will be considered a success even if an interceptor and dummy warhead failed to smash into each other 144 miles above the South Pacific. 'This is not a pass-fail test,' said Lt. Gen. Ronald Kadish, director of the Pentagon's Ballistic Missile Defense Organization. 'Success would be if we learned a lot and gained confidence for the next step.'"[24] Carefully scripted, the kill vehicle did intercept the target in that test. By December 2002, there were eight ground-based interceptor tests: five "successes" and three failures. After a test failure in December 2002 and renewed concerns from skeptics about technical feasibility and exorbitant government expenditures, the Pentagon simply "postponed" further testing. The next test was not held until December 2004, after the presidential election. It failed too, attributed to "an unknown anomaly." According to Lieutenant General Henry Obering, the new director of the Missile Defense Agency, a "glitch" caused the test failure.[25] After the December 2004 failure, Senator Jack Reed (D-Rhode Island), a member of the Senate Armed Services Committee, questioned whether money spent by the Pentagon on missile defense might be better spent elsewhere, especially given the mounting costs of operations in Iraq and Afghanistan. By contrast, a spokesman for program advocate Senator John Kyl (R-Arizona) said that "one bum test" would not alter support for the program.[26] But even General Obering, in an apparent moment of candor later in 2005, revealed a little skepticism, stating that the system had a "greater than zero" chance of working.[27]

Throughout 2005, delays and testing failures plagued the program, though interceptors had been deployed to Alaska in 2004. David Duma, acting Director of Operational Test and Evaluation for the Pentagon, reported in his FY2005 Report, issued in January 2006, that "while the system currently being deployed 'may have some inherent defensive capability,' its battle management system 'has not yet demonstrated engagement control' and that 'there is insufficient evidence to support a confident assessment of [even] limited defensive operations.'" He also admitted that planned tests will "lack operational realism." A January 2006 Congressional Research Service report confirmed Duma's negative assessment and stated there was no evidence of a learning curve in the tests.[28]

The interceptors were declared operational in July 2006, not because of technical breakthroughs or achievements, but coinciding with the North Korean attempt to launch the intercontinental Taepo-Dong 2 missile. "U.S. Northern Command brought the 100th Missile Defense Brigade (Ground-Based Mid-course Defense) to operational level for the first time in response to the July 2006 North Korean missile crisis."[29] But declaring it operational does not make it so. While the interceptors were "activated," meaning they could be launched, for a capability to be declared operational usually implies that the full system has been fully and successfully tested, itself requiring that the military have operational plans for integrating the system into its planning. Those issues have not been fully resolved.

Like its predecessor the Taepo-Dong 1, the North Korean missile crashed into the ocean forty seconds after launch—call it the "Go-Wrong 2"—but North Korea's determination to launch it succeeded only in lending credence to the arguments of U.S. missile-defense advocates. The United States should be grateful that the North Korean rocketry performed so poorly, otherwise it might have been forced to fire an interceptor, only to reveal that the emperor has no clothes. The whole affair was an unsteady game of chicken in which North Korea test-fired a missile it was not sure could fly while the United States activated a system it was not sure could catch the missile. In the end, it was the North Koreans who failed, but it could as easily have been the United States.[30] The action taken by the United States in declaring the system operational "appears to be a public relations ploy designed to create the perception that the administration is defending the country against a possible missile attack from North Korea."[31] General Obering, meanwhile, as his position would warrant, was optimistic and positive about the program. "Does the system work? The answer is yes to that. . . . Is it going to work against more complex threats in the future? We believe it will."[32]

The entire issue of missile-defense tests and what constitutes success versus failure is worth further consideration because it seems that what constitutes a success changes, creating a shell game for those trying to technically assess the program. Multiple organizations keep track of missile-defense tests. Chronologies are available at the websites of organizations including the Center for Defense Information (CDI), the Missile Defense Agency (MDA), and the Missile Defense Advocacy Alliance.[33] How successes are tallied, however, varies. Regarding the test in September 2007, MDA said it was the sixth successful intercept out of ten tests.[34] The Missile Defense Advocacy Alliance website heralded it the seventh successful test.[35] Center for Defense Information analysts, however, calculated the test to be the seventh successful test out of thirteen attempts —a very different ratio than implied by the others.[36] The problem is that MDA disavows flight tests where the interceptor fails to leave the launch pad due to engineering problems, such as occurred in December 2004 and February 2005. Those tests simply "don't count," though in a real world situation they certainly would, with potentially catastrophic results. During a test in May 2006, the test did not go off because the target did not fly where it was supposed to, indicating both how scripted the tests are and how test results are manipulated to appear in the most flattering light.

A Center for Defense Information analysis entitled "Missile Defense by the Numbers" examined the tortured logic of determining a successful test, how the goal posts for determining success keep changing, and the unrealistic nature of the tests themselves. The report's author, Victoria Samson, stated:

Perhaps the strongest question mark comes from MDA's assertion that the last successful test flight intercept of the GMD system now should not be included in the overall success column. This was the September 2006 test where the Pentagon scored its first GMD flight test intercept in just under four years. Oddly enough, it was trumpeted at the time as an intercept and a success. Now, however, MDA is backtracking and stating that because an intercept wasn't the primary objective of the September 2006 test, it should not be included in the whole tally. If that is indeed the case, then MDA's much-vaunted GMD system, the one that takes the lion's share of the missile defense budget, the one that the United States is looking to expand to Eastern Europe, and the one that is souring relations with Russia, last scored an intercept five years ago, in July 2002—hardly a program that is barreling along, success after success.[37]

The analysis went on to examine how countermeasures, those measures that opponents can take to thwart missile defense, are increasingly being dropped from the tests to improve the chances of success. Whether any country bold enough to fire a missile at the United States would also be similarly accommodating is doubtful.

The first intercept attempt for the GMD program occurred in October 1999 and included a simple decoy, decoys being among the simplest of potential countermeasures that adversaries could use. Eventually, by the 2002 tests, three decoys were included. After that, however, the numbers of decoys deployed dropped off. "This is an important point to make, as one of the biggest frailties of the missile-defense system is its inability to determine in a cloud of objects which is the threat missile and which is a harmless decoy."[38]

Other systems are under development as well. Two boost phase systems are being developed by the MDA: the Airborne Laser and the Kinetic Energy Interceptor. The Navy's Aegis ballistic missile-defense system is a mid-course system, though the MDA sometimes talks about it as an ascent system, meaning early midcourse, because it is deployed close to North Korea and would have to intercept a missile early in its flight. The Aegis is the most advanced of these three systems. According to a report MDA sent to Congress in 2007, these programs also have problems, including countermeasures potentially being even more challenging than those associated with the mid-course phase.[39] According to some reports as well, the already operational Russian TOPOL SS-27 missile is immune to currently considered antiballistic missile defenses:

The missile is capable of making evasive maneuvers as it approaches its target, enabling it to evade any terminal phase interceptors. It almost certainly also carries countermeasures and decoys to decrease the chances of a successful targeting. The missile is shielded against radiation, electromagnetic interference and physical disturbance; previous missiles could be disabled by detonating a nuclear warhead within ten kilometers. This vulnerability is the basis behind the use of nuclear ground-based and orbital interceptors, to detonate or damage the missile before it reaches its target. However, the SS-27 is designed to be able to withstand nuclear blasts closer than 500 m, a difficult interception when combined with the terminal phase speed and maneuverability. While the boost phase is the most vulnerable time for the SS-27, it remains protected. Hidden safely within missile silos and mobile launchers, a successful boost-phase interceptor would have to be fired from near or within Russian borders or from space. And the SS-27 is also designed to survive a strike from any laser technology available, rendering any current space-based laser useless.[40]

That the Russians are capable of such a system demonstrates the clear limits to the feasibility of missile defense.

For missile-defense advocates, technical feasibility, including challenges to the test success record, simply do not matter and challenges are seen as "belittling" the system. After the September 2007 test and the CDI analysis, Peter Huessey, president of GeoStrategic Analysis, published an editorial in the *Washington Times*, stating: "The United States recently tested a missile-defense system. The interceptor from Vandenberg USAF base in California smashed into a target launched from Alaska in a demonstration of the technological prowess of U.S. industry. A message was sent to North Korea that any rocket launched at Los Angeles is going to be destroyed—in other words, that nuclear blackmail was off the table."[41] The article goes on to chastise the CDI analysis as asserting "that there is no need for a missile defense against Iranian or North Korean rockets because both are no threat to either the United States or our European allies."[42] Perhaps Huessey was reading a different analysis—the CDI report focuses on the technical success and failure rate of system tests, not threat assessments of need. His editorial, on the other hand, ignored technical issues and instead focused on the 1995 NIE as a rationale for the program, though the 1995 NIE at the time it was released was seen as a roadblock to national missile defense and was used by the Clinton administration to focus more on TMD than NMD. Advocacy for missile defense, as stated in Chapter 1, hinges on factors other than program feasibility.

"Rods from God" and Other Assorted Space Weapons

The first problem in addressing the contentious issue of space weapons is just defining the term. Numerous definitions for space weapons are found in the literature, across a wide range of perspectives. Basically, they can be categorized into three types. The narrowest definitions hold that space weapons are those systems in which the destructive component resides in orbit. A slightly broader category includes both terrestrial and space-based systems directed at space-based and terrestrial targets. The broadest category includes fundamentally all space systems: any dual-use capability, including sensors and propulsion contributing to space-weapons capabilities, systems contributing to force enhancement such as GPS and communications satellites, and systems passing through space, such as ICBMs or even the Space Shuttle. The first category is so narrow it excludes a number of ground-based or air-based programs that would result in the same effect as space-based programs, such as destruction of a satellite. The last category is so broad, however, that it offers little utility. Many systems fitting into the category are already in existence and deployed, making the question of whether space should be weaponized moot.

Nevertheless, definitions set the framework for discussion and analysis. And while disagreement on definitions should not be an excuse for avoiding discussion on issues such as space weapons, it often is used, and sometimes deliberately, as a red herring. Decades ago, it was just as difficult to define an ICBM for treaty purposes, but it was accomplished. ICBMs were defined as a weapons delivery system with a range of at least 5,500 kilometers and a ballistic trajectory over most of its flight path. Which basing modes were permissible were specified, and limits were placed on launch weight, throw weight, and rapid reloading capability. Provisions were also made for inspection. If definitions could be developed for ICBMs, there is no reason they cannot be formulated for space weapons. Self-serving proclamations about the impossibility of defining space weapons are found even in government documents. In a January 2008 memo from Brian Green, Deputy Assistant Secretary of Defense for Strategic Capabilities,[43] Green noted that "the last five Administrations have not been able to overcome the complexities of defining a 'space weapon.'" The line of argument used by space-weapons advocates contends that you cannot talk about limiting, prohibiting, or otherwise regulating space weapons until you define them. But, their circular reasoning goes, since it's impossible to define space weapons, discussion must end.

For the purposes of discussion here, space weapons are defined as: Any ground-based system designed or operated for the purpose of physically disabling or destroying the space segment of a space system, or any space-based system designed or operated for the purpose of physically disabling or destroying targets in space, on the ground, or in the atmosphere. Note that all types of weapons are covered by this definition, explosive, kinetic, and directed energy. If such a definition were used as part of a treaty, the definition is not so broad as to ban every rocket or payload that can reach space. However, if behavior such as testing makes it clear that an operator was going to use some otherwise innocuous piece of hardware as a weapon, this change of purpose could be considered a violation and subject to sanctions. This definition also does not cover jammers, which are hard to verify. But jammers do not inflict permanent damage or cause space debris, and there are a variety of ways to counter them, so it is acceptable to deal with them separately. While the United States does not *officially* have a space-weapons program nor endorse the development of space weapons, work is being done toward developing technology that would well fall into this definition of space weapons.

The second issue is the dual-use nature of the technology. Dual use has two connotations: technology appropriate for use by either the military or for civilian purposes, and technology that can be used for either offensive or defensive purposes. Both generate considerable space security issues because space technology is at least 95 percent dual use. So, satellites developed for crop monitoring—in China, the United States or anywhere—can also be used for monitoring troop movements.

Rockets used for lifting communications satellites to broadcast CNN, Fox News, and Al Jazeera use the same fundamentals of rocket science required to launch missiles carrying warheads. And those same communication satellites that can broadcast the news can also be useful to the military.

More to the point for this discussion is technology that can be used both offensively and defensively. Missile defense, as already pointed out, is technically better suited for use as an ASAT weapon. Small satellites for scientific missions or other missions that can be maneuvered can be used as a kinetic-kill ASAT against other satellites if sufficiently sophisticated, as pointed out with the Chinese BX-1 example. Intent is difficult to decipher and depends largely on trust, something largely lacking in the politics of space security nowadays.

It is also important to point out what we do not know. The Center for Defense Information, which specifically monitors defense budgets for programs that could fall into the category of space weapons, points out that classified programs are an "unknowable known": "Between FY06 and FY07, the unclassified top line budgets of some classified programs with MDA, Defense Advanced Research Project Agency (DARPA) and the Air Force increased almost 60 percent. In the FY 2008 budget, these top line figures, too, are classified . . . The distribution of money within these classified budgets to space-related weaponry research is unknown."[44] What we do know, however, is that there are programs that could result in the development and deployment of space weapons.

Programs of specific concern include the Space-Based Interceptor Test Bed, the Near Field Infrared Experiment (NFIRE), Experimental Spacecraft System (XSS), the Autonomous Nanosatellite Guardian for Evaluating Local Space (ANGELS), and the Starfire Optical Range. All are either funded or repeatedly have shown up on the President's request list. While others such as the Hypervelocity Rod Bundles program—dubbed Rods from God—get more attention (and a cover on the June 2004 *Popular Science*), it is still in the conceptual stage, far short of the point at which hardware is being built or tested. Nevertheless, it has advocates. Michael Goldfarb, writing in support of the program in the *Weekly Standard*, describes the system.

The system would likely be comprised of tandem satellites, one serving as a communications platform, the other carrying an indeterminate number of tungsten rods, each up to twenty feet in length and one foot in diameter. These rods, which could be dropped on a target with as little as fifteen minutes notice, would enter the Earth's atmosphere at a speed of 36,000 feet per second—about as fast as a meteor. Upon impact, the rod would be capable of producing all the effects of an earth-penetrating nuclear weapon, without any of the radioactive fallout. This type of weapon relies on kinetic energy, rather than high-explosives, to generate destructive force. . . . Clearly the rods are a first-strike, offensive weapon.[45]

TABLE 2. Selected Space Programs in the President's FY 2008 Defense Budget Request

PE[a]	RI	Program	Service	2006	2007	2008	"+/−"	Note
0603040lF	26	Advanced Spacecraft Technology Experimental Satellites Series (XSS)[b]	USAF	86.3 27.2	101.1 27.5	**78.7** **28.9**	−22.4 1.4	This PE "develops, integrates, and demonstrates . . . spacecraft payloads, space craft protection, spacecraft, and launch vehicles," among other technologies. The Integrated Space Technology Demonstration sub-element, which is believed to fund XSS, develops microsatellites (10–100kg) for "space situational awareness and/or tactical satellite concepts." While the FY 2008 request does not specifically mention the microsats for "autonomous proximity operations," the FY 2007 request does.
0602601F	11	Space Technology Spacecraft Protection Technology	USAF	103.6 2.1	103.5 1.9	**109.6** **2.5**	6.1 0.6	This PE is believed to include ANGELS. Efforts under this project include: (i) "develop key satellite threat warning technologies and tools for high value satellite asset defense" and (ii) "develop high value space asset defensive capabilities."

Table 2. Selected Space Programs in the President's FY 2008 Defense Budget Request (Continued)

PE[a]	RI	Program	Service	2006	2007	2008	"+/−"	Note
0603438F	45	Space Control Technology Space Range Defensive Counterspace Offensive Counterspace	USAF	14.6 4.5	30.1 5.8	**37.6** **12.1**	7.5 6.3	This incubation project supports a range of space control activities from technology development and prototyping to simulations and exercises. USAF notes "Consistent with DoD policy, the negation efforts of this program *currently* [emphasis added] focus on negation technologies which have temporary, localized, and reversible means."
0604857F	61	Operationally Responsive Space	USAF		35.4	**87**	51.6	This program encompasses research and development on quick-reaction launch vehicles and satellites. This, together with the Common Aero Vehicle (see below), constitutes the USAF contribution to DARPA's Falcon program.

0604856F	60	Common Aero Vehicle (CAV)/ Hypersonic Technology Vehicle	USAF	26.5	33.2	**32.8**	−0.4	CAV is being designed as a hypersonic glide vehicle that will dispense conventional weapons, sensors, and payloads worldwide
0603287E	33	Falcon/Hypersonic Cruise Vehicle	DARPA	38.6	51.5	**50**	−1.5	from and through space within one hour of tasking. In 2004, Congress barred any work to "weaponize" the CAV, and as a result the program was restructured and has been renamed Hypersonic Technology Vehicle.
0604421F	76	Counterspace Systems	USAF	28.2	50.3	**53.4**	3.1	This is the principal account for funding offensive and defensive counterspace systems and command and control. Efforts currently focus on two systems: (i) a ground-based mobile jammer (CCS) and (ii) a method for detecting attacks on satellites (RAIDRS).
		Counter Satellite Communications System		6.0	16.0	**18.0**	2.0	
		Rapid Identification Detection and Reporting System		17.5	22.1	**28.1**	6.0	
		Offensive Counterspace Command and Control		4.7	12.3	**7.3**	−5.0	

TABLE 2. Selected Space Programs in the President's FY 2008 Defense Budget Request (Continued)

PE[a]	RI	Program	Service	2006	2007	2008	"+/−"	Note
0305173F	197	Space & Missile Test Evaluation Center	USAF		4.7	**3.1**	−1.6	This program began in FY 2007. The main objective is to "transition R&D space vehicle technology with residual military utility to operational status for immediate real world support and to perform initial operational utility assessment for future acquisition programs." While the FY 2007 request noted that the program would provide "rapid support of counter-space systems missions," the FY 2008 budget does not.
0603985C	85	BMD System Space Program	MDA	0	0[c]	**27.7**	27.7	FY 2007 funding for NFIRE was "deemed insufficient for the current schedule"; the second mission has been delayed. According to MDA, "Near term funding for the space test bed program will be used to refine concepts and prepare to conduct focused experiments demonstrating the viability of the concepts."
		Near-Field Infrared Experiment			36.0	**36.0**	0	
		Space Test Bed				**10**	10.0	

ID	#	Program	Agency					Description
603894C	84	Multiple Kill Vehicles (MKV)	MDA	48.4	144.4	**271.2**	126.8	The MKV has been mentioned in the past as the preferred interceptor for a space-based missile defense.
0603175C	30	Ballistic Missile Defense (BMD) Technology Micro Satellite Experiment	MDA	147.3	193.3	**118.6**	−74.7 (cancelled)	"At the conclusion of FY 2007, this task will have demonstrated the ability of domestic industry to design and develop components needed to develop future space sensing and target capabilities using micro satellites." The program has been cancelled for FY 2008.
0603287E	33	Tiny, Independent Coordinating Spacecraft (TICS)	DARPA	48		**6.0**	1.2	Will develop technologies to permit delivery of "small, hard-to-detect nano satellites" into "any common operational orbit" with "little or no warning." "Such systems could perform rapid response reconnaissance on any spacecraft with times to mission orbit measured in just hours." The nanosatellites, housed on a "mothership," would further employ "advanced robotic technologies to allow satellites to reconfigure on demand."

TABLE 2. Selected Space Programs in the President's FY 2008 Defense Budget Request (Continued)

PE[a]	RI	Program	Service	2006	2007	**2008**	"+/−"	Note
0603287E	33	Front-end Robotics Enabling Near-term Demonstration (FREND)	DARPA	9.1	13.2	**14.4**	1.2	Designed to "autonomously grapple space object out outfitted with custom interfaces" in GEO. Provides the potential for spacecraft salvage, repair, rescue, reposition, de-orbit and retirement, and debris removal.

[a] PE stands for Program Element number which represents a discrete budget line item and pot of funding.

[b] Experimental Satellite program is founded as "3834 Integrated Space Technology Demonstrations" with some elements, such as command and control software contained within "2181 Spacecraft Payloads."

[c] This figure is zero because NFIRE was not funded through this Program Element in FY 2007.

Notes: NFIRE was shifted between Program Elements yet again this year, and for FY 2008 is scheduled to receive funding from two programs: PE 603175C (BMD Technology) and PE 0603893C (Space Tracking and Surveillance Program). Total NFIRE funding for FY 2008 is $36 million. The Space-Based Test Bed and NFIRE, among others, will be managed by the Missile Defense Space Experiment Center (MDSEC).

Source: Theresa Hitchens, Victoria Samson and Sam Black, "Space Weapons Spending in the FY 2008 Defense Budget," 21 February 2007, http://www.cdi.org.

Goldfarb acknowledges "myriad technical and political hurdles to deployment," but he and others remain supportive, though scientists point out that it would cost fifty to one hundred times as much as a similar attack from the ground,[46] if technically viable. That suggests an attachment based more on emotion than rationality.

Even at the conceptual stage though, other countries pay attention. A 2006 article in a New Zealand newspaper characterizes the head-scratching puzzlement felt even in many friendly countries about U.S. plans in space. "Advocates dream of having futuristic space weapons straight out of Flash Gordon. In its Transformation Flight Plan of November 2003—which reveals what sort of weapons might be deployed in the future—the Air Force introduced Rods From God, a hypersonic cruise vehicle that would fire uranium, titanium or tungsten cylinders at targets at 11,585km/h, a vision that defies physics."[47] Countries like China feel they can not afford to just wonder about U.S. intentions and must assume that if the United States is considering a concept like Rods from God, it must have a mission in mind for it once developed. After all, that's the way the system was supposed to work before capabilities-based planning, as articulated in the 2001 QDR, replaced threat-based planning and opened the door to the unrealistic "we want it all" approach.

The Space-Based Test Bed program, recommended by Senator Kyl[48] after the Chinese ASAT, is intended to investigate the potential utility and technical feasibility of adding a space-based missile-defense layer, to complement the ground-based mid-course intercept system already declared operational. The FY 2008 request for funding was to conduct proof-of-concept activity toward providing options regarding future deployment decisions. The program has been on MDA's wish list for some time, but Congress keeps derailing funding due to MDA's unambiguous intent to deploy weapons in space. While in FY 2007, MDA had intended to ask for $45 million to begin work in FY 2008, that was delayed and the FY 2008 request asked for only $10 million. Proponents such as Senator Kyl argued that "The United States better get serious about defending our eyes and ears in space."[49] Opponents, such as ardent critic Senator Byron Dorgan (D-North Dakota) said the funds could be "better used elsewhere as threats to U.S. space assets are lower compared with the prospects of weapons of mass destruction being smuggled into the country."[50] The $10 million request was not approved for FY 2008, but these programs are like telemarketers: they never stop calling or just go away.

NFIRE is a small satellite capable of maneuvering—a capability the United States considers highly nefarious and dangerous in the hands of the Chinese. Officially part of the Pentagon's search for a boost phase missile-defense system, it has gone through multiple iterations. At one time the configuration included a kill vehicle, a capability that MDA initially flaunted. "In February 2003, when the Pentagon's Missile Defense Agency reported to Congress on its upcoming research, it expressed pride in the kill vehicle, even if the one on the first NFIRE test would be a nonmaneuvering one: "The Generation 2 kill vehicle (KV) will be integrated into the experiment payload," the report stated, adding that such platforms would be "the first KVs with the performance to reliably achieve boost phase intercept."[51] Later, at Congressional hearings, MDA backpedaled:

"It is my understanding that this portion of the program would enable MDA to develop technology that can be applied to space-based weapons," Sen. Daniel Akaka, D-Hawaii, told Air Force Undersecretary Peter Teets. "My question to you is, is the NFIRE program intended to pursue space-weapons capabilities?"

"It is true that the kind of capability that NFIRE will have could, with a different concept of operations, be used as a space-based weapon capability," Teets replied. "But there's no such concept of operations that I'm aware of that is under consideration at this point in time. . . . A modified kill vehicle had to be used for the test," Teets said, because "I don't know how else you can do that—I mean, if you're going to get close to it, you're not going to do it with an airplane."[52]

Congress stripped NFIRE of the kill vehicle in 2004, and a German-built laser communications terminal was added instead. Nevertheless, MDA has not given up on trying to get it back, though so far it has been unsuccessful. Experiments for FY 2008 include having it fly by an accelerating booster missile at ranges less than ten kilometers.

Clementine 1 was a satellite sent to map the lunar surface in 1994. Considered a potential model for future missions, it was a sensor technology demonstration for the old SDIO and carried NASA equipment to conduct a never-done-before lunar survey, representing a cost-effective way to achieve civil and military goals simultaneously. Clementine 2 was to be a follow-on mission, with a 1998 launch to intercept three Near Earth Objects and hit each with a small high-speed probe. In 1997 though, President Clinton used the Line Item Veto to delete $30 million in funding for Clementine 2 from the FY 1998 budget. Clinton was not an advocate for the development of space weapons, and there were concerns regarding the potential for the technology to be tested also to be used as an ASAT. Some people considered Clementine 2 a Trojan Horse: the Air Force and SDIO were trying to develop ASAT technology while claiming other purposes. The XSS, however, is based on technology from the old Clementine 2 program, again showing that these programs never really die.

An Air Force program, the first two XSS satellites were launched in 2003 and 2005. XSS is a microsatellite program: microsats weigh between ten and five hundred kilograms (22–1,100 lb.) and therefore are cheaper to both build and launch. Their missions were to conduct "proximity operations" in LEO, meaning that they were to attempt to fly close to other satellites. Ostensibly, the satellites are a step toward developing the capability to refuel, resupply, repair, and reposition satellites from space. They are 300-pound, dishwasher size microsatellites, launched on Minotaur rockets, which are refurbished Minuteman missiles. But, "in addition, USAF budget documents show that the XSS program is related to P 0603605F Advanced Weapons Technology, which is dedicated to research on laser and microwave weapons. Thus, the XSS program could evolve into a space-based kinetic-energy and/or a directed-energy ASAT program."[53] One defense official, speaking on the condition of anonymity in 2003 stated, "XSS-10 and -11 [were] both designed for the same mission. XSS-11 can be used as an ASAT weapon."[54] A follow-on satellite demonstration is called for in FY 2009 according to the FY 2008 budget.

The ANGELS program was first announced in 2005. Originally it was intended as a nanosatellite program: nanosatellites having a wet mass[55] between one and ten kilograms (2.2–22 lb.). The ANGELS experiment was conceived as a tiny—that is, "nano"—satellite that would be placed in an orbit near a larger satellite so it could watch for signs of trouble (hence the "guardian" aspect of its name). However, in November 2007, the goals for the ANGELS program were changed significantly. The Air Force decided to drop plans for development of a prototype spacecraft to escort larger satellites and decided instead to work toward a broader space monitoring experiment toward enhanced SSA (Space Situational Awareness). Orbital Sciences Corp. was awarded a $30 million contract to develop the ANGELS spacecraft, scheduled to launch in 2010.

Originally the spacecraft was expected to cost $20 million and weigh ten kilograms, but both figures expanded as engineers began to grasp the complexity of the technology involved. The ANGELS spacecraft now is expected to weigh about sixty-five to seventy kilograms. That is still smaller than its predecessor, the 140-kilogram XSS-11 microsatellite. ANGELS will also feature more advanced electro-optical sensors and autonomous operations capabilities than XSS and will operate at geostationary altitudes, far higher than XSS-11's low Earth orbit.[56] Changing the mission to SSA also lessens the attention the program generates.

The Starfire Optical Range is a USAF facility located in New Mexico run by the Air Force's Directed Energy Directorate Optics Division. The high-powered equipment there creates what *Esquire* magazine called in 2006 "BIG FREAKIN' LASER BEAMS in Space."[57] It is a "world-class 3.5-meter telescope, weighing 275,000 pounds, its two-ton primary mirror cast in a one-off spinning oven, its bundles of cables like a dragon's veins, in overall complexity approaching a living being."[58] It serves purposes from seeing into space for SSA to helping the Japanese determine what was wrong with an ailing satellite. Using the telescope, as the satellite passed overhead, Starfire was able to determine that its solar panels had failed to deploy.

Experiments are funded under the Advanced Weapons Technology budget line, which also incorporates solid-state laser development with "weapons-class power" for applications including a ground-based laser. While some applications are useful for SSA and tracking satellites, Starfire experiments include "compensated beam propagation" which scientists say may go beyond the needs of SSA. In FY 2007, ASAT operations were openly stated as among the project's goals.

Don't Worry, Be Happy?

Former Air Force Brigadier General Simon ("Pete") Worden—once known as Colonel Vader in space circles and now head of NASA Ames Research Center in California—is an innovator, a risk-taker, and a pragmatist, the latter due in part to having to master the maze of Washington bureaucratic politics.[59] He led the successful Clementine 1 and had hoped to lead the cancelled Clementine 2 programs, demonstrating with Clementine 1 that big things could be accomplished with relatively small budgets. With a doctorate in astronomy, General Worden was not the typical Air Force general. Writing in 2006 about U.S. efforts to develop a space-weapons program, Worden stated: "There's just one problem. A massive U.S. space-weapons program does not exist. Not only has there not been a space weapons push, but overall U.S. military use of space is in sharp decline."[60] More than a little frustration showed through in Worden's comments about Pentagon mismanagement of earlier space programs, suggesting that the Pentagon is "incapable of delivering any space capability, let alone a space weapon." Technology development is part of the problem, money is another. Worden goes on to say: "Space-weapons advocates (and there are some in the military) have little chance when every space penny goes to funding overruns on such programs as the Space-Based Infrared System (intended to detect and track ballistic missiles) and Future Imagery Architecture (a planned constellation of reconnaissance satellites)—programs that are both five times more expensive than initially estimated."[61]

Clearly, programs that include or could advance the U.S. space-weapons capabilities exist in various stages from research and development to the nominally operational missile-defense system. Some analysts and commentators consider that "bad" and counterproductive to U.S. interests. Others consider their insufficient funding as the problem—that there is no "massive" program—ostensibly leaving the United States vulnerable to potentially having its eyes blinded and ears deafened in space.

A 2005 editorial in the *Washington Times* exemplifies the latter view. Entitled " 'Death Stars' and Other Bogeymen," it discusses the need for weapons in space. "This . . . notion has some arms-control enthusiasts in a frenzy, talking of American 'death stars.' Call them the Bush-as-Darth Vader crowd."[62] The article then references historical analogies, as pointed out in Chapter 1 as a favorite but inappropriate tactic because of physical differences between space and air versus land and sea as battlespaces, to demonstrate necessity. "All this reminds us of the late nineteenth-century British reluctance to adopt the machine gun, which helped the Germans slaughter them on battlefields in World War I, or the attitude of Meiji Japanese or late imperial Chinese rulers, who scorned Western technology and ended up prey to it. In each case a country paid a dear price for eschewing military applications of new technologies. In our case, the price could be a disabling of our satellite communications and intelligence-gathering capabilities in a war."[63]

James Oberg points out that problems can also stem from uninformed reporters. He cites one author who wrote about NFIRE for ABC News on-line though having no prior experience with space, having apparently specialized primarily in "lifestyle" subjects.[64] Bias can also play into the problem, especially when advocates try to disguise themselves as analysts.

Still others see no problem at all, but for all the people on both ends of the spectrum susceptible to hype. Dwayne Day states:

Unfortunately, a lot of people outside this community fall for the rhetoric with regularity. The press reports these speeches and the occasional wild study as if they represent Pentagon plans. Conservatives believe that if an Air Force general states the need for an antisatellite weapon or an expensive piece of hardware it must be vital. Moreover, so-called "peace and justice" groups claim that the sky is falling and we are about to enter the era of space militarization. The gulf between rhetoric and reality is filled with a lot of clueless people.[65]

There are, however, a considerable number of scientists and experts trying to breach the gulf between rhetoric and reality, but find few listeners. Indeed, the most clueless people appear to be those who disregard questions of feasibility regarding the programs they propose.

Day goes on to point out the absurdity of requests such as that from General Tommy Power in 1962 for "a manned spacecraft propelled into orbit by nuclear bombs exploded underneath it" (called Orion), or General Homer Boushey's 1958 declaration that the United States needed "to put nuclear missiles on the Moon in order to serve as the ultimate deterrent."[66] That those missiles would have arrived at their targets three days after the war was over seemed of no relevance to General Boushey (who, by the way, was a fighter pilot). Reality, according to Day, is "a few Air Force generals advocating pie-in-the-sky plans, often involving space weaponry. The problem is that most of the programs in rhetorical military space do not abide by the laws of physics, few of them abide by the laws of bureaucratic and international affairs, and none of them abide by the laws of fiscal reality."[67]

Day's thesis seems to be that as long as there is a disconnect between speechmakers and budget realities, there is really no reason to worry. There are two problems with that thesis: the rhetoric is gaining support beyond those madcap Air Force Space Command generals and finding its way into U.S. policy, and the rest of the world takes it seriously. It is the threatening message that the United States is sending about its intentions in space, inadvertent or not, that must be considered next since. As RAND analyst Karl Mueller stated, space weapons are inherently political.

Chapter Four
Strategic Communications
What Message Is the United States Trying to Convey?

> I know you believe you understand what it is you think I said, but I
> am not sure you realize that what I said is not what I meant.
> —Attributed to Robert McCloskey, Richard Nixon,
> and Alan Greenspan, among others.

The United States has lost its edge on engaging the world. Though Secretary of State Madeleine Albright referred to the United States as the
"indispensable nation" in the 1990s, Walter Russell Mead pointed out
in 2004 that "within months of September 11, the indispensable nation
was becoming the indefensible nation."[1] For a variety of reasons, nations
both allies and potential competitors began to see the United States as
the chief threat to world peace. While that attitude has lessened somewhat since 2004, the world no longer sees the United States as the heroic
defender of peace and freedom it once did. Beyond policies and actions
in the Middle East, U.S. rhetoric in general, and specifically as exemplified in our relations with China and in the National Space Policy, has
been detrimental. Both tone and content have unnecessarily challenged, sometimes confused, and sometimes even belittled other countries. There is often a "do as we say, not as we do" message in U.S.
rhetoric as well, as exemplified by the purposeful destruction by the
United States of one of its own satellites in 2008. That event spoke vol-
umes to other countries about U.S. intentions in space, and will likely
result in a counterproductive ratcheting up of programs elsewhere
aimed at developing capabilities to hold the United States at bay in
space. These issues create two sets of problems for the United States
regarding space: communicating its intents to the rest of the world,
especially the advanced nations with space capabilities of their own, and

communicating its intents to China, as America's presumed greatest threat.

The timing of this U.S. tumble from grace could not be worse. As the lone remaining superpower it is critical that, if it must be seen as a hegemon, it be seen as a benevolent hegemon rather than a rogue hegemon. Unfortunately, the latter image evoked by the war in Iraq has proved hard to shake. A 2007 public opinion poll conducted as part of the Pew Global Attitudes Project indicated that "Anti-Americanism is extensive, as it has been for the past five years."[2] Much of that anti-Americanism may have its foundation in the worldwide lack of confidence in George W. Bush that the poll identified. But more broadly, "Global distrust of American leadership is reflected in increasing disapproval of the cornerstones of U.S. foreign policy"[3]—at least some of which will endure the change of administration. Damage to the U.S. image through foreign policy decisions will be compounded by fallout from the 2008 financial meltdown which began in the United States. Francis Fukuyama, in an article entitled "The Fall of America, Inc.," states: "even as Americans ask why they're having to pay such mind-bending sums to prevent the economy from imploding, few are discussing a more intangible, yet potentially much greater cost to the United States—the damage that the financial meltdown is doing to America's 'brand.'"[4]

Perhaps the only good news in the survey is that China's image, recently ascending, has slipped significantly among the publics within many of the major nations of the forty-seven total nations surveyed. A Pew Research Center Poll taken in 2005 had shown China, an authoritarian communist dictatorship, was viewed more favorably than the United States in eleven of the sixteen countries surveyed, including Britain, France, Germany, Spain, the Netherlands, Russia, Turkey, Pakistan, Lebanon, Jordan, and Indonesia. India and Poland saw the United States in a more favorable light than China, and Canada was about evenly split.[5] In 2007 however, "Large majorities in many countries think that China's growing military is a bad thing, and the publics in many advanced nations are increasingly concerned about the impact of China's economic power on their own countries."[6] In the United States, the growth of the Chinese military in general often translates into specific assumptions about China having hostile intentions toward the United States in space. While prudence is always the preferred route in security considerations, there are a variety of tools available to the United States to minimize the risks associated with the assumptions, but the United States is currently using only one: military hardware. That sends a powerful message to China and others, likely to create a self-fulfilling prophesy about Chinese intentions.

Communicating with China

According a Zhang Hui, a research associate at Harvard University's Kennedy School of Government, China has carefully studied U.S. space policy and actions, and drawn conclusions about U.S. intentions for the future.

China has seen much evidence to suggest the movement by the administration of U.S. President George W. Bush toward space weaponization is real. A number of U.S. military planning documents issued in recent years reveal the intention to control space by military means. In practice, the United States is pursuing a number of research programs to enable the development of space weapons, which could be used not only to attack ballistic missiles in flight but also to attack satellites and targets anywhere on Earth. Chinese officials have expressed a growing concern that U.S. plans would stimulate a costly and destabilizing arms race in space and on Earth, with disastrous effects on international security and the peaceful use of outer space. This would not benefit any countries' security interests.[7]

Any discussion of U.S.-China space relations is inherently grounded in U.S.-China relations more generally.[8] China is a rising power with a rapidly increasing military. That makes it a potential threat, or perhaps a "near-peer competitor" which must be monitored for the future. China's rising status also provides strong justification for the U.S. military to buy lots of big platforms (ships, tanks, planes) that it so covets and that keep the defense budgets in astronomical ranges, even without the war against terrorism and Iraq. On the other hand, these considerations must be juxtaposed against the need for China's help dealing with the megalomaniac who runs North Korea, keeping the nuclear lid on India/Pakistan, terrorism, and managing a globalized economy.

Bush administration officials reached out to China repeatedly, including U.S. Secretary of State Condoleezza Rice, who stated in June 2005 that "The U.S. welcomes the rise of a confident, peaceful, prosperous China and wants China as a global partner."[9] U.S. Deputy Secretary of State Robert Zoellick extended Secretary Rice's message in September 2005, talking about how China could become a "responsible stakeholder" in the international system.[10] Zoellick's successor, John Negroponte, reiterated the importance of the U.S.-China relationship in a 2008 press roundtable in Beijing.

Technically China is not an ally of the United States and we use the term "strategic" usually when we're referring to dialogues with countries that have formal alliances with the United States. So that's the technical reason that we refer to it as the Senior Dialogue rather than the Strategic Dialogue. Let me emphasize here that the relationship with China is very, very important. It is as important as any relationship we have with any country. It is a long-term relationship, it is one that I can say from a personal perspective since I have worked on the U.S.-

China relations off and on since 1972, has come a long way since 1972, and it is
a relationship that I think on both sides which has to be cultivated and nurtured
very carefully.[11]

It is not just the State Department that stresses the importance of the
U.S.-China relationship. At a 2007 press conference with Defense Secretary Robert Gates and the vice chairman of the Joint Chiefs of Staff, General James Cartwright, Gates addressed a question on whether he saw
China as a friend, ally, challenger, competitor, or even adversary. "I don't
consider China an enemy," Gates said, "and I think there are opportunities for continued cooperation in a number of areas. And I still would
like to see—I still think it's important for us to develop the strategic dialogue with China where we sit down and talk about how we see the threat,
how each of us perceives the threat and the purpose behind our modernization programs and so on."[12] Cartwright followed up with a point he
has touched on several times—the importance of communication. "It's
the lines of communication and developing them so that we don't misinterpret, in both the ship case and the ASAT and the Taiwan piece. I had
my counterpart here two weeks ago and sat down, and that was the key
dialogue between the two of us, [that] we do not have good enough
lines of communication so that we don't misinterpret or misunderstand
each other's actions. And that's important in this relationship."[13]

While the Bush administration was known for its attention to "staying
on message," outside of the highest levels of the U.S. government, a consistent message regarding China seems illusive. In fact, there has also
been a recent resurgence in what many analysts, particularly outside the
United States, see as U.S. China-bashing,[14] based on concerns from mor-
alistic neoconservatives, economic protectionists, defense types concerned about China's arms buildup (and needing a worthy peer-
competitor to justify the U.S. defense budget), and fundamentalist
Christians irate over atheist China's repressive ways. As Charles Free-
man, a former senior trade official in the Bush administration, has
noted, it's not easy to manage a relationship with China when both Democrats and Republicans in the United States are "screaming" about
alleged Chinese misdeeds.[15]

The concerns of these groups usually surface, through Congress, at
lower levels and in functional areas. Subsequently, at the highest level
the United States has attempted to convey to Chinese elites a willingness
to work with them. Translating that general willingness to work together
into meaningful dialogue in functional areas has been problematic
because at those levels the United States tends to want to delve into specifics uncomfortable for Beijing. In U.S.-China Defense Consultation
Talks and Military Maritime Security, for example, the United States

seeks transparency—which China inherently avoids—on specific capabilities, deployment, and spending. China, on the other hand, is more interested in engaging in function-area dialogue to better understand the U.S. strategic intent on issues such as U.S. support for Taiwan, the U.S.-Japan military alliance, the North Korean nuclear issue, and space. Consequently even when dialogue infrequently occurs, both sides can end up frustrated by lack of progress on their goals. Clearly, there is a great deal of work to be done.

Part of the difficulty with assessing China is that it is largely a country opaque to outsiders,[16] and deliberately so. This attitude toward opaqueness predates and extends beyond a military "abhorrence"[17] of transparency traceable back to Sun Tzu. Inherent cultural proclivities are exacerbated by China's closed political system, and even further intensified in space-related areas by often excessive security concerns common to authoritarian states.[18] But in the end, it is the inherently dual-use nature of space technology itself that multiplies the already difficult aspects of analyzing Chinese intentions in space. A submarine has few uses outside the military sector. The same is not true regarding a satellite. Consequently, cultural proclivities, dual-use technology, and a multitude of peripheral issues make determining the intended use of Chinese space technology a 10,000-piece puzzle.

Especially without dialogue, which has been virtually nonexistent on space issues between the United States and China since the sensationalist 1999 Cox Committee report alleging Chinese theft of U.S. secrets regarding nuclear weapons and missile design,[19] deciphering Chinese intent regarding space becomes considerably more difficult than surveying known capabilities. Further, China is constantly changing, and it is sometimes difficult for analysts to keep up with its changes, structural, political, and cultural. In reviewing testimony about the Chinese space program from a May 2008 hearing of the congressionally chartered China Economic and Security Review Commission (USCC), for example, Dr. Gregory Kulacki, China program manager for the Union of Concerned Scientists, discovered three significant factual errors. Given that the USCC issues an annual report on China that is highly regarded by Congress, a memo was sent to the USCC detailing the errors. Whether or not the memo was considered by the commission is unknown.[20] Language and translation issues can pose problems as well. The United States, for example, consistently calls for increased transparency, or openness, from the Chinese. Chinese officials, however, note that the word transparency, translated into Mandarin, carries a connotation of espionage. Increasingly, it has been suggested by both Chinese and American analysts that perhaps "clarity of intent" would be a preferable term for use between the two countries.

Analysis on China must be based on information from a variety of official and unofficial sources, with interpretations falling along a spectrum. Underestimating capabilities and best-case intent evaluations risk being unprepared to deal with the threats posed; overestimating capabilities and worst-case intent evaluations can lead to actions which produce unintended negative consequences that ultimately can increase the potential threat to U.S. capabilities. Balance is no doubt difficult, but the United States has leaned heavily toward the latter during the Bush administration.

America's Message?

At a November 2007 presentation for the Carnegie Endowment for International Peace, Gregory Kulacki made a critical point in conjunction with discussion on China's ASAT test. According to Kulacki, "The problem is of crosscultural communication, heading in both directions—not only is China bad at predicting how things will look to the U.S., the U.S. is bad at understanding Chinese motivations."[21] With direct dialogue between China and the United States minimal, there is considerable reliance on figuring out each other's intent from written sources (some more reliable than others), innuendo, and speculation.

James Mulvenon's 2007 article entitled "Rogue Warriors? A Puzzled Look at the Chinese ASAT Test" is an example of the pure speculation that takes place on the U.S. side, often by necessity. "Though little data exists about the internal machinations of the Beijing authorities, this article attempts to posit possible explanations for the apparent lack of bureaucratic coordination on the issue and assess the potential implications for Chinese civil-military relations."[22] Mulvenon ends up basing his three self-described speculative scenarios on what was *not* said in Chinese documents rather than what was said, and pointing out the problems created by what the United States has long considered as a lack of transparency on the part of the Chinese. "The 2006 defense white paper did not proactively or pragmatically announce China's intention to test space weapons for the purposes of greater transparency. While a sin of omission (deletion of mention of opposition to the weaponization of space) is slightly closer to a spirit of transparency than sins of commission (continuing to defend the principle while testing a weapon that renders the principle meaningless), the case of the ASAT test highlights Beijing's significant challenges in managing international perceptions of China's rise, especially if that rise is coupled with a perception (correct or not) that the military dimension of that rise may not be completely under civilian control."[23]

Gregory Kulacki and Jeffrey Lewis have challenged U.S. interpretations of the Chinese ASAT test and the lens through which U.S. analyses are conducted. They argue that U.S. analyses "view China as a unified, rational decision-maker, rather than a complicated bureaucracy in which conflicting interests compete for attention and resources, and mistakes can be made."[24] Kulacki, who has resided part-time in China for over twelve years and is well connected into multiple Chinese space communities, said "that his Chinese colleagues' explanation of the development and testing was wildly divergent from American interpretations"[25] and pointed out that most U.S. assessments have not considered accounts from those actually involved with the development of the systems.

Direct rather than indirect or speculative communication between the United States and China has proved important repeatedly. As pointed out in Chapter 1, China deliberately flew two nonimpact ASAT missions before their hit in January 2007. When the United States did not protest against those preliminary tests, the Chinese apparently interpreted that to mean that the United States did not object. A message was sent by the United States that was, perhaps, not intended.

Clearly, "message" and clear communication are important, and challenges abound. The one place where there is opportunity to clearly communicate a message is policy statements. While a certain amount of strategic ambiguity can be argued as desirable to maintain flexibility, policy statements are usually considered an opportunity to let others know general direction and goals. Therefore, it is appropriate to take a closer look at the message potentially conveyed by the 2006 NSP from its language. This is especially important given that there was a ten-year gap between the Clinton NSP issued in 1996 and the Bush NSP issued in 2006. Unless the Obama administration repeals it immediately, which is highly unlikely if for no other reason than space policy has never been a high priority for a new administration, then the 2006 policy is likely to be around for a long while.

The 2006 National Space Policy: The Empire Strikes First?

Unfortunately, the policy suffers from multiple "language" issues. For example, ambiguity makes it difficult for readers to discern with certainty the message being conveyed. Intentionally or not, the language seems designed to fog important issues under a canopy of imprecision, perhaps in an attempt to tamp down potential objections from those in Congress and others interested in the direction of U.S. space policy. While the words "space weapons" are never uttered, they can be heard if one listens closely.[26] Additionally, principles presented at times seem almost contradictory, which is likely a function of integrating long-held principles of U.S. space policy, including principles from the 1996 Clinton policy, with principles from Defense Department and Air Force policy documents that became increasingly mainstream under the Bush administration. Inclusion of language from these documents understandably resulted in ambiguous language being interpreted with more weight on militaristic and nationalistic perspectives.

The very first principle in the policy, for example, harkens back to values held since the Eisenhower administration. It states: "The United States is committed to the exploration and use of outer space by all nations for peaceful purposes, and for the benefit of all humanity." That is reassuring. But the following sentence is not. "Consistent with this principle, 'peaceful purposes' allow U.S. defense and intelligence-related activities in pursuit of national interests." "National interests" is a term not used in the 1996 national space policy, but is used in, for example, the *Air Force Doctrine Document 2–2.1, Counterspace Operations.* Imagine, for a moment, what the American reaction would have been in, say, 1972, had the Soviet Union made a similar declaration. National interests are, of course, whatever governments deem them to be, and in the Soviet case, those interests might have including spying on the United States. This is not to say that the Americans do not have a good case for arguing for the unimpeded use of space for the kind of observation and communication that would hamper rogue states and terrorists. We do. And we should make it clear we will not accept limits on our ability to protect ourselves. But to state flatly that all defense and intelligence purposes fall under the "peaceful use of space" is to invite other nations—say, Russia or China—to claim exactly the same right. The peaceful uses of space do in fact include observation and warning of attack, but the language of the administration's policy is so broad that it reads more like a blanket claim to hegemony in space rather than a reasonable demand that we, like any nation, be allowed to traverse the skies in our own defense.

Subsequent to the Chinese ASAT test, Congressman Terry Everett (R-Alabama) has been a vocal advocate for a comprehensive strategy for space protection and funding for hardware to protect our hardware. In a 2008 op-ed, he raises the issue of "peaceful use" as challenged by that test.

We have long viewed the use of space as a privilege for all nations so long as that access is peaceful. This policy has existed since the Eisenhower Administration and has been reinforced through subsequent international agreements. It is therefore unacceptable for any nation or nonstate actor to have the power to "hold at risk" American satellite systems or any other nation's systems, thereby placing all of the commercial, civil and military uses of space at risk.[27]

All true, but the new definition of "peaceful" as given in the 2006 NSP seems to include anything any country does in conjunction with defense-related activities—or at least so China could argue. Further, with the vast majority of space technology dual use and thereby of potential military value, what exactly could a country like China do that the United States would not consider threatening? The inability of many people in the national security community to stand in anyone else's shoes to consider a different perspective is a serious analytic flaw. In fact, defining terms in the Outer Space Treaty such as "peaceful" has been part of the agenda being pushed through the United Nations for years as part of the efforts to avoid the weaponization of space, and the United States has been the biggest obstacle. The policy of allowing any country to use space for peaceful purposes has existed since the Eisenhower administration, and has been reinforced through subsequent international agreements—but now the United States is abrogating some of those agreements and refusing to consider new ones. It is widely agreed that it is unacceptable for any nation or nonstate actor to have the power to hold satellites at risk, but space control implies that the United States would have exactly that power. If that is not what space control implies, what does it mean? It is perhaps no wonder others are confused by our language and our apparent do-as-we-say-not-as-we-do attitude.

Along with being disturbingly ambiguous, the tone of the policy is clearly more unilateralist, more militaristic, and sometimes borders on mean-spirited. The Planetary Society, which bills itself as the world's largest space interest group, described the language of the policy as "frankly, scary. . . . It is belligerent and bellicose, and reminiscent of a schoolyard bully." Consider specific policy language.

The very first section of the NSP, "Background," states: "In this new century, those who effectively utilize space will enjoy added prosperity and security and will hold a substantial advantage over those who do not." While true, more tactful language, rather than almost taunting language, might have been used. According to some individuals who worked on the interagency drafting process of the NSP, much of the more troubling language was not inserted until late in the game (after more than twenty-five drafts). Why it was inserted then is not clear.

Comparisons are often made between the 1996 NSP and the 2006 NSP, evidencing the clear change in tone, and sometimes substance as well. Whereas the 1996 NSP stated that the United States "rejects any limitations on the fundamental right of sovereign nations to acquire data from space," the 2006 document states that it "rejects any limitations of the fundamental right of the *United States* to operate in and acquire data from space" (emphasis added). Whereas in the past the right to acquire data from space extended to all nations, now it appears only to be granted to the United States, with the right to operate in space additionally granted *to the United States.* But if universality is part of morality, and if the United States can claim complete freedom to operate in space, does not this right then extend to every other nation on Earth as well? Other countries will most certainly claim so. "Freedom of action in space," the NSP goes on to say, "is as important to the United States as air power and sea power." That statement is drawn directly from the Secretary of Defense's cover memo to July 1999 DoD Directive 3100.10, "DoD Space Policy," and it is patently true.[28] But does that mean that other countries can then demand similar rights and expectations regarding their security in space as well? To assert a right in the international community is to assume that others can assert a similar right as well.

A key principle in the new policy states: "The United States considers space systems to have the rights of passage through and operations in space without interference. Consistent with this principle, the United States will view the purposeful interference with its space systems as an infringement on its rights." In other words, the United States considers space to be like the high seas. And yet, when it is in America's national interest, the United States acts against vessels in the maritime commons (when it—rightly—forces North Korean ships to submit to inspection). But does such an absolute declaration of a sovereign right really help the cause of cooperation in space? Even on Earth, the high seas are not immune to international governance; why should space be any different? Comparisons between space and air, land and sea are used when convenient to further the cause of space hegemony, forgotten when not.

In response to questions from the press and in related public statements at the United Nations and elsewhere, the Bush administration did clarify that this right of passage applies to all nations, not just the United States. However, the United States is emphatic that these rights it enunciates cannot and will not be guaranteed by international law but by the threat of force. Specifically, an additional principle in the 2006 policy states:

The United States considers space capabilities—including the ground and space segments and supporting links—vital to its national interests. Consistent with this policy, the United States will: Preserve its rights, capabilities, and freedom of action in space; dissuade or deter others from either impeding those rights or developing capabilities intending to do so; take actions necessary to protect its space capabilities; respond to interference; and deny, if necessary, adversaries the use of space capabilities hostile to U.S. national interests.

This principle provides a rationale for development of new capabilities. Additionally, in other parts of the document, the passage on right of access is apparently superseded, or contradicted, by other policy priorities.

Even more generally, all governments are charged with protecting national sovereignty and that is accomplished through various tools, usually including a military. Therefore, with space providing valuable force enhancement advantages, as demonstrated by the United States, space will intrinsically be viewed as part of military modernization for all countries. Does the United States see space use for military purposes as a tool that should be available only to the United States or those it chooses to approve? Apparently so. Should some countries be allowed to use radar or radios and others not?

Perhaps the clearest message in the 2006 policy concerns arms control. Whereas the 1996 policy stated, "The United States will consider and, as appropriate, formulate policy positions on arms control and related measures governing activities in space," the 2006 policy says, "The United States will oppose the development of a new legal regime or other restrictions that seek to prohibit or limit U.S. access to space. Proposed arms control agreements or restrictions must not impair the rights of the United States to conduct research, development, testing, and operations or other activities in space for U.S. national interests." That statement takes the statement from the 2001 Space Commission chaired by Donald Rumsfeld—"the United States must be cautious of agreements intended for one purpose that, when added to a larger web or treaties or regulations, may have the unintended consequences of restricting activities in space"[29]—one step further. Basically, no new restriction on any use of space that the United States deems essential to its national interests, which can be defined as anything, can be imposed. So, while space weapons are not specifically referenced, they are also not excluded, rather like the "sin of omission" Mulvenon chided the Chinese about.

Gratefully, international cooperation is given a nod, with the Secretary of State given the lead in "diplomatic and public diplomacy efforts, as appropriate, to build an understanding of and support of U.S. national space policies and programs and to encourage the use of U.S. space capabilities and systems by friends and allies." Within that context, Congressman Everett raised the issue of international cooperation to counter the Chinese threat.

Like other issues of the day, space protection demands international cooperation. The best pressure we can apply to China, and any others who might threaten our space capabilities, is multilateral pressure. We should be engaging the international community—our NATO allies are a good start—to put more pressure on China to explain its test and its intentions. This is an opportunity for the United States and our allies to lay claim to the peaceful use of space and put pressure on those who might have different intentions.

But Congressman Everett's words would likely be read with at least some measure of curiosity by a non-U.S. audience. While most space-faring nations took China to task after its ASAT test and no country condoned Chinese actions, the United States is viewed as a space threat as much as or more than China, and not particularly amenable to international cooperation on issues it objects to, regardless of the views of other countries, even if there is an overwhelming consensus.

In 2000, the United Nations General Assembly voted on a resolution called The Prevention of an Arms Race in Outer Space (PAROS). The resolution was adopted 163 for, zero against, three abstentions—the Federated States of Micronesia, Israel, and the United States.[30] In 2003, 174 nations voted "yes" on a resolution calling for negotiations toward preventing an arms race in space. Only four countries abstained: Micronesia, the Marshall Islands, Israel, and the United States.[31] Then in December 2005, 160 countries voted in favor of adopting resolution A/Res/60/54, Preventing an Arms Race in Outer Space, with Israel abstaining and the United States *the sole country to vote against it.* What message have those votes sent with regard to the U.S. attitude toward international cooperation on the peaceful use of outer space?

Additionally, many countries, including NATO countries, have robust space relations with China, including both commercial and governmental activities. French satellite operator Eutelsat Communications Group took steps in 2008 toward using Chinese rockets for future launches.[32] The European Space Agency is working with China on an earth observation program called "Dragon." These countries share the common view of space security through an economic, globalization lens as much as a military lens, and see development of dual-use technology as a wise investment of scarce resources. None want to see China aggressively pursue a space-weapons capability, but none want to see the United States take that road either.

Unfortunately, the more friends and allies hear and understand about the U.S. policy, the less comfortable they are with it. The *Times* of London perhaps best summed up the international perspective on the 2006 NSP in its 19 October 2006 article entitled "America Wants It All—Life, the Universe, and Everything,"[33] where it stated that space was no longer the final frontier, but the fifty-first state of the United States. It went on to say that, "The new National Space Policy that President Bush has signed is comically proprietary in tone about the U.S.'s right to control access to the rest of the solar system." While this statement may well be wrong, depending on how ambiguous passages are interpreted and policy contradictions reconciled, the importance lies in the perception.

Similar views were expressed in other international media outlets. According to the *Asia Times* (Hong Kong), "The policy sends unmistakable signals to Russia, China and India . . . that the United States intends to monopolize its long-standing space presence by militarizing it."[34] State-owned Rossiya Television in Moscow stated, "The universe has an owner. . . . America assumes the sole right to deny access to space to any country hostile to U.S. interests . . . not a single space project conceived on Earth can be deemed valid without a U.S. presence . . . any space project from whatever country must be examined by experts from the State Department and the Pentagon and only then will the States decide whether to let it go ahead or to launch a counter mechanism . . . blatant contravention of the international Outer Space Treaty."[35] Is this the message that the United States intended to send or one that it thinks will yield the kind of cooperation Congressman Everett talked about?

While most attention focuses on U.S.-China space relations, or lack thereof, there should be concerns about Russia as well. The negative Russian response to the NSP and to U.S. plans for missile defense sites in Europe, as well as President Vladimir Putin warning that he will aim missiles at Ukraine if that nation joins NATO, and generally souring U.S.-Russia relations (as dramatically demonstrated by Russian bombers buzzing the USS *Nimitz* in February 2008), all raise other important space questions for the future. After the Space Shuttle retires in 2010, the United States will be reliant on Russia for ongoing manned spaceflight needs for some time, until the new manned vehicle is ready. During that period, however long it turns out to be, the United States will be paying Russia for its services, and dependent on those services.

In a 2008 interview, even before the Russia-Georgia military confrontation in August, Congressman Dave Weldon (R-Florida) noted that the direction of the U.S.-Russia relationship has not been improving, which does not bode well for the future of space cooperation. He stated: "Russia is not a reliable partner. If our past experience . . . serves as any guide, relying on the Russians will cost us much more money than we anticipate. And frankly, I'm increasingly uncomfortable giving unnecessary leverage to a country that's been supplying military weaponry to Ahmadinejad's Iran and Chavez's Venezuela."[36] Subsequent to the confrontation, this bad situation got even worse, particularly regarding the ISS.

A law passed in 2000 known as the Iran, Syria, and North Korea Non-Proliferation Act bans the United States from buying Russian space technology unless the president determines steps are being taken by Russia to prevent the proliferation of nuclear and missile technology to any of those countries, specifically Iran. In 2005, Congress waived the ban to allow NASA to enter into a $719 million contract with the Russians for use of the Soyuz as a shuttle to the ISS through 2011. However, a waiver extension needs to be passed to guarantee access after 2011. Before the confrontation, the waiver would have been difficult. After the confrontation, on 13 August 2008, Senator Bill Nelson (D-Florida) stated "It was a tough sell before, but it was doable simply because we didn't have a choice. We don't want to deny ourselves access to the space station, the very place we have built and paid. It's going to be a tougher sell now unless there are critical developments during the next forty-eight to seventy-two hours."[37] A senior House Republican staffer took an even less optimistic view, characterizing the waiver as "dead on arrival. Nobody thinks it's going to happen, and the reality is there is no backup plan for the space station."[38] Ideally, the ISS will remain a symbol of international cooperation even during times of political strife and the Obama administration seems to back that view; Obama urged Congress to grant the required waiver even while still a candidate.[39]

Russia is also busy rebuilding much of what had become its moribund space infrastructure and space program generally. Chinese analyst Zhong Jing notes that "Russia, another space power, has identified space capabilities as vital to maintaining the country's status as a world power. Its '2006–2015 Space Exploration Plan,' whose main task is to launch more than seventy new satellites in the next ten years, was approved on 14 July 2005."[40] Space funding there increased by 13 percent in 2008, not including funding for the military.[41] Russia is determined to reinvigorate the dual-use Glonass satellite navigation system and will build a new launch site in Russia's Far East. Though difficulties have been encountered with the whole "rejuvenation" effort and more can be expected,[42] whether Russia is or could become a space threat to the United States remains a valid question. What is the intended message to Russia about the future?

Actions Speak Louder Than Words

In January 2008, the U.S. government announced that an errant top-secret spy satellite designated US-193,[43] malfunctioning since its launch in 2006, was expected to fall out of the sky sometime between late February and early March. That it was malfunctioning meant it could not be controlled upon reentry. Initially, American officials said there was little to worry about because satellites fall from orbit relatively frequently and whatever hardware does not burn up on reentry into the atmosphere is most likely to fall harmlessly into the ocean, since approximately 70 percent of Earth is covered by water. In fact, Gordon Johndroe, a spokesman for the National Security Council, noted to the press that 328 satellites had come down in the past five years without injury to anyone.[44] Johndroe was correct. Satellites fall to Earth when defunct, and

while most of the hardware burns up during reentry, some 10 to 40 percent of the hardware can survive intact. But there is only one known
instance of a person being hit from falling space debris. Lottie Williams,
a woman walking alone in Tulsa, Oklahoma, was hit on the shoulder in
1997, but not seriously injured.

There were some things different about US-193 and its reentry
though. First, because the satellite had never functioned properly, it carried a full tank of toxic hydrazine fuel. Second, most defunct satellites
can still be controlled when they are de-orbited, so ground personnel
can more or less assure that debris will largely fall into unpopulated
areas. Third, the satellite technology, while it had not worked properly,
was considered top-secret.

Then, toward the end of January, government reports began to
change. Pentagon officials began to state that they were monitoring the
situation, and they were examining "potential options to mitigate any
possible damage this may cause."[45] In retrospect, it is clear that even
then more than just consideration of options was already underway. On
14 February, NASA Administrator Mike Griffin, Deputy National Security Adviser James Jeffrey, and General James Cartwright, vice chairman
of the Joint Chiefs of Staff, announced at a press conference that the
United States intended to intercept and destroy US-193 with a missile,
as a matter of public safety. According to James Jeffrey:

What makes this case . . . different, however, and in particular for the president
in his consideration, was the likelihood that the satellite, upon descent to the
Earth's surface, could release much of its thousand-plus pounds of hydrazine
fuel as a toxic gas. The likelihood of the satellite falling in a populated area is
small, and the extent and duration of toxic hydrazine in the atmosphere would
be quite limited; nevertheless, if the satellite did fall in a populated area, there
was a possibility of death or injury to human beings beyond that associated with
the fall of satellites and other space objects normally, if we can use that word.
Specifically, there was enough of a risk for the president to be quite concerned
about human life.[46]

The United States offered advance word of its intent, notifying other
nations through diplomatic channels and the United Nations.

The plan was to use a modified SM-3 missile launched from the Aegis
cruiser USS *Lake Erie*. Those missiles are part of the U.S. missile defense
program, though formerly it would have been considered part of TMD,
rather than NMD. The missile intercepts its target at a relatively low altitude, during what would be considered its terminal phase, rather than
higher where the plague-ridden mid-course technology focuses. The
SM-3 has a much more successful test track record than the mid-course
interceptors housed in California and Alaska.[47] The modifications made,
which in fact had been under way for over three weeks, were largely soft-

ware modifications. The Navy intended to take up to three shots at the satellite if needed and the cost of the mission was estimated as between twenty to sixty million dollars. Chances of success for the missile to hit the satellite were given by some analysts as fifty-fifty. The interceptor had been tested on targets with much slower closing speeds than those estimated for the satellite. However, the 5,000 pound, bus-size satellite provided a much bigger target for the interceptor than those used in past tests.

Public safety was the stated government concern that justified using missile defense technology to destroy a satellite. At the press conference Mike Griffin spoke to the issue of public risk.

The analysis that we've done is as certain as any analysis of this type can be. The hydrazine tank will survive intact, and in fact the hydrazine which is in it is frozen solid, as it is now. Not all of it will melt, okay? So you will land on the ground with a tank full of slush hydrazine that would then later evaporate. The tank will have been breached—not probably, but the tank will have been breached, because the fuel lines will have been ripped out of the main spacecraft, and so that hydrazine will vent.

If it lands in a populated area—the general referred to an area the size of a couple of football fields, and loosely that's what our analysis shows—it's hard to find areas that have any significant population to them where you could put a toxic substance down across a couple of football fields and not have somebody at risk. And so we didn't want to create a situation like that. So in brief, the tank will survive, it will be breached, the hydrazine will reach the ground, and that's not an outcome we want to see.

Detailed information regarding how the government reached these conclusions was, however, not provided to the public or international community, though doing so would have posed no risk to national security.[48] Doing so would have allowed independent verification. That verification was important, because according to calculations done within scientific communities in the United States and undoubtedly abroad, the risk was minimal, generating considerable skepticism about the real motivation behind the U.S. decision to target the satellite. More and better communication could have tamped down that skepticism. After all, the net result of the shot, regardless of motivations, was a de facto antisatellite test and as television personality Bill Nye, the Science Guy, is credited with pointing out, "One test is worth a thousand expert opinions."

Why skepticism? First of all, the NASA administrator stated unequivocally that the tank would survive reentry, though breached. On what basis was that assumption made? Basic information on hydrazine states that it autoignites (spontaneously catches fire) at temperatures that could reasonably be expected during reentry; that it is sensitive to static discharge, which could be expected during reentry; and that sealed containers may rupture and explode when heated.[49] It would, on its own, turn into the fireball that was instead generated by impact with a Navy missile. Why these basic scientific premises would not apply in this particular instance was not addressed. Second, if it did miraculously survive intact, what were the chances that debris would scatter on land rather than over the ocean? And if it landed on land, what were the chances it would land in a populated area? And if it landed in a populated area, what were the chances of people being hurt or injured—and was that assuming that everyone stood still and breathed in the toxic vapors or that they did what reasonable people might do, and leave the impact site? According to MIT research professor Geoffrey Forden, there was a 3 percent chance that an individual somewhere in the world would be injured by the hydrazine, if any fell to Earth. For a Los Angeles resident, for example, that would mean the risk of being harmed was one in a billion. Forden and his colleagues also concluded that the chances of the toxic gas making it to Earth were close to zero, based on the amount of pressure on the tank during reentry being about fifty times the gravitational force on Earth.[50] Jonathan McDowell, a Harvard astrophysicist, separately concluded the risk of being hit by a piece of the satellite was about one in a million. "The chances the hydrazine will land within hundred yards of someone if the tank makes it through Earth's atmosphere, he said, are higher: about two in hundred. But, 'if people just walk away from it, they won't be harmed at all,' he said."[51] A well-regarded study by Aerospace Corporation regarding space debris stated that "the risk that an individual will be hit and injured is estimated to be less than one in one trillion. To put this into context, the risk that an individual in the U.S. will be struck by lightning is about one in 1.4 million."[52] Real-life incidents back up McDowell's conclusions about the risk from hydrazine. A major hydrazine rail spill between Los Angeles and Santa Barbara in 1991 did not lead to any casualties, and it is regularly trucked around the country by the government.[53] While scientists may well disagree over methodologies and specifics, not knowing the basis for the government's conclusions prohibits statistical verification of any kind, and allows skepticism to develop.

With skepticism come attempts to develop alternative theories about motivations. There was, for example, speculation that the spacecraft carried a plutonium power source[54] that could have dispersed radioactivity on the ground, but an increase in the global background of PU-238 would have been detected even if the Pentagon blew it up on reentry, and none was. More plausibly, there was speculation that the Pentagon's real concern focused on big pieces of the top-secret, cutting edge satellite technology (believed to be part of the Future Imagery Architecture and cited in Chapter 3 as grossly over budget and technologically plagued, as the failure of this satellite verifies) landing in foreign locations or ending up on eBay. That concern is understandable—but not the motive the government gave. More prominent from skeptics was the concern that whether as a primary or secondary motive, the government wanted to test its antisatellite capability and have an opportunity to perhaps bolster support for missile defense—the crippled satellite providing an opportunity for target practice that was just too tempting not to take.

The cost of the "shootdown,"[55] was estimated beforehand at between $40 to $60 million. The missiles themselves cost about $10 million and if three had been used, that would put the upper end cost for the missiles at $30 million, with a considerable portion of the rest of the estimated cost dedicated to data gathering. With only one missile fired, the final cost was estimated at $30 to $40 million, so clearly, a considerable amount of money was spent gathering data.

During the runup to the shootdown, a supportive editorial asked the question "Why not take a shot?"[56] That is the crux of the strategic communication issue. Other countries have had concerns that the U.S. space policy is taking a more aggressive, unilateral posture generally and that missile defense had the technical ability to be used as an ASAT weapon specifically. "Taking a shot" validated these concerns.

The Russian Foreign Ministry issued a statement on 16 February suggesting that public safety was a "thinly veiled excuse" for destroying US-193 and that the United States was actually conducting an ASAT test—perhaps to flex U.S. muscle, as a tit-for-tat to the Chinese, to gather valuable test data, to gather support for yet another increase in the missile defense budget, or some combination of all of those reasons. After the test, an analyst at the Russian Academy of Sciences' Institute of Space Research stated that the "most likely reason for the destruction of US-193/NROL-21 was to test antisatellite weapons on the quiet. . . . The Americans have long stopped worrying about Russia's 'symmetrical' responses to U.S. military power," the analysis continued. "Not so China. . . . This seems to be why U.S. President George W. Bush decided to destroy US-193: to test a new type of strategic weapons and check the feasibility of a national antimissile shield in an antisatellite role."[57]

The Chinese were not pleased either, but remained circumspect before the destruction of the satellite, still smarting from the (rightful) international condemnation suffered after their 2007 test. While ground-based, kinetic-kill technology was used by both the United States and China to destroy their respective defunct satellites, the Chinese satellite was at a much higher altitude than the U.S. satellite, creating significantly more and longer-lasting orbital debris, and was done without clear and direct notice to other countries. After the test, China said it was monitoring potential debris dangers created by the strike and urged the United States to provide more data.[58] Secretary Gates responded that the United States was prepared to share some details to ease concerns about potentially dangerous debris.[59]

A newspaper article in the *Tehran Times* used the destruction of US-193 not only to examine U.S. intentions regarding space weapons, but to dredge up issues such as U.S. use of Agent Orange in Vietnam as well.

The operation to shoot down the orbiting spacecraft was clearly designed to send a message to both Russia and China, America's two major competitors in the race for military domination in space. Interestingly, the SM-3 missile used to shoot down the satellite forms the terminal phase of the antiballistic missile system currently being developed by the Bush Administration. . . . Whatever the motivation for shooting down the satellite, the demonstration of America's ability to destroy satellites will now make it very difficult to convince other countries that they shouldn't develop a similar antisatellite capability and increases the likelihood of a new arms race in space between the three main players . . . once you start shooting down satellites in space, for whatever reason, other countries are sure to follow, and before long, there will be mayhem and havoc in the heavens.[60]

Not surprisingly, the shootdown garnered as much or more global press coverage and analysis as it did in the United States, and like that related to the 2006 U.S. National Space Policy, often more critical or at least skeptical.

It is interesting that the Iranian analysis assumed a space arms race between the United States, Russia, and China and advocated against such. An editorial in a South Asian publication piled on to the space arms race theme and hinted that other countries might feel compelled to join in as well as a result of the U.S. test.

Indian president A. P. J. Abdul Kalam's contention that India has the capability to intercept objects in space and destroy them within a radius of 200 km has ignited a strategic dilemma. The issue has gained significance after the U.S. successfully shot down one of its own collapsing satellites at a height of 233 km. The fear that India will be left lagging in one more global arms race and pay a heavy ex-post price looms on the minds of the country's strategic elites. Although Washington described its operation on Feb. 20 as a life-saving strike to prevent a rogue satellite from crashing on to earth, the hush-hush manner in which the entire event took place set the cat among the pigeons. . . . It makes sound diplomatic sense to couch a provocative military action in humanitarian garb by whipping up public anxiety about a loose cannon that could randomly take lives. Most analysts believe that the affair was a barely disguised demonstration of U.S. military preparedness in an emerging new Cold War with China and Russia. China's critical reaction to the American kinetic warhead smacks of rank opportunism and holier-than-thou prickliness. After all, it was Beijing that fired the first salvo in this category of space weaponization through a direct kinetic hit on one of its satellites in January 2007 at a height of over 800 km. Washington's show of muscle is a tit-for-tat response to Beijing's much-hailed muscle flexing as a new great power in space.[61]

While international coverage and analyses of the test were largely critical or at least skeptical of U.S. motives, the story was covered differently in the United States.

An editorial in the *New York Times* spoke of "conspiracy theories" and said "small, paranoid minds wondered if the government was not being completely forthright about its motives."[62] But a statement immediately following the event by Defense Secretary Robert Gates that "the operation speaks for itself"[63] in terms of resolving doubts about the viability of missile defense technology only bolstered skepticism. The lead sentences in the coverage of the satellite destruction in both the *Washington Post* and *Los Angeles Times* spoke not of public safety, but missile defense and antisatellite weapons. "The successful U.S. missile strike against a failing spy satellite 133 miles above the Earth on Wednesday bolstered the credibility of America's long-troubled missile defense system, according to military experts," said the *Los Angeles Times*.[64] "The unprecedented downing of an errant spy satellite by a Navy missile makes it clear that the Pentagon has a new weapon in its arsenal—an antisatellite missile adapted from the nation's missile defense program," stated the *Washington Post*.[65] Flush with its success, military rejoicing over resolving dire public safety issues seemed to fade to the background.

Just before 10:30 P.M. Eastern time on 20 February, the Navy fired a single missile and hit the satellite at an altitude of about 150 miles as it traveled more than 17,000 miles per hour. Even beforehand, it was pretty clear where the Navy hoped to bring the satellite down from a NOTAM (Notice to Airman) order issued by the U.S. government on 18 February, warning of possible hazards in an airspace off the coast of Maui, Hawaii. The location chosen to intercept the satellite raised eyebrows as well. If concern about debris motivated the shootdown to begin with, would not the idea be to keep the debris as far away from population centers or shipping lanes as possible?

General Cartwright had stated prior to the event that modifications made to the missile to allow it to find and impact the satellite were "not transferable to a fleet configuration"[66] as an assurance that this was not an ASAT test. Certainly modifying all the SM-3s would not be desirable, as that would negate its capabilities to intercept missiles. But given that the modifications involved software, rather than hardware, some number of missiles could be modified for ASAT use or, now that the software has been developed *and tested*, downloaded as needed.

Announcing intentions on 14 February and striking the target on 20 February left precious little time for debate, expressions of concern, or protest. A Presidential order had been issued and it was going to be carried out. The House Armed Services Committee (HASC) offered a statement in support of the event[67] and not surprisingly, the Missile Defense Advocacy Alliance issued a supportive statement as well.[68] It is unlikely that the decision to destroy US-193 was undertaken lightly or with nefarious intent. When initial government statements were made that the satellite posed little risk, that was the working reality. But the military is always charged to consider worst-case scenarios and ways to deal with those scenarios. For whatever reason or by whatever process, one of those scenarios worked its way through the bureaucratic channels high enough and with enough momentum and clout for President Bush to eventually approve the action with Defense Secretary Robert Gates, rather than the usual military commander, given responsibility for issuing the actual order to proceed. It is not even clear that the military or the NRO was fully supportive of the idea. It could have been an idea intentionally generated from a think tank, a contractor, or a congressional staffer. After the satellite was destroyed, HASC Chairman Ike Skelton (D-Missouri) praised the military for shooting down the satellite, but reiterated that "this action should not be construed a standard U.S. policy for dealing with problem satellites."[69] HASC Strategic Forces subcommittee chair Ellen Tauscher (D-California) went out of her way at a 27 February 2008 hearing to praise the shootdown.[70] But a senior member of the House Homeland Security Committee, Representative Edward Markey (D-Massachusetts), was more critical. Focusing on the long term, he said, "the geopolitical fallout of this intercept could be far greater than any chemical fallout that would have resulted from a wayward satellite."[71]

With the destruction of the satellite, the United States may well have opened a Pandora's Box of "thinly veiled excuses" from other countries in the future. What if, for example, China and Russia announced that they were initiating a joint technology development program to mitigate the danger to human life from the 100 percent risk, based on irrefutable historical evidence, that Earth will be hit by a damaging asteroid or meteor in the future. They say they will do this as a "moral imperative," much as the United States bills missile defense. Part of this program will be the targeting and destruction of some defunct satellites in orbit. They also say they will announce these events before they occur, and execute them in ways to minimize the creation of space debris. Would the United States be okay with that? I do not think so. But it has now lost the moral high-ground to object. In fact, it set the precedent.

Subsequent to the destruction of US-193, some focus shifted to Washington's refusal to consider space arms race proposals put forth the previous week by China and Russia. "The United States, the world's top space power, has often accused other countries of vigorously developing military space technology. But faced with the Chinese-Russian proposal to restrict space armaments, it runs in fear from what it claimed to love."[72] Physicist and best-selling author of *Physics of the Impossible,*[73] Professor Michio Kaku supported China's position. "With a certain amount of justification, the Chinese claim there is a double standard . . . this latest move can be seen as provocative, since the United States has refused to renegotiate and strengthen the 1967 outer space treaty."[74]

If there is a silver lining from the satellite strike, it is that besides the bad precedent potentially set for "thinly veiled excuses," a positive precedent for prenotification has been set—by the United States. De facto, the United States, which has been adamantly against any rules of any kind that restricted its flexibility in space, has created and potentially bound itself as well as other countries to following certain rules on prenotification in the future. Sharing data with China adds to transparency as well, though given the U.S. government's reluctance to provide answers to questions about the analysis leading to the decision to target the satellite, the transparency seems quite limited. While the biggest outcomes of the satellite strike will likely be bolstering support for *national* missile defense and demonstrating that the United States has an operational antisatellite weapon capability, while still denying such and so appearing both hypocritical and aggressive, prenotification rules and any global increase in transparency regarding space activity is good and should be promoted further.

A Better Approach?

Strategic communication is the intersection between rhetoric, policy, action, and politics. It is an inherently difficult and messy business. Nevertheless, a few aspects are intuitively obvious. First, effective communication requires that all involved parties be able to both send and *receive* messages. Currently, the United States communicates largely by broadcasting through a loudspeaker with little attention paid to how it is received nor listening for incoming signals. That's not effective communication.

U.S. policymakers need to realize that more attention is paid to U.S. space policy abroad than at home. Ham-fisted, militaristic rhetoric and actions perhaps intended to demonstrate strength to a domestic audience, perhaps intended to goad Congress into providing more money for more hardware, or perhaps intended to bully China, may seem an effective approach, but might also be counterproductive if establishing the United States as the international leader in space is part of the ultimate U.S. "space supremacy" goal. While the Bush administration tried to stress continuity of space policy over change, the arguments simply have not held up.

The 2007 Report of the Defense Science Board Task Force on Strategic Communications states a heightened awareness that success in strategic communications depends on four key propositions:

Deep comprehension of identities, attitudes, cultures, interests, and motives of others

Awareness by leaders and practitioners that *what we do* matters as much *as what we say*

Institutionalized connections between a wide variety of government and civil society partners in the United States and abroad

A durable model of strategic direction that adapts quickly, transforms stovepipes, integrates knowledge and functions, and builds next generation skills and technologies.[75]

All of these, of course, presuppose a determined message that the United States wants to convey. So far, regarding space, the United States is failing miserably in all regards.

That is not to say that the Defense Department does not "get it" that its Darth Vader sounding language can be counterproductive. However, it seems only willing to issue directives on language to be used in public discussions—what we say—rather than reexamine policies—what we do. A 25 January 2008 memo from Brian Green, Deputy Assistant Secretary of Defense for Strategic Capabilities, says: "Public outreach and international engagement are key elements of the Department of Defense's efforts to promote safe and responsible use of space and are essential to achieving National Space Policy Goals. The Department of Defense must continue to convey a clear and consistent message on space protection." Whether the department has ever conveyed a clear and consistent message is debatable. Nevertheless, toning down rhetoric appears the primary emphasis of the directive. For example, space control activities are to be presented as ensuring "capabilities are available to deny adversaries the use of space advantages to ensure our terrestrial forces and homeland remain safe." The memo also places U.S. activities in the context of reacting to Chinese activities, rather than predating China's ASAT test. "Our space capabilities face a wide-range of threats including radio frequency jamming, laser blinding and antisatellite systems. The maturation of these threats, including China's antisatellite capability, requires a broad range of capabilities, from diplomatic to military, to protect our interest in space."[76]

What those diplomatic capabilities might involve remains unclear though, as the memo restates the least ambiguous aspect of the National

Space Policy: "The U.S. does not agree that new legal regimes or arms control agreements related to space "weaponization" would be helpful in protecting U.S. national security interests."[77] If, however, there are limits to how much or how well hardware can protect hardware in space, and there are, then options beyond hardware should be considered. A closer look at options and objections to diplomacy and arms control is therefore in order.

Chapter Five
Diplomacy and Arms Control
Limits and Opportunities

Arms control has to have a future, or none of us does. But it doesn't necessarily have to come in big packages of six-hundred-page treaties.

—Stanley Hoffmann

The U.S. attitude regarding arms control in space has been absolutely clear—"talk to the hand," as one European described it. The 2001 Rumsfeld Commission Report on the management of space assets began the evolution toward the current U.S. position, stating that the "United States must participate actively in shaping the [international] legal and regulatory environment for space activities," and "protect the rights of nations to defend their interests in and from space," but "should be cautious of agreements intended for one purpose that, when added to a larger web or treaties or regulations, may have the unintended consequences of restricting future activities in space."[1] While that document hinted at a new U.S. attitude toward space arms control and treaties, the U.S. position was unambiguously stated in the 2006 U.S. National Space Policy: "The United States will oppose the development of new legal regimes or other restrictions that seek to prohibit or limit U.S. access to or use of space."[2] Through various documents, the United States has now articulated plans for warfighting "in, from, and through"[3] space. Yet an effective military means of protecting U.S. assets against a number of potential threats to critical U.S. space-based assets is not just elusive, but likely impossible. Equally important, any means that results in the creation of more space debris—as space weapons would—would be counter to U.S. and global interests. And it is not just the arms-control community or paranoid individuals who feel that way.

In a 2002 article, James Clay Moltz, the author of *The Politics of Space*

Security: Strategic Restraint and the Pursuit of National Interests, stated multiple reasons for skepticism toward space weapons within parts of the military that are still valid today.[4] First, the testing and deployment of space weapons can compromise the very space assets they are supposed to protect. That lesson was learned through early testing over the West Coast and the Pacific, when both power grids in Hawaii and U.S. satellites in orbit were adversely impacted. As Moltz writes, "But even more sobering for the military [than knocking out power grids in Hawaii] was the disabling of several recently launched military reconnaissance and communication satellites. The Pentagon had, in effect, 'blinded itself' and had to scramble to replace the precious assets it had destroyed."[5] The Chinese ASAT test in 2007 raised the specter of the problem again, and likely those in the Air Force responsible for Space Situational Awareness had their own qualms about shooting down US-193 given that models for debris dispersion had proven less than 100 percent correct in the past. Beyond debris, there are the reliability issues raised in Chapter 3. The military is not keen on depending on obscenely expensive hardware launched into an extremely harsh environment only to be then left untended for indefinite periods. The cost issues are not inconsequential either and ultimately may be the factor that stops the development of space weapons, including national missile defense.

Articles written by military authors expressing their skepticism are found in such hardly dovish journals as *Aerospace Power Journal* and the *Naval War College Review.* In 1998, Lieutenant Colonel Bruce M. DeBlois focused first on the technical reasons why space weapons are not viable, and then returned to political reasons why the United States should not deploy space weapons. In the latter context, DeBlois said, "The idea of putting weapons in space to dominate the globe is simply not compatible with who we are and what we represent as Americans."[6] In 2000 Major Howard D. Belote argued in *Aerospace Power Journal*[7] that pro-weapons zealots, as he called them, often miss the contextual picture— that U.S. actions will generate reactions in other countries. Lt. Col. Christopher Petras, the chief legal counsel for international air operations for NORAD, suggested in 2003 that legal ground for an agreement on space debris might be found. "A cursory review of relevant positions of the law of armed conflict suggests that there is at least a foundation for dialogue with respect to an agreement that would prohibit the use of weapons that cause widespread, long-term, and severe contamination of the commons of space with debris."[8] Navy Captain David C. Hardesty wrote in 2005 "that space-based weapons, though in the short term increasing military capabilities, are in the long term very likely to have a negative effect on the national security of the United States."[9] His key argument against space weapons was that their vulnerability ultimately overrides their advantages. Yet, the U.S. position continues to favor protection of space technology through the development of more technology, rather than arms control.

In fairness, until recently the arms-control community has not really done a good job of realistically dealing with the hawkish space hegemons currently dictating U.S. space policy. The United States has been tacitly and then overtly against more multilateral treaties in general, and the options offered by the space arms-control community have focused largely on treaties. That has created a deadlock. "Unfortunately, each side has become so entrenched in the validity of their own ideological belief that the channels of communication between the two sides have been all but closed."[10] That situation must change.

International Forums

There are two key international forums concerned with the use of space for peaceful purposes, the Conference for Disarmament (CD) in Geneva and the UN Committee on the Peaceful Uses of Outer Space (COPUOS) headquartered in Vienna. Within both of these, and even within NATO, there has been a "dialogue of the deaf" between Washington and other countries on space issues. While there are political issues contributing to the difficulties in generating meaningful discussions within the CD and COPUOS, nevertheless Washington has achieved largely what it wanted from these efforts. Nothing. It has largely maintained the flexibility to do whatever it wants, whenever it wants in space, despite overwhelming and consistent views from other countries that they desire more parameters for internationally acceptable actions than currently are defined and agreed upon.

Committee on the Peaceful Uses of Outer Space

COPUOS was formed shortly after the first artificial satellite was launched. The General Assembly of the United Nations decided to establish an ad hoc Committee on the Peaceful Uses of Outer Space, made a permanent committee in 1959, to consider four issue areas:

The activities and resources of the United Nations, the specialized agencies and other international bodies relating to the peaceful uses of outer space;

International cooperation and programs in the field that could appropriately be undertaken under United Nations auspices;

Organizational arrangements to facilitate international cooperation in the field with the framework of the United Nations; and

Legal problems which might arise in programs to explore outer space.[11]

Starting with a membership of twenty-four countries and growing to sixty-nine members, COPUOS was basically created for the purpose of governing the clearly promising realm of space. It was intended to study and address the legal issues engendered by the exploration of outer space.

Soon after the inception of COPUOS, the UN General Assembly adopted the Declaration of Legal Principles Governing the Activities of States in the Exploration and Use of Outer Space in 1963, to facilitate "broad international cooperation in the scientific as well as in the legal aspects of the exploration and use of outer space for peaceful purposes."[12] Thus the origins of the space regime from a legal perspective can be traced to that declaration, as well as several general principles stated in five treaties, including the paramount Outer Space Treaty, a number of related arms-control treaties, and some general principles of international law, some of those found in the United Nations Charter. Andrew Park has succinctly outlined those especially relevant to the weaponization issue:

Although international space law has derived many of its policies from the basic principles set forth by COPUOS, few in the international space law community would argue that the OST is the most significant legal text governing the realm of outer space. Part of the reason the OST—which entered into force in October 1967—is so revered is that it not only became the first treaty to govern access to space, but more pertinently, it was the first to address the issue of space weaponization. The fundamental premise of the OST is that space is not open to national appropriation but should be reserved for the pursuit of the common interest of mankind and for "peaceful purposes." The underlying goals of the OST are to avoid colonial competition in space and to avert an extension of the Cold War's dangerous military rivalry. The OST provides the framework for international order in outer space, introducing principles that have since been elaborated on in later treaties. However, due to the few number of states that are capable of operating in space, the OST has been largely untested, and its principles have been by and large aspirational.

Other agreements are relevant to the weaponization debate, and while they must be acknowledged, they primarily serve as a backdrop for the legal regime created by the OST. In particular, the Limited Test Ban Treaty of 1963 banned nuclear weapons testing in outer space while subsequent treaties and declarations regulated different forms of military activity in space. Finally, four other General Assembly resolutions are worth noting to fill out the remainder of the landscape of the weaponization issue: the Declaration on International Cooperation in the Exploration and Use of Outer Space for the Use and Benefit and in the Interest of All States, the resolutions on Direct Television Broadcasting, on Remote Sensing of the Earth from Outer Space, and on the Use of Nuclear Power in Outer Space.[13]

In 2007, the Outer Space Treaty turned forty. That anniversary provided the impetus for analysts to consider "where next" and "to what end?" Some, such as Philip Ball, are skeptical about a positive future, suggesting that "the OST is an agreement forged in a different political climate from that of today" and that while "the commitments of the OST need urgently to be updated and reinvigorated . . . right now there seems rather little prospect of that happening."[14] Others are more positive and proactive. Sergei Orzhonikidze, director-general of the United Nations office at Geneva, said, "For the past four decades the 1967 Outer Space Treaty has been the cornerstone of international space law. The treaty was a great historic achievement, and it still is."[15] Russia, with China, introduced a new draft treaty toward preventing an arms race in space in Geneva on 14 February 2008.[16] The treaty was immediately rejected by the United States.

In all fairness, while the U.S. attitude toward arms control has been dismissive at best, the Chinese and the Russians have not been completely sincere in their arms-control dealings either. They have offered treaty drafts, knowing they would be refused by the United States, while until recently themselves, or at least the Chinese, often refusing to accept discussions of even a voluntary code of conduct or "transparency and confidence building measures" unless they are directly linked to weapons-ban treaty negotiations.[17] In general, the Chinese have and continue to be very reluctant to discuss space subjects, and also seem to have the same kind of my-way-or-the-highway attitude as the United States regarding space weaponization, resulting in gridlock.

The OST was never meant to be a comprehensive end-all treaty. It was conceived as a living document which would need further clarification on such seemingly simple items as defining "peaceful" vis-à-vis supporting "peaceful uses of outer space" to considering new issues as they became apparent. But for all the reasons outlined in Chapter 2, further elaboration never occurred, except in select areas. One of those areas is space debris.

Because the creation of space debris is in nobody's interest, international cooperation is furthest along on that issue. The United Nations and the Inter-Agency Space Debris Coordination Committee (IADC) have been working for several years to develop international debris mitigation guidelines, work which finally reached fruition in June 2007. The IADC includes the space agencies of China, France, Germany, India, Italy, Japan, Russia, Ukraine, the United Kingdom, and the United States, plus the European Space Agency. Ironically, China was scheduled to host the 2007 IADC meeting in Beijing between 23 and 25 April. After China tested its ASAT weapon in January 2007 and created the largest space debris mess ever, they cancelled the IADC meeting only days before it was to be held to avoid certain and deserved condemnation. Scores of international delegates had to cancel their reservations at the last minute, making a bad public relations situation even worse for the Chinese. While a treaty banning space weapons has been a nonstarter, progress has been made in space debris mitigation which could ultimately serve the same purpose.

Primarily through NASA, the United States has been a leader in international mitigation efforts. In fact, the United States first wrote and released its own guidelines in 1997, calling for measures such as designing satellites and rocket stages to limit the debris released when placing satellites in orbit, and depleting propellant from nonoperational satellites or stages to reduce the risk of explosions.[18] Following the U.S. lead, in 2001 COPUOS asked the IADC to develop and submit a set of voluntary guidelines for potential adoption by both COPUOS and the United Nations. The guidelines were initially expected to be approved by COPUOS in 2004 but due to the reservations of several countries, most notably Russia and India, the negotiations were prolonged. Finally, a less technically specific version of the guidelines were adopted by the COPUOS Scientific and Technical Subcommittee in 2005, and those were approved by the larger body during its fiftieth anniversary session in 2007.[19] Included in the guidelines is a provision pledging signatories to refrain from the deliberate creation of space debris or destruction of satellites, noting that if you have to destroy something, it should be done at very low altitude.[20] The guidelines, however, are not legally binding and lack enforcement mechanisms. There is no legal restriction on the testing or use of ASAT weapons which create enormous amounts of debris, as demonstrated by early U.S. tests and the more recent Chinese test. The debris created by the testing and/or use of ASAT weapons which destroy satellites by colliding with them at high speed could—with one test—overwhelm the voluntary reductions agreed to in the IADC guidelines reductions. Keep in mind that the amount of large debris created by the Chinese ASAT test was essentially the same as was reduced by debris mitigation efforts over the previous decade. The debris created by destruction of that satellite, with a mass of less then one ton, is significantly less than would be produced by the destruction, for example, of a ten-ton spy satellite.[21]

Because the United States has the most space assets, civil and military, its interest in protecting them is understandably high. It is also the only nation capable of tracking and monitoring space debris, through the Air Force's Space Surveillance Network. Exercising that capability provides SSA—knowing what is going on in space—is critical as orbits become increasingly populated, debris increases, and space activity generally increases. Until recently, the United States generously shared data on space debris with commercial operators and foreign governments, to avoid collisions and damaging impacts with debris in space. Because of both budget difficulties within NASA and due to the increasing turn toward unilateralism and militarism in space policy, the Air Force now controls the data and it is shared on a much more restrained basis. Again, one must wonder what message that action sends to other countries. It should also be pointed out though that the U.S. military still largely supports efforts to mitigate the creation of debris. As stated, those in the Air Force responsible for SSA were likely not happy about the intentional destruction of US-193.

Conference on Disarmament

The Conference on Disarmament has evolved from a series of earlier Geneva-based negotiating forums. It was established in 1979 "as the single multilateral disarmament negotiating forum of the international community."[22] The CD reports to the General Assembly and its budget is part of the UN budget. With an official membership of sixty-five members, other UN Member States also participate in the CD's substantive discussions. The early success of the CD, and its predecessors, is evidenced in its negotiation of such major multilateral arms limitations and disarmaments agreements as the Treaty on the Nonproliferation of Nuclear Weapons, the Convention on the Prohibition of Military or Any Other Hostile Use of Environmental Modification Techniques, the seabed treaties, the Convention on the Prohibition of the Development, Production and Stockpiling of Bacteriological (Biological) and Toxin Weapons and on their Destruction, the Convention on the Prohibition of the Development, Production, Stockpiling and Use of Chemical Weapons and on their Destruction, and the Comprehensive Nuclear Test Ban Treaty. The CD currently focuses on issues regarding weapons of mass destruction of any kind, and prevention of an arms race in outer space. While it has clearly had considerable success in the former, it has a lackluster track record on the latter.

The last CD success occurred in 1996 with the Comprehensive Test Ban Treaty. Since that time, CD efforts on all subjects have been largely stuck in gridlock, owing considerably to the consensus style decision-making it employs. While that style served the organization well in the past so as not to waste its time in areas of narrow interest, it has now become a de facto veto tool. In 1996, the CD expanded by twenty-three countries to its current size. According to Stephen Rademaker, a Republican who has held high-level positions on Congressional staffs and within the White House, the increase in size led to the CD becoming "a debating society, not a negotiating body."[23]

According to Rademaker, as the conference has become more and more ideologically diverse, it has also become increasingly gridlocked, to the point that "governments have begun to downgrade their participation in the forum."[24] He put special emphasis on the standoff between U.S. efforts to push a fissile material cutoff treaty (FMCT), and other countries' refusal to deal with the FMCT unless the United States agrees to participate in PAROS talks, which the United States has resisted. Still other countries have pushed for negative security assurances, which are guarantees by nuclear-weapons states that they will not use nuclear weapons against states that have formally renounced them. All this, he says, "provides little basis for optimism that the CD is going to be able to rise to today's challenges."[25] And there are many challenges, some generated by the United States.

At the CD meeting on 13 February 2007, Christina Rocca, speaking for the United States, took the opportunity to speak out against the Chinese ASAT test. She observed "that there was an inherent contradiction between the political efforts in the Conference vis-à-vis outer space, as well as the work on mitigation of space debris in the Committee on the Peaceful Uses of Outer Space and the Interagency Space Debris Coordination Committee, on the one hand, and the action taken on 11 January this year. All space-faring nations deserved an explanation for that discrepancy."[26] One year and two days later, on 15 February 2008, Ambassador Rocca took the floor again, this time to announce U.S. intentions to destroy US-193, "in the interests of transparency . . . [and] consistent with the provisions of the 1967 Outer Space Treaty and in the spirit of international cooperation."[27] The skepticism that action generated in some countries has already been stated, regardless of U.S. prenotification of its intent. The Canadian press was among those running analyses of the view that "in last week's space spectacular, a U.S. missile did more than turn a dead satellite into bits of space scrap. It also blew another hole in hopes that the world's countries would forge a treaty making outer space a weapons-free realm."[28]

Even more recently, in March 2008, Paula DeSutter, Assistant Secretary of State for Verification, Compliance and Implementation delivered remarks on whether an outer space arms-control treaty would be verifiable to the George C. Marshall Institute at the National Press Club in Washington, D.C. Her remarks are notable in the consistency of the three messages that the Bush administration maintained on the particular issue of space arms control, as opposed to other areas of space policy. The first is that there "is no—I repeat, no—ongoing arms race in space."[29] This mantra is repeated so often it is reminiscent of Obi Wan's hand-waving intonation "these are not the droids you are looking for" in *Star Wars: Episode 4.* Only in the present case it is not Obi Wan employing the Jedi mind trick, convincing everyone to go about their business and ignore what is going on. It is those supporting the weaponization of space. Second, Ambassador DeSutter again dredges up the red herring argument that the inability to define a space weapon makes further discussion on the subject impossible. As already discussed in Chapter 3, that argument simply does not hold up. Third, and ironically, after reciting a list of technical parameters that would need to be applied to any technical means of treaty verification—technical parameters that one can only *wish* would also be applied to missile-defense and space-weapons evaluations—she concludes that "unfortunately, even with all of these tools, undetected and undetectable cheating remains quite possible."[30] In other words, technology cannot provide a 100 percent guarantee against cheating. That is undoubtedly true. Why is it, however, that space hawks seem always to profess the belief that technology can provide the solution to any problem and address any need—except in the area of treaty verification? It seems to be the *only* area where they use the word "impossible."

Finally, Ambassador DeSutter refers to and agrees with George C. Marshall Institute President Jeff Kueter's earlier statement that "Few criticize the U.S. decision to attempt the destruction of a fully fueled, disabled spy satellite before it crashes to Earth. Using missile-defense assets to further minimize the risk of harm is commendable."[31] Overseas newspapers and skeptical analyses from the scientific communities seemingly do not count as criticisms. Apparently because the largely technically uninformed public did not take to the streets over the intentional destruction of US-193 and Congress, presented with a fait accompli between the short time of announcement and mission execution, decided not to step in front of a moving train, that equates to approval. Ambassador DeSutter's remarks succinctly characterize the U.S. position, which is not the dominant international position. Regardless of motivations or approval, escalation of negative space activity continues, to the chagrin of most countries.

Canada, for example, has taken an active, even leading role, in trying to break the stalemate on space arms-control issues. Its ambassador to the UN, Paul Meyer, offers a different perspective on the CD, one that reeks of frustration. Of the conference's inability to make progress in any areas since 1996: "This disappointing state of affairs in turn reflects CD members' inability to agree on what issues they should take up and how they are to be treated. . . . At the root of this failure are differing national priorities, interests, and threat perceptions among the CD member states."[32] The way to fix that, from his Canadian perspective, is clear: "A CD work program that would be both substantive and generally acceptable would have three components: a negotiating mandate for an FMCT, a discussion mandate for PAROS, and a discussion mandate for nuclear disarmament under which rubric the topic of negative security assurances could be subsumed."[33] Ambassador Meyer points out as well that there is wide support for PAROS, as indicated by the 2005 vote of 166 countries in favor of a supporting resolution, and the United States standing alone in objection, with Israel abstaining.[34] He concludes by noting the critical nature of arms control, especially now given the grave dangers faced, and optimistically concludes that "there is nothing wrong at the CD that a little concerted diplomacy cannot fix."[35]

Michael Krepon, the director of the Stimson Center, after years of working within the Washington Beltway, offers a pragmatic approach not reliant on doing the same things over and over and expecting a different result. Krepon argues that the focus should be placed on something less formal than treaties, such as codes of conduct, since treaties are hard to negotiate and adamantly rejected by the Bush administration in any event. "The pace of . . . deliberations might well be quickened with well-structured workshops between technical experts and diplomats on the key elements of the prospective code."[36]

Code of Conduct/Rules of the Road

What is a code of conduct? In its simplest form, a code of conduct is a set of rules outlining the responsibilities or proper parameters of operation for individuals, organizations, or entities. Hence they are also sometimes referred to as "rules of the road," with driving used as an analogy: drivers (in the United States) stay to the right, obey speed limits, use lights when driving at night, etc. There are precedents for developing codes of conduct in instances where treaties or more formal agreements are impractical. These include the Incidents at Sea Agreement (1972), Prevention of Dangerous Military Activities (1989), International Code of Conduct Against Ballistic Missile Proliferation (2002), and the Proliferation Security Initiative (2003).[37] In the security realm, codes of conduct are intended to prevent dangerous military-related practices on the ground, in the air, and at sea. For example, even during the Cold War both Washington and Moscow recognized the utility of setting up practices to avoid incidents at sea that could have quickly escalated. That led to the Incidents at Sea Agreement, requiring the navies of both countries to avoid collisions and respect the principle of noninterference with each other's ships. Subsequently, the navies of more than thirty other countries have adopted similar agreements. A similar agreement for space seems appropriate, especially given the eagerness with which space hegemons compare space to other battlespaces. Specific to space, "a code of conduct is needed to insure the safe operation of satellites while at the same time increasing cooperation in space, thereby reducing tensions that might lead to conflict in space."[38]

The argument most commonly used against a code of conduct for space is that bad actors do not follow rules. That is true. But rules that have been agreed to make it easier to identify those rule-breakers and build coalitions to censure them. Every kind of rule is sometimes broken, but that does not negate the importance of having rules and making sure that everyone understands them. Further, the idea that an act of cheating or rule-breaking could cripple the United States to such a devastating extent that consideration of even voluntary rules cannot even be considered has been largely dispelled. MIT scientist Geoffrey Forden has provided the technical analysis that convincingly demonstrates that the current threat from the Pentagon's apparent greatest space threat, China, even extrapolated some years out, is marginal and able to be countered by the U.S. without space weapons. He suggests that an ASAT testing ban could assure that situation is maintained even longer, and a code of conduct would go a long way toward that end-state as well.[39]

The Henry L. Stimson Center in Washington has drafted a Model Code of Conduct for responsible space-faring nations.[40] It was created by experts from NGOs in Canada, France, Japan, Russia, and the United States in October 2007, with the objective of preserving and advancing the peaceful exploration and use of outer space. It begins by recognizing the salience of several articles of the United Nations Charter, and reinforcing the principles of the Outer Space Treaty. Article 2(4) of the United Nations Charter obligates members to refrain in their international relations from the threat or use of force against the territorial integrity or political independence of any state, or in any other manner inconsistent with the purposes of the United Nations. Article 42 of the Charter provides authority under which the UN Security Council may mandate action by air, sea, or land forces as necessary to maintain or restore international peace and security. Article 51 of the Charter recognizes the inherent right of self-defense of all states. So the code attempts to build on past legal agreements and advocate additional ones, but to do so incrementally, beginning with voluntary guidelines.

The Code of Conduct drafted through the Stimson Center suggests specific rights and responsibilities for space-faring nations.

RIGHTS OF SPACE-FARING STATES:
The right of access to space for exploration or other peaceful purposes.
The right of safe and interference-free space operations, including military support functions.

The right of self-defense as enumerated in the Charter of the United Nations.

The right to be informed on matters pertaining to the objectives and purposes of this Code of Conduct.

The right of consultation on matters of concern and the proper implementation of this Code of Conduct.

RESPONSIBILITIES OF SPACE-FARING STATES:

The responsibility to respect the rights of other space-faring states and legitimate stakeholders.

The responsibility to regulate stakeholders that operate within their territory or that use their space launch services in conformity with the objectives and purposes of this Code of Conduct.

Each state has the responsibility to regulate the behavior of its nationals in conformity with the objectives and purposes of this Code of Conduct, wherever those actions occur.

The responsibility to develop and abide by rules of safe space operation and traffic management.

The responsibility to share information related to safe space operations and traffic management and to enhance cooperation on space situational awareness.

The responsibility to mitigate and minimize space debris in accordance with the best practices established by the international community in such agreements as the Inter-Agency Debris Coordination Committee guidelines and guidelines of the Scientific and Technical Subcommittee of the United Nations Committee on the Peaceful Uses of Outer Space.

The responsibility to refrain from harmful interference against space objects.

The responsibility to consult with other space-faring states regarding activities of concern in space and to enhance cooperation to advance the objectives and purposes of this Code of Conduct.

The responsibility to establish consultative procedures to address and resolve questions relating to compliance with this Code of Conduct, and to agree upon such additional measures as may be necessary to improve the viability and effectiveness of this Code of Conduct.[41]

Not surprisingly, the Code has been endorsed by numerous international delegation representatives.[42] The delegation statements of Italy, Switzerland, the European Union, and Canada to the 2007 Conference on Disarmament all endorsed at the very least the idea of discussing a code of conduct as an interim step toward PAROS, and the French Foreign Minister, Philippe Douste-Blazy, has expressed support for the idea of a code of conduct.[43] Representative Jane Harman (D-California) endorsed the idea in a *Space News* op-ed on 9 April 2007. Representative Ellen Tauscher (D-California) spoke of the need for "common norms and acceptable rules of behavior in space" to the *Washington Times* in February 2007. The same month David McGlade, CEO of Intelsat, supported dialogue on rules of the road to *Space News*, indicating industry's recognition of the need for a stable space environment. The space industry trade publication *Aviation Week & Space Technology* stated that "Washington should consider whether crafting codes of conduct for space might lead to many of the benefits that advocates of a space arms-control treaty wish for, but without as many technical difficulties and risks" in 2007.[44] The *Economist* also issued a similar endorsement in 2007.[45] Perhaps most importantly, the military seems to be recognizing the benefits of a code of conduct as well.

Whither Optimism?

In October 2006 General James Cartwright, then the top U.S. military officer in charge of space operations, stated that he was using the Joint Space Operations Center to "ensure U.S. satellites, as well as international partners in space, adhere to common 'rules of the road' . . . In the space arena, when the United States detects that something has gone wrong, the first questions typically asked are, 'Gee, was it our satellite that wandered off course? Was it someone else's?' "[46] General Cartwright's replacement as Commander of U.S. Strategic Forces, former astronaut General Kevin P. Chilton, echoed his feelings about a code of conduct at his confirmation hearing. Chilton said, "I think as a government, we should examine the potential utility of a code of conduct or 'rules of the road' for the space domain, thus providing a common understanding of acceptable or unacceptable behavior with a medium shared by all nations."[47] Two critical elements for future consideration are clear from both General Cartwright and General Chilton's statements.

First, there is increasingly a need for enhanced space situational awareness. Russian General Vladimir Popovkin, head of Russia's space forces, also reinforced that notion, as well as a code of conduct. " 'It's necessary to legalize the game rules in space,' Popovkin said, warning that the complexity of space weapons could trigger a war. Satellites could fail for technical reasons, but their owner might think they were incapacitated by an enemy and be tempted to retaliate, he said. 'If that happens, a nation might ask a legitimate question: Could it be the beginning of an effort to deafen and blind it?' Popovkin said."[48]

Second, a free-for-all in space is in nobody's best interest. The American and Russian publics seem to concur. Most Americans and Russian think their governments should cooperate toward preventing an arms race in space, according to a study released in 2008 of 1,247 Americans and 1,601 Russians, carried out by WorldPublicOpinion.org in conjunction with the Center for International and Security Studies at the University of Maryland.[49] The study also found strong support for unilateral restraint, a treaty that would keep space free of weapons and treaties that would prohibit countries from attacking or interfering with each others' satellites and from testing or deploying weapons designed to attack satellites. If the military continues to push for some sort of code or rules, there is a good chance something can be done. Those chances were bolster with the election as well, as candidate Barack Obama was the only presidential candidate that supported a space code of conduct, according to a 2008 survery of presidential candidates by Washington's Council for a Livable World.[50] A treaty seems unlikely for the near future, but if the United States even agrees to dialogue that would be internationally welcomed progress.

Chapter Six
Globalizing Space

We cannot solve our problems with the same thinking we used when we created them.

—Albert Einstein

Fundamentally, globalization is all about connectivity. While initially globalization was considered primarily a concept applied to financial markets, it has since been recognized to have multiple dimensions: economic, cultural, environmental, and security-related among the most important. Consequently, everything and anything related to connectivity has become a commodity. Case in point: in March 2008, Verizon and AT&T paid over $16 billion for radio spectrum licenses at a Federal Communications Commission auction, evidencing the value of those commodities.[1] Satellites are a multibillion-dollar international commodity, and they are key in providing connectivity to remote and previously inaccessible areas of the world. Consequently, everybody wants them and everybody wants to protect their own, but the avenues being pursued by the United States toward the latter goal increasingly appear counterproductive.

Without connectivity, individuals, corporations, institutions, countries, and regions can be left behind—"roadkill" in the globalization era.[2] Being left behind is perilous, both for those unfortunates who suffer from being left behind and for those who will feel their angry backlash. Thomas P. M. Barnett, in his book *The Pentagon's New Map*, says, "Globalization is a condition defined as mutually assured dependence."[3] The 2008 financial meltdown required concerted global action to stop the downward spiral; one country alone, even the United States, couldn't do it. Globalization has replaced the Cold War as the defining framework surrounding international relations, but has yet to be recognized as such in the realm of space security. Barnett goes on to argue that those areas of the world that are not connected will be the future security hot spots, what he calls "the gap." That premise has a long pedigree.[4] If globalization is mutually assured dependence, then each involved entity becomes a stakeholder and it behooves them to maintain their ability to stay connected.

In 2007, the U.S. Navy put forth a new U.S. maritime strategy called "A Cooperative Strategy for Twenty-First Century Seapower."[5] According to analyst Taylor Dinerman, in an article linking the strategy goals to space, its goal is to link all, or nearly all, of the world's navies. Further, it seeks to link these navies not to increase overall kinetic firepower, but to create a global sensor and communications network to provide round-the-clock transparency toward secure and free access to global oceans for all seafaring countries. It is a visionary strategy that reflects the realities of globalization. Dinerman further states, "Today, only the U.S. navy has the hardware, the people, the expertise, and the vision to create what will be a new kind of global service, similar in some ways to GPS. In this case [referencing the new Maritime Strategy], unlike the satellite navigation system, most of the hardware will be owned and operated by non-U.S. actors."[6] Its inclusionary framework toward cooperative rather than inherently competitive goals makes total sense, but is, nevertheless, somewhat revolutionary. Rather than focusing on "platforms"— those things navies buy from which to launch ordinance at each other—it focuses on shaping the future maritime environment toward one favorable to the United States.

If the idea of cooperating toward a more secure future holds true on the seas, and it appears that the Navy thinks it does, then consideration of how it might work in space at least deserves consideration. Assuring that countries are connected in as many ways as possible is to everyone's benefit—in space as on Earth—but yet space remains the last bastion of Cold War-like politics.

We have seen that the domination of space is not viable because of technical, economic, and politically realities. Making use of globalization—mutual dependence—and giving other countries a vested interest in space security is a more plausible and potentially effective alternative. Indeed, globalization can become a complementary factor in security planning. "Shared interests in protecting the Internet, for example, have created a large unofficial and official coalition of parties for which uninterrupted access is vital. The United States serves as the link among all cyberspace-vested interests and other technically based domains, including space. . . . Protecting space assets can become an international rather than an exclusively U.S. interest."[7] Rather than seeing other countries' activities in space—activities that cannot be stopped in any event—as a threat, they should be used as grounds from which to build coalitions of those interested in maintaining uninterrupted access and use. In fact, some people and organizations argue that "space sustainability" is a better term than space security, because it focuses on global development and environmental protection on Earth and in space, the global commons again, through regulations that would foster good behavior, set boundaries for space activities, and create disincentives for bad behavior, rather than on military approaches.[8] That is a far better option than the my-way-or-the-highway approach that has been tacitly employed. The politics of globalization, including features of liberal internationalism such as multilateral mechanisms and diplomacy, must replace the Cold War-like politics which has recently dominated space relations.

Global Realities

Space technology is already globalized, available to almost any interested buyer. Differences between suppliers are found primarily in degree of technological maturity, sophistication, and cost. Satellite technology has been globally understood and available since the 1960s and the advent of the Communications Satellite Corporation (COMSAT), a U.S. organization specifically set up to drive the commercial diffusion of satellite technology internationally. Launch technology was more closely held by the United States, but since physics is understood in Tokyo, Beijing, Paris, Moscow, and elsewhere as well as it is in Pasadena, that genie could not be kept in the bottle. Arianespace, a European consortium with shareholders in ten European countries, has held over 50 percent of the world market for launching satellites to geosynchronous Earth orbit since 2007—a market dominated by the United States in earlier times. Further, in this era of globalization joint ventures are often the way that international business is conducted. International Launches Services is a joint venture between a U.S. firm and two Russian firms. Sea Launch, a spacecraft launch service using a mobile sea platform, is jointly owned by U.S., Russian, Ukrainian, and Norwegian companies. The bottom line is that the United States still holds very few monopolies on space technology. It can perhaps influence how fast countries acquire sophisticated technologies, but in increasingly few cases can it deny technology to a country because that country will simply find and be able to buy it elsewhere.

At the Schriever Air Force Base website, GPS is referred to as "the world's only global utility."[9] Perhaps it is more accurate to say that GPS *and* the Internet are currently the only two global utilities, still signifying their unique and important nature, as it can be reasonably argued that the Internet is a global utility as well. Because GPS is so valuable not just to the United States, but to all countries, its satellites are likely among the least at risk to destruction of all those satellites in orbit.

Air Force Lt. General Michael Hamel, commander of the Space and Missile Systems Center, told reporters in March 2008 that one of the reasons China's 2007 ASAT test was so alarming was that it highlighted the strategic vulnerability of the U.S. military vis-à-vis GPS satellites.[10] The circumstances under which China would actually destroy GPS satellites, however, and potentially place global use of the system at risk in areas from financial systems to civilian aircraft and cell phone networks, would have to be incredibly dire as worldwide condemnation would certainly follow. General Hamel then went on to talk about disruption of GPS signals through jamming and disruptive wave forms. Those same concerns about jamming and hacking were voiced by Air Force officials at the National Space Symposium in Colorado Springs, Colorado, in April 2008.[11]

The possibility of disrupted GPS signals is far more likely than blown up GPS satellites. The annual DoD report, "Military Power of the People's Republic of China," submitted to Congress on 25 May 2007, claimed that China acquired jammers from the Ukraine in the late 1990s capable of jamming GPS.[12] Since then China has probably developed its own jammers as well. But jamming is a technical threat the United States has contended with long before GPS and knows how to address. According to Lt. Col. Stormy Martin, who oversees navigation programs at Space Command, "The Air Force solution for the future . . . is switching over to a dedicated military signal that will be harder for would-be jammers to identify and pumping up the volume of the GPS signal so it will be heard by receivers like a politician barking his message over the protests of an angry crowd."[13] Doing that will cost money, likely close to a billion dollars, but feasibility is then a matter of budget prioritization, not technical wizardry. The point is that shared value offers the GPS satellites more protection against kinetic attack than space weapons could ever offer. It should also be noted that when the GPS Selective Availability signal (the degraded signal originally made available for civilian use) was turned off in May 2000, instantly making GPS more accurate for all, the decision to do so was largely based on global commercial interests creating strong pressure for this change—an early example of globalization and military proprietorship colliding, with globalization winning.

The European desire for its own navigation satellite system, called Galileo, and U.S. fears about its military potential again illustrate the dilemmas created when dual-use technology and globalization collide. Whereas Europe has considered Galileo primarily in terms of it potentially creating 150,000 new jobs and generating revenue estimates that seem to be doubling almost annually, for the United States GPS is ultimately a military system, owned and operated by the Air Force. And it is because of that U.S. perspective and military ownership of GPS that Europe consequently fears that the United States might deny others access to GPS in the event of hostilities and feels it cannot afford to rely exclusively on that system. This vicious circle of political fear and subsequent government actions that generate more political fears must stop.

In the private sector, visits to space and space exploration and development are no longer considered the purview of NASA or even other nations. Sadly, the adage that the fastest way to kill a new idea is to give it to NASA is gaining credence, though at least some of NASA's "issues" come from being the stepchild to Washington's current obsession with military space activity. Nor does nationality dictate who gets to go to space. Rather, it's all a matter of money, or as the *New York Times* put it, "Thrillionaires: The New Space Capitalists."[14]

Entrepreneurs including Briton Richard Branson of the Virgin Group, John Carmack, the creator of computer games like Doom and Quake, and thirty-something Elon Musk, the founder of PayPal, are all involved with building rockets. South African-born Musk is credited with saying, "When people ask me why I started a rocket company, I say, 'I was trying to learn how to turn a large fortune into a small one.'"[15] Why do they want to build rockets? Like the original explorers of the American West, they are not quite sure, but they are confident that the rewards will be worth it. The new vehicles being built are "meant to open space to a new generation of spacefarers who are more creative than classically trained astronauts" according to designer Burt Rutan. "And that will bring with it a new way of looking at space travel, just as personal computing opened up the use of computers from a military and academic tool to something that transformed the world." The newcomers, Rutan predicts, will bring "breakthroughs that will come, that will tell us why we're doing this and what can we do with it."[16]

While waiting for these rocketry breakthroughs to be made, some "thrillionaires" are buying seats on those vehicles already available. A Virginia-based firm called Space Adventures has already arranged for multiple individuals to visit the International Space Station on a paying basis. American millionaire Dennis Tito was the first to broker a ride to ISS in 2001, after shrill protests from NASA, including charges that he was "un-American" because he paid the Russians to take him into orbit. South African businessman Mark Shuttleworth followed in 2002, American scientist-turned-entrepreneur Gregory Olsen in 2005, Iranian-American businesswoman Anousheh Ansari in 2006, billionaire Simon Simonyi in 2007, and Richard Garriott, a video-game mogul and son of former NASA astronaut Owen Garriott, in 2008. These individuals see the future of space in terms of tourism and development.

While the risks of space development are inherently high due to the harsh environmental conditions of space that must be overcome, the potential rewards are beyond estimation. Private dollars will go, however, where the risk is manageable and efforts are being taken to promote stability. Again, economic considerations may well be the card that trumps U.S. military ambitions to dominate space.

Threats and Opportunities

Beyond the "long war" against terrorism, China is viewed as the greatest potential threat to the United States, as a near-peer competitor. Increasingly, however, questions are being asked about the circumstances under which China would risk war with the United States, clearly jeopardizing everything it has accomplished in the past twenty years. Taiwan scenarios immediately come to mind, as Taiwan is unquestionably China's "fall on their sword" issue. No Chinese leader can afford to be the one who let Taiwan slip away. Except for Taiwan though, risk scenarios become much more complicated and the potential for anticipated conflict lessens, largely because of globalization.

According to former trade publication *Aviation Week & Space Technology* editor William B. Scott and Michael J. Coumatos (together coauthors of *Space Wars: The First Six Hours of World War III*),[17] the chances of conflict in space are slim because of financial connectivity between the potential contenders. "Absent an all-out war, however, there is little reason for China to conduct a preemptive attack on U.S. satellites. The economies of China and the U.S. are inextricably intertwined. In 2006, according to *Business Week*, the U.S. imported $287.8 billion in Chinese goods. . . . And China holds billions in U.S. debt. History shows it's difficult to fight those with whom one trades extensively. Would China's leaders risk trillions of dollars, as well as the roughly eighty million Chinese jobs linked to exports, by shooting down a U.S. satellite, possibly triggering a war? . . . In short, a shooting war in space would be a financial disaster for both China and the U.S."[18] So while economics does not negate the potential for war, it does raise the cost.

Originally, the Chinese government embraced globalization tentatively, as its only means of badly needed economic development to keep its 1.3-plus billion population placated with the authoritarian communist government. Subsequently, however, it has accepted globalization and the interdependence that inherently accompanies it with increasing enthusiasm. While the government in Beijing has felt the need to "manage" the internal and external vulnerabilities created by globalization,

Beijing also sees the growing tide of globalization as a means to counter U.S. hegemony.[19] A similar premise might be used by the United States to counter the numerous vulnerabilities to space assets inherently created by the physical environment.

In August 1998, North Korea attempted to launch a small satellite into orbit. It was not successful; nothing was tracked in orbit, though U.S. and other sensors were clearly looking. Yet, even after failure was clear, the North Koreans deftly reported 100 successful orbits, apparently oblivious to international recognition that the emperor had no clothes, so to speak. In February 2008, Iran fired a rocket into space, claiming it was a precursor to the intended launch of a satellite called Omid (Hope) into orbit in 2009. Iran's attempted satellite launch got a considerable amount of press coverage in the global press. The video of the launch seemed to show a relatively small, one-stage missile apparently incapable of placing a satellite in orbit. Iran tried again in August 2008 to launch a satellite into orbit, this time using a multistage rocket. Though Iran again claimed it was successful, the United States reported the second stage of the rocket failed.[20] While both could be precursors to something that could eventually launch Omid into orbit, the 2009 timetable seems exaggerated. Clearly, however, the Iranians see becoming a space-faring nation as a goal to aspire to. Rather than condemn them for this, the United States, as the leader in space hardware, assets, technology, and achievements to date, ought to try to use that to our advantage.

Both the North Korean and Iranian launches were referred to by the United States as threatening missile tests. In 1998 State Department spokesman James Rubin stated that North Korea now had "the capability to deliver a weapons payload," thus "confirming the inherent capability to threaten its neighbors."[21] In 2008, White House spokesman Gordon Johndroe "stated unequivocally that the test was threatening."[22] In the case of both North Korea and Iran, it is likely that each country would like to have the capability to lift satellites into orbit, a capability that can be argued as their right. But the technology used to lift satellites into orbit is inarguably dual-use and whether the primary reason for the launch or not, the 1998 and 2005 launches provided North Korea and Iran the opportunity to test technology that could be useful for offensive purposes. If it is argued that motivation does not excuse de facto results, then the intentional destruction of US-193 was a de facto ASAT test. If it is perceived that China and the United States are testing ASATs, other countries, like India, may feel justified in claiming ASAT capabilities as well—and potentially test that capability—or risk being left behind. Equally important, trying to stop the use of already globalized space technology—technology that can be argued as essential to the economic health and therefore the national security of a country—is futile. Even potentially nefarious technology cannot be "un-invented."[23] Therefore, the only realistic chance of turning threats into opportunities seems to be through the interdependence that inherently accompanies globalization.

Naturally, the Pentagon will not be willing to cede the protection of its valuable space assets to arguments based primarily on economics, nor should it. But that doesn't mean that more kinetic approaches based on military dominance must prevail either. Michael Krepon has suggested that "Presidential space policy usually emphasizes one of three preferences: active diplomacy to reduce threatening developments in space, active pursuit of military options to counter perceived threats, or a policy of contingent restraint."[24] It is important to recall that contingent restraint prevailed from Eisenhower until Reagan. The pursuit of military options came to the fore more recently, during the George W. Bush administration, when the Pentagon began having a far greater influence on space policy.

A 2008 Council of Foreign Relations report, by Bruce W. MacDonald, states the options slightly differently. "In shaping a future military space regime, the United States can choose to pursue one or some combination of three doctrinal options: diplomacy, space deterrence, and space dominance."[25] With outright dominance demonstrated as not a viable option, MacDonald goes on to offer a better suggestion. He supports a deterrence-based approach derived from nuclear-weapons deterrence concepts successfully employed during the Cold War, but that were later hastily abandoned in post-9/11 Washington because it was felt that those concepts did not apply to fighting terrorism or dealing with rogue states. While recognizing the differences between nuclear and space deterrence, and the need for a much more nuanced approach with space, he nevertheless makes a strong case.

If the United States can resist the urge to overreach, it may be able to achieve a more stable, less costly military space posture and doctrine that could maintain a measure of U.S. space superiority, based on the strategic nuclear balance precedent. The United States could preserve space superiority relative to China, deriving more benefit from space than China does and retaining more offensive capability, though China would still keep its ability to deter the United States from attacking China's growing space capability. Such a capability appears well within China's reach, in spite of Washington's wishes otherwise.

Over the long term, deterrence-based superiority would be grounded in the reality of the difficulty in maintaining dominance in space, and the fundamental vulnerability of space-based weapons both to other space-based weapons as well as to ground-based counterspace weapons, especially directed-energy weapons. Deterrence-based superiority would be less costly to maintain than dominance and could be substantially more stable under the proper conditions, though neither achievement not maintenance would be simple.[26]

Beyond the military capabilities that would be required to support such a posture, including jammers and other forms of reversible electronic and electro-optical systems, healthy U.S.–China relations in general, including dialogue and resisting the urge toward provocative rhetoric, and confidence-building measures (CBM) would also be necessary.

Still, diplomacy alone is likely not enough in this post-9/11 world. It is a necessary, but not sufficient means to protect American security in space. But military goals need to be realistic and achievable, and the best U.S. hope in space lies in returning to a posture of contingent restraint, combined with deterrence-based superiority and denial deterrence (i.e., convincing an opponent that his attack will not succeed through redundancy and other capabilities for reconstituting essential space capabilities). This would by no means be an easy approach and would in fact require considerable focus for both planning and implementation. But it would provide the U.S. military with an economical and technologically viable strategic framework for protecting space assets, something glaringly lacking in U.S. policy for some time.

A Way Forward

At least one space warrior has already become an advocate of cooperation as a way to build space security. Retired Air Force General Pete Worden is now director of NASA's Ames Research Center. Worden believes "space cooperation is already serving as 'glue' to forge coalitions and keep people working together. As one of the few truly global media, space capabilities should realize their full potential as the basis for 'soft power' influence. This does not exclude economic competition among cooperating players—indeed shared interests in allowing commercial developments are a foundational element of space soft power."[27] Consequently, in his role as director at Ames, he has built a number of collaborations, including a signed agreement with the University of Stuttgart and a project with the Korea Advanced Institute for Science and Technology. Worden says these collaborations focus on the core areas of Ames expertise, particularly small spacecraft science missions, so they are win-win for all parties. Additionally, Ames is hosting the 2009 summer session of the International Space University, an institution built around the goal of fostering space cooperation.

Coming from someone with both a technical and a military background, perhaps most interesting is Worden's response to being asked what advice he would give the Bush administration's successor on how best to protect U.S. space assets.

Space should be recognized as a cornerstone of national economic, societal values and security interests. These can be protected through a combination of forging shared global interests AND military options. The latter can best be assured through maintaining multiple backups for contingencies. At the head of this list is the ability to rapidly reconstitute lost or destroyed assets and to respond to an aggressor in asymmetric ways. The latter means not responding to an attack on space systems with a tit-for-tat counterattack. Searching for some other response, perhaps an economic or alternate strategic response could better deter further aggression than a strictly military option.[28]

By any standard, Worden's advice is balanced and reasonable. Unfortunately, however, politics trumps balance and reason on a regular basis.

Hopefully, the Obama administration will begin with a serious evaluation of current space policies and courses of action. Parameters for an evaluation of the military and security issues, including space weapons, might be drawn from the former chairman of the military Joint Chiefs of Staff and Secretary of State Colin Powell's 1992 *Foreign Affairs* article on committing armed forces to a dangerous situation that have become known as the Powell Doctrine. Powell provided a set of questions relevant to considering committing weaponry to space. "Is the political objective we seek to achieve important, clearly defined and understood? Have all other nonviolent policy means failed? Will military force achieve the objective? At what cost? Have the gains and risks been analyzed? How might the situation that we seek to alter, once it is altered by force, develop further and what might be the consequences?"[29]

Such an evaluation is long overdue. And while it may seem unnecessary to state that the evaluation should be done by technically competent individuals without an agenda or vested interest in the outcome, it is necessary. Officials from both Boeing and Lockheed Martin, first and second in terms of contractors doing business with the Pentagon, offered in April 2008 to investigate the feasibility of a space-based layer for ballistic missile defense for the U.S. government.[30] One need not be Carnac the Magnificent to predict what their findings would be. Even with a technically sound, unbiased evaluation, however, change will likely be slow.

While most Americans want to think most states are actually purple rather than distinctly red and blue, the reality is that politically acceptable centrist positions are still elusive on many issues. Though the administration of George W. Bush ended its term with low public approval ratings, a change of administrations will not inherently bridge all partisan divides. And while the Obama administration will likely— one hopes—be less bombastic and more circumspect in both its domestic and international rhetoric and better at strategic communication, it is going to have a very difficult course maneuvering too far one way or the other on most issues. That means we must assume overall past trends—though not necessarily specific policies or programs—will continue.

What does that mean for space? Even if the Obama administration took a hard turn from the current course of action and decided that a treaty banning space weapons was the right thing to do, it still likely would not happen for some time. Though Europe has continually moved toward liberal internationalism, a world governed by international institutions and multilateral treaties, the United States has shied away, even during the Clinton years. From the Kyoto Protocol to the International Criminal Court, the United States has simply refused to bind itself to multilateral agreements, fearing infringement on its sovereignty. With the Bush administration's embrace of unilateral primacy and savaging of liberal internationalism, the United States stopped even considering or pretending to consider similar agreements (hence changing its 2007 PAROS vote from "abstain" to "no"). John Bolton, who served for a time as the Bush administration's ambassador to the United Nations, once wrote that "globalists" were bringing "harm and costs to the United States . . . [by] belittling our popular sovereignty and constitutionalism, and restricting both our domestic and our international policy flexibility and power."[31] While the chauvinistic and bellicose attitude Bolton and hence the United States became known for, especially at the United Nations, has dissipated over time, it is nevertheless doubtful that the Congress of the United States will easily embrace any multilateral treaties, including space treaties.

Missile defense presents its own set of problems. Even if the Obama administration wanted to refocus U.S. efforts onto theater missile defense, technically feasible and politically acceptable to most countries, it would likely have a difficult time doing so. Republicans would have to renege on their "moral obligation" arguments and too many Democrats have voted too much money to national missile defense over the years, attempting not to look soft on defense rather than taking the tough stance, to suddenly change course. So we will likely continue to throw good money after bad for awhile at least, though expansion can be stopped and increased external program oversight instituted toward requiring technical milestones be met or programs cancelled.

In the best of all worlds, the United States might craft a "Grand Bargain" with China regarding space, one where both sides would make big concessions, for potentially for big gains.[32] Missile defense, or perhaps deployment options and space weapons, or at least the deliberate creation of space debris, should both be on the table for consideration in such a grand bargain. That would require an enormous act of political skill and courage on the part of the new administration.

Short of a grand bargain, the areas that potentially hold the most promise for incremental change are those where common interests and joint gains can lead to a willingness to take on if not institutional obligations, then at least to refrain from activities to the detriment of all. Rules of the road generally, including transparency, confidence building measures, and space debris specifically come to mind as ripe for speedy and positive attention by the United States; areas where the United States can and should take the lead. Reforming export control regulations as well—given the realities of globalization, is another area where inactivity by yet another administration would be not only inexcusable but counterproductive.

Returning to a strategy that acknowledges the differences between the space environment from air, land, and sea, and the difficulties imposed by those differences would be a step toward rationality. Equally important, it would allow the United States to again employ cooperative space activities as one of its strongest smart policy tools. The role of global leadership has been thrust upon the United States as the sole remaining superpower. Thankfully, it is eminently qualified to respond. Leadership should not be underrated; it is a commodity as important to security as any tank or gun. It is generated as much through smart power as through military might, something it took the United States too long to realize in Iraq.

Increasingly on space issues, our leadership is being challenged. According to an 2008 index looking at forty factors such as government spending and numbers of spacecraft built, the United States remains dominant in space, outpacing its nearest competitor, Europe, by almost two to one.[33] But a study using that index also found that "India and China, along with Russia, Japan and Europe are all set to reduce the dominance that U.S. has over space activities."[34] Perhaps even more disturbing than countries seeking to increase their own capabilities is that countries are increasingly and deliberately choosing not to work with the United States, witness French companies advertising their satellites as "ITAR free"[35] (meaning they contain no U.S. parts and so are not encumbered by draconian U.S. export rules) nor to emulate the United States, as in not voting with the United States on PAROS votes. The militarized attitude of the United States has served to isolate the United States in international cooperative ventures. The choice made by the United States to focus on keeping all military options open in space has harmed the United States in other areas.

With Neil Armstrong's historic first step on the Moon, the United States established itself as the leader of humanity off the planet Earth. Space is already inherently globalized. The United States must acknowledge other nations exploring and utilizing space as potential collaborators and view partnerships with them as opportunities to exhibit our leadership in the global commons. Further, America must lead by example, or it will find itself alone if not by choice, then by consequence of its own actions. Leadership without willing followers becomes hollow at best and more perilously, coercive.

Most of all, the United States must move beyond mantras. It is disingenuous for American policymakers to say "we mean no harm" with its space policies, programs, and rhetoric when in fact from any perspective but that of the United States "harm" to others can either be inferred as a potential consequence or be seen as irrelevant to the United States. The United States has taken a lone wolf attitude to its peril for too long. A multitude of consequences issuing from globalization make that attitude impossible to sustain. It is no longer enough to try to control the security dilemma that exists and is growing in space; it must be actively scaled back and dealt with from an entirely different perspective, toward making incremental but effective changes.

Einstein famously remarked that "Any intelligent fool can make things bigger, more complex, and more violent. It takes a touch of genius—and a lot of courage—to move in the opposite direction." With the new administration, now is the time for change.

Notes

Preface

1. Hawai'i Research Center for Futures Studies, http://www.futures.hawaii.edu.
2. Arthur C. Clarke, *Profiles of the Future* (New York: Harper & Row, 1962).
3. See Center for Strategic and International Studies Commission on Smart Power website: "America must revitalize its ability to inspire and persuade rather than merely rely upon its military might. Despite the predominance of U.S. hard power, there are limits to its effectiveness in addressing the main foreign policy challenges facing America today. America's standing in the world is diminished, and although there have been discrete "soft power" successes—most notably the progress against HIV/AIDS and malaria, and the creation of the Millennium Challenge Corporation—many of the traditional instruments of soft power, such as public engagement and diplomacy, have been neglected and fallen into disrepair." http://www.csis.org/smartpower.
4. See Mike Moore, *Twilight War: The Folly of U.S. Space Dominance* (Oakland, Calif.: Independent Institute, 2008).

Chapter 1. Space: The Final Cold War Frontier

1. Joan Johnson-Freese, "Getting Our Bearings: GPS," *Yale Global On-Line Magazine*, 23 May 2003. http://www.YaleGlobal.Yale.edu.
2. http://www.af.mil/library/posture/AF_trans_flight_plan-2003.pdf.
3. U.S. Air Force, *Counterspace Operations, Air Force Doctrine Document 2–2.1*, 2 August 2004.
4. http://www.dtic.mil/doctrine/jel/new_pubs/jp3_14.pdf.
5. Jeff Sessions, "Missile Defense, A National Priority," *Strategic Studies Quarterly* 2, no. 2 (Summer 2008): 25, 27.
6. See, for example, David Wright, Laura Grego, and Lisbeth Gronlund, *The Physics of Space Security: A Reference Manual* (Cambridge, Mass.: Union of Concerned Scientists, 2005). http://www.amacad.org/publications/rulesSpace.aspx.
7. See Joan Johnson-Freese, *Space as a Strategic Asset* (New York: Columbia University Press, 2007), chapter 1, for a discussion on security dilemmas and space. See also Mike Moore, "Call Their Bluff," *Space Review*, 28 January 2008. http://www.thespacereview.com/article/913/1.
8. *Space Report: 2007 Update*, Space Foundation, 6. http://www.TheSpaceReport.org.
9. Includes Department of Defense, National Reconnaissance Office,

National Geospatial Intelligence Agency, and Missile Defense Agency. *Space Report: 2007 Update*, Space Foundation, 5. http://www.TheSpaceReport.org.

10. Peter B. de Selding, "EC Report Calls for Doubling Security Space Spending," *Space.com*, 4 April 2005. http://www.space.com/spacenews/archive 05/Spacesec_040405.html.

11. *Space Report: 2007 Update*, Space Foundation, 10. http://www.TheSpace Report.org.

12. See Nancy Gallagher and John D. Steinbruner, *Reconsidering the Rules for Space Security* (Cambridge, Mass.: American Academy of Arts and Sciences Occasional Paper, 2008), 5. The Union of Concerned Scientists' satellite database can be accessed at http://ucsusa.org/global_security/space_weapons/satellite_dat abase.html.

13. See Ludwig von Mises, *Human Action: A Treatise on Economics*, 4th ed. (Irvington-on-Hudson, N.Y.: Foundation for Economic Education, 1996), chapter 24.

14. William J. Broad, "From the Start, the Space Race Was an Arms Race," *New York Times*, 25 September 2007, F10.

15. The full title was Treaty on Principles Governing the Activities of States in the Exploration and Use of Outer Space, Including the Moon and Other Celestial Bodies. For text see Department of State website http://www.state.gov/t/ac/trt/5181.htm.

16. Another twenty-seven countries have signed the treaty but have not yet completed ratification.

17. Bruce M. Deblois, Richard L. Garwin, Scott Kemp, and Jeremy Maxwell, "Space Weapons: Crossing the U.S. Rubicon," *International Security* 29, no. 2 (Fall 2004): 50–84.

18. Karyn Charles Rybacki and Donald Jay Rybacki, *Advocacy and Opposition* (Boston: Allyn and Bacon, 2008), 4–5.

19. Everett C. Dolman, *Astropolitik: Classical Geopolitics in the Space Age* (Portland, Ore.: Frank Cass, 2001).

20. Gallagher and Steinbruner, *Reconsidering the Rules*, 2.

21. James Carroll, "Preventing an Arms Race in Outer Space," *Boston Globe*, 12 May 2008, A15.

22. Gallagher and Steinbruner, *Reconsidering the Rules*, 3.

23. The Honorable Jon Kyl (R-Ariz.), "China's Anti-Satellite Weapon and American National Security," Heritage Lectures, Heritage Foundation, no. 990, 29 January 2007.

24. Jerry Sellers and Wiley Larson, "Communications and Data Handling," in *Keys to Space*, ed. A. Houston and M. Rycroft (New York: McGraw Hill, 1999), 8–13.

25. See John Hyten and Robert Uy, "Moral and Ethical Decisions Regarding Space Warfare," *Air & Space Power Journal* 18, no. 2 (Summer 2004): 51–61.

26. Barry D. Watts, *The Military Use of Space: A Diagnostic Assessment* (Washington, D.C.: Center for Strategic and Budgetary Assessments, February 2001).

27. For example, Lieutenant Colonel Todd Freece, USAF, has argued that too much time is spent looking for and preparing for conventional attack scenarios, which he calls "bears," rather than smaller but potentially equally disruptive "bee stings." He says, "One of the most difficult problems for the U.S. space strategy to address will emerge from the intersection of three trends: (1) the growing number of individuals able to purchase and operate satellite communications equipment for criminal or political activity, (2) the rise in global commu-

nication networks as a way for disparate organizations to find and synchronize with one another, and (3) the application of swarming tactics against U.S. military or commercial space systems by nonstate actors. Individually, a single 'bee sting' of interference does not diminish the capacity of U.S. space systems to function by any substantive amount. If, however, the 'bee sting' occurs while U.S. space systems are supporting a key operation, the success of the supported effort may be jeopardized much like a driver is distracted by a hornet trapped in the car with him while he is attempting to negotiate traffic. Finally, simultaneous attack by hundreds of 'bees' from widely distributed locations could paralyze significant segments of U.S. military, civil and commercial satellite communications networks. The challenge of overcoming a swarming attack on space systems is enormous." See "Bees, not Bears: Addressing Unconventional Threats to the U.S. in Outer Space," unpublished paper, written at the Naval War College, 25 January 2007.

28. Jammers, which interfere with satellite communications and can be directed at the satellite or the ground station, are sometimes also considered ASATs. For the purposes of discussion here, however, the focus is on those technologies which damage or destroy hardware in orbit.

29. Some material in this section is based on Gene Milowicki and Joan Johnson-Freese, "Strategic Choices: Examining the U.S. Military Response to the Chinese Anti-Satellite Test of 11 January 2007," *Astropolitics* 6, no. 1 (January–April 2008): 1–21.

30. Feng Yun, a 1,650-pound satellite in a polar, low-Earth orbit, traveled at an altitude of approximately 860 kilometers (533 statute miles). The vehicle is believed to have been boosted into orbit by a four-stage solid-fuel launch vehicle launched from a mobile launcher (which would make it difficult to track down in a conflict) at the Songlin test facility near Xichang in Sichuan province.

31. See Union of Concerned Scientists, "Debris from China's Kinetic ASAT Test, May 2007. http://www.ucsusa.org/global_security/space_weapons/debris-from-chinas-asat-test.html; Carl Hoffman, "Battlefield Space," *Popular Mechanics* (July 2007): 77–78.

32. Christopher Stone, "Chinese Intentions and American Preparedness," *Space Review*, 13 August 2007. http://www.thespacereview.com/article/930/1 (accessed 7 September 2007).

33. Hoffman, "Battlefield Space," 81.

34. Nicholas L. Johnson et al., "The Characteristics and Consequences of the Break-Up of the Fengyun-1C Spacecraft," IAC-07-A6.3.01 (presented at the 58th International Astronautical Congress, Hyderabad, India, 24–28 September 2007).

35. Hoffman, "Battlefield Space," 81.

36. Ibid.

37. Bonnie Glaser, "U.S.-China Relations: Old and New Challenges: ASAT Test, Taiwan, and Trade," *Comparative Connection*, 11 April 2007. http://www.csis.org/media/csis/pubs/0701qus_china.pdf.

38. Ibid.

39. "China Confirms Anti-Satellite Missile Test," *Guardian*, 23 January 2007. http://www.guardian.co.uk/china/story/0,,1996689,00.html (accessed 28 September 2007).

40. Joseph Kahn, "China Shows Assertiveness in Weapons Test," *New York Times*, 20 January 2007.

41. See comments in Vago Muradian, "China Attempted to Blind U.S. Satel-

lite with Laser," *Defense News*, 28 September 2006, http://www.defensenews.com/story.php?F = 2121111; Kim Willenson with Evert Clark, "War's Fourth Dimension," *Newsweek*, 29 November 1976.

42. "Top Commander: Chinese Interference with U.S. Satellites Uncertain," *Inside the Pentagon*, 12 October 2006.

43. "Satellite Laser Ranging in China," UCS Technical Working Paper, 8 January 2007. http://www.ucsusa.org/global_security/space_weapons/chinese-lasers-and-us-satellites.html.

44. "DoD Continues Satellite Blinding Investigation," 5 January 1976, 18.

45. Richard Fisher, Jr., "Closer Look: Shenzhou-7's Close Pass by the International Space Station," 9 October 2008. www.strategycenter.et/research/pub IS.191/pub_detail.asp.

46. David Wright and Gregory Kulacki, "Chinese Shenzhou 7 'Companion Satellite' (BX-1)," 21 October 2008. http://www.ucsusa.org/nuclear_weapons_and_global_security/space_weapons/technical_issues/chinese-shenzhou-7-satellite.html.

47. Shirley Kan, "China's Anti-Satellite Weapon Test," Congressional Research Service, Order Code RS22652, 23 April 2007, 3–4.

48. Michael R. Gordon and David S. Cloud, "U.S. Knew of China's Missile Test, But Kept Silent," *New York Times*, 23 April 2007.

49. Mary Fitzgerald, "China's Predictable Space 'surprise,'" *Defense News*, 12 February 2007. See also Mary C. Fitzgerald, Statement on "China's Military Strategy for Space," before the U.S.-China Economic and Security Review Commission, 30 March 2007.

50. Jeff Kueter, Statement before the House Oversight and Government Reform Committee, Subcommittee on National Security and Foreign Affairs, 23 May 2007.

51. Phillip C. Sanders and Charles D. Lutes, "China's ASAT Test: Motivations and Implications," The Institute for National Strategic Studies, National Defense University, June 2007. See also Ashley J. Tellis, "China's Military Space Strategy," *Survival* 49 (September 2007): 41–72. His analysis was critiqued by Michael Krepon, Eric Hagt, Shen Dingli, Bao Shixiu, and Michael Pillsbury in "China's Military Space Strategy: An Exchange," *Survival* 50 (February 2008): 157–98.

52. Dean Cheng, "China's ASAT Test: Of Interceptors and Inkblots," *Space News* 18 (February 2007): 17, 19.

53. "A Different View of China's ASAT Test," 13 November 2007. http://www.carnegieendowment.org/events/index.cfm?fa = eventDetail&id = 1074&&prog = zch.

54. Theresa Hitchens, "Statement," U.S. Congress, House, Committee on House Oversight and Government Reform, Subcommittee on National Security and Foreign Affairs, Weapons in Space, 23 May 2007, 8.

55. "Chinese Anti-Satellite Alarms Washington," *Aviation Week & Space Technology*, Aerospace Daily & Defense Report, 19 January 2007. http://www.aviationweek.com/aw/generic/story_channel.jsp?channel = space&id = news/CHIS01197.xml (accessed 9 September 2007).

56. Frank Mooring, Jr., "Chinese ASAT Test Called Worst Single Debris Event Ever," *Aviation Week & Space Technology*, 11 February 2007. http://www.aviationweek.com/aw/generic/story_generic.jsp?channel = awst&id = news/aw021207p2.xml (accessed 9 September 2007).

57. http://space.au.af.mil/stratcom/spacemissions.htm.

58. Robert S. Dudney, "Chinese Advances Worry U.S. Tacticians," *Record,* 12 June 2007. http://www.therecord.com/NASApp/cs/ContentServer?pagename = record/Layout /Article/ (accessed 12 June 2007).

59. "Air Force Chief: 'Killing Another Nation's Satellite is an Act of War,'" *World Tribune,* 4 May 2007. http://www.worldtribune.com/worldtribune/ WTARC/2007/ea_china_05_04.html (accessed 9 September 2007).

60. Geoffrey Forden, "Viewpoint: China and Space War," *Astropolitics* 6, no. 2 (May 2008): 138–153.

61. Geoffrey Forden, "After China's Test: Time for a Limited Ban on Anti-Satellite Weapons," *Arms Control Today* 37, no. 3 (April 2007): 19–24. http://www.armscontrol.org/act/2007_04/Forden.asp.

62. Peter Buxbaum, "Air Force 'Shocked' by Chinese Actions in Space," *Federal Computer Week,* 24 September 2007.

63. Loring Wirbel, "U.S. Officials Downplay General's Assessment of China ASAT test," *EE Times,* 12 April 2007. http://www.eetimes.com/showArticle.jht ml?articleID = 199000714.

64. "Fallon: U.S. Shouldn't Be Shocked at Chinese Anti-Satellite Test," *Inside the Pentagon,* 22 March 2007, 1.

65. Department of Defense, *Annual Report to Congress, Military Power of the People's Republic of China, 2007,* 31 May 2007, 20.

66. Geoffrey Forden, "How China Loses the Coming Space War," *WIRED,* 10 January 2008, part 1. http://blog.wired.com/defense/eye_on_china/index .html.

67. Bill Gertz, "U.S. Satellites Dodge Chinese Missile Debris," *Washington Times,* 11 January 2008. http://www.washingtontimes.com/apps/pbcs.dll/arti cle?AID = /20080111/NATION/444629685/1001.

68. Michael Sirak, "Air Force Mulls Path Ahead for Protecting Satellites," *Defense Daily,* 25 September 2007.

69. See Union of Concerned Scientists, "Countermeasures: A Technical Evaluation of the Operational Effectiveness of the Planned U.S. National Missile Defense System," April 2000. http://ucsusa.org/global_security/missile_ defense/countermeasures.hmtl.

70. Hoffman, "Battlefield Space," 78–79.

71. David Coffee, "Communication Satellite History," updated 7 December 1999, http://imi.jou.ufl.edu/projects/Fall99/Coffee/HISTORY.HTM (accessed 13 November 2007); IEEE, "Alouette—ISIS Satellite Program, 1962," updated 2007, http://www.ieee.org/web/aboutus/history_center/alouette .html (accessed 13 November 2007); Space History Division, "Ariel 1," updated 18 August 1999, http://airandspace.si.edu/spacecraft/SS-ariel1.htm (accessed 13 November 2007).

72. See Barry D. Watts, *The Military Uses of Space: A Diagnostic Assessment* (Washington, D.C.: Center for Strategic and Budgetary Analysis, 2001), 19.

73. "A Different View of China's ASAT Test," 13 November 2007. http:// www.carnegieendowment.org/events/index.cfm?fa = eventDetail&id = 1074&& prog = zch.

74. Amy Butler, "Secret Steps: U.S. Government Mobilizes to Deal with ASAT Problem," *Aviation Week & Space Technology,* 15 October 2007, 39.

75. NRO, an organization whose name was even classified until 1992, designs, builds, and operates intelligence satellites for the U.S. government. As such they focus on supplying information to warfighters and policy-makers and therefore, while they reach for cutting edge technology (such as the failed US-

193 satellite discussed in Chapter 4), they are also very mission-focused and pragmatic.

76. See John Zaller, *The Nature and Origins of Mass Opinion* (Cambridge: Cambridge University Press, 1992).

77. See http://www.creationmuseum.org.

78. Susan Jacoby, *The Age of American Unreason* (New York: Pantheon Books, 2008).

79. See Patricia Cohen, "Dumb and Dumber: Are Americans Hostile to Knowledge?" *New York Times*, 15 February 2008.

80. Sarah Lai Stirland, "Scientists Push Presidential Candidates for Positions on Science," *WIRED*, 13 December 2007.

81. Lawrence M. Krauss, *The Physics of Star Trek* (New York: Harper Paperbacks, 1996).

82. Stirland, "Scientists Push Presidential Candidates."

83. "Modest Support for Missile Defense, No Panic on China," Pew Research Center for the People and the Press, 15–28 May 2001. http://people-press.org/reports/print.php3?PageID = 53.

84. *Quadrennial Defense Review Report* (Washington, D.C.: Department of Defense, 2001), 13–14, 17.

85. Michael Fitzsimmons, "Whither Capabilities-Based Planning?" *Joint Forces Quarterly* 44 (First Quarter 2007): 101.

86. Fitzsimmons, "Whither Capabilities-Based Planning?" 103.

87. See John Newhouse, *War and Peace in the Nuclear Age* (New York: Knopf, 1989), 205.

88. Robert Foelber, "The Limits of Arms Control," Heritage Foundation Reports, 26 July 1983.

89. Keith Payne and Colin Gray, "The Star Wars Debate: Nuclear Policy and the Defense Transition," *Foreign Affairs* 62, no. 4 (Spring 1984): 820–842.

90. Everett C. Dolman, "Space Power and U.S. Hegemony: Maintaining A Liberal World Order in the Twenty-First Century." http://www.gwu.edu/~spi/spaceforum/Dolmanpaper%5B1%5D.pdf, 7.

91. James Oberg, *Toward a Theory of Space Power* (Washington, D.C.: George Marshall Institute, Washington Roundtable on Science and Public Policy, 2003), 2, cited in David C. Hardesty, "Space Based Weapons: Long Term Strategic Implications and Alternatives," *Naval War College Review* 58 (Spring 2005): 45–68.

92. DoD Directive 5101.2, "DoD Executive Agent for Space," 3 June 2003.

93. See Jeffrey D. Spencer and James Cashon, "Space and Air Force: Rhetoric or Reality?" AU/ACSC/023/1999–04. http://www.fas.org/spp/eprint/99–023.htm.

94. See F. W. Peters and Michael E. Ryan, *The Aerospace Force: Defending America in the Twenty-First Century*, White Paper (Washington, D.C.: Department of the Air Force, 2000). http://www.af.mil/shared/media/document/AFD-060726–029.pdf.

95. Master Sergeant Mitch Gettel, "Air Force Releases New Mission Statement," *Air Force Print News*, 8 December 2005. http://www.af.mil/news/story.asp?storyID = 123013440.

96. George R. Mastroianni, "Occupations, Cultures, and Leadership in the Army and Air Force," *Parameters* 35, no. 4 (Winter 2005–2006): 76.

97. Mastroianni, "Occupations, Cultures, and Leadership," 82.

98. Ibid.

99. http://www.airforce.com/achangingworld. In another of the videos that includes a simulated antisatellite hit, a banner underneath says "It takes SPACE DOMINANCE to defend America in a changing world."

100. Thom Shanker, "Sharpened Tone in Debate over Military Culture," *New York Times*, 23 April 2008, 13.

101. Martin France, USAF, "Planetary Defense: Eliminating the Giggle Factor." http://www.airpower.au.af.mil/airchronicles/cc/france2.html.

102. Dr. Michael F. Stumborg, "Air Force Space Command: A Transformational Case Study," *Air & Space Power Journal* 20, no. 2 (Summer 2006): 79–90. http://www.airpower.maxwell.af.mil/airchronicles/apj/apj06/sum06/stumborg.html

103. John P. Kotter, *Leading Change* (Boston: Harvard Business School Press, 1996), 33–158.

104. Taylor Dinerman, "United States Space Force: Sooner Rather than Later," *Space Review*, 27 February 2006. http://www.thespacereview.com/article/565/1.

105. The Commission to Assess United States National Security Space Management and Organization was established pursuant to Public Law 106–65, the National Defense Authorization Act for Fiscal Year 2000, Section 1622.

106. Joan Johnson-Freese, "Moving Beyond Rhetoric: Transitioning to an Air and Space Force," *Space Policy* 16 (November 2000): 249–259.

107. "Senator Opposes Pentagon Plan to Downgrade Space Command," *Space Daily*, 5 March 2006. http://www.spacedaily.com/reports/Senator_Opposes_Pentagon_Plan_To_Downgrade_Space_Command.html.

108. "Senator Opposes Pentagon Plan."

109. http://www.af.mil/factsheets/factsheet.asp?fsID=155.

110. Dwayne Day, "General Power vs Chicken Little," *Space Review*, 23 May 2005. http://www/thespacereview.com/article/379/1.

111. Lt. Col. Raymond W. Staats, USAF and Major Derek A. Abeyta, USAF, "Technical Education for Air Force Space Professionals," *Air and Space Power Journal* 19 (Winter 2005): 56.

112. http://www.losangeles.af.mil.

113. Trisha Schmalz, "Space Officers Can Add 'W' to Specialty Code," 27 March 2007. http://www.afspc.af.mil/news/story.asp?id=123067227.

114. Grant Loeb, "Strategic Defense: How Much Will It Really Cost?" Backgrounder 607, Heritage Foundation, 2 October 1987. http://www.heritage.org/Research/NationalSecurity/bg607.cfm.

115. "Analysis of the Costs of the Administration's Strategic Defense Initiative 1985–89," Staff Working Paper, May 1984. http://www.cbo.gov/ftpdoc.cfm?index=4961&type=0.

116. Frida Berrigan and William D. Hartung, "The Empty Promise of Global Missile Defense," 1 August 2002. http://www.commondreams.org/views02/0801-06.htm.

117. Michael Cabbage, "Star Power Helps Tout Missile Defense," *Orlando Sentinel*, 19 October 2004.

118. Cabbage, "Star Power Helps."

119. General Accounting Office, "Missile Defense: Review of Allegations about an Early Missile Defense Flight Test," Letter and report to Senator Charles E. Grassley and Representative Howard L. Berman, GAO-02–125, February 2002; Missile Defense: Review of Results and Limitations of an Early Missile Defense Flight Test, GAO-02–124.

120. 23 March 1983. http://www.cnn.com/SPECIALS/cold.war/episodes/ 22/documents/starwars. speech/.

121. Gallagher and Steinbruner, *Reconsidering the Rules*, 33.

Chapter 2. The Evolution of U.S. Space Policy

1. Thomas M. Nichols, *Eve of Destruction: The Coming Age of Preventive War* (Philadelphia: University of Pennsylvania Press, 2008); George H. Quester, "Two Hundred Years of Preemption," *Naval War College Review* 60 (Autumn 2007): 15–28.

2. For a chronology of missile-defense activities from 1945 to 2002, see Missilethreat.com, a project of the Claremont Institute. http://www.missilethreat .com/overview/pageID.265/default.asp.

3. Dwight D. Eisenhower, *Waging Peace* (Garden City, N.Y.: Doubleday, 1965), 556.

4. Reprinted in Stephanie Feyock, compiler for the National Security Space Project, *Presidential Decisions: NSC Documents* (Washington, D.C.: George C. Marshall Institute, 2006), 1.

5. Reprinted in Feyock, *Presidential Decisions*, 18.

6. See Bhupendra Jasani and Maria A. Lunderius, "Peaceful Uses of Outer Space: Legal Fiction and Military Reality," *Security Dialogue* 11, no. 1 (1980): 57–70; Latoya Tate, "The Status of the Outer Space Treaty at International Law During 'War' and 'Those Measures Short of War,' " *Journal of Space Law* 32 (Summer 2006): 1; Philip Ball, "Time to Rethink the Outer Space Treaty," *Nature* (online), 4 October 2007. http://www.nature.com/news/2007/071004/full/news .2007.142.html.

7. Appendix: "Treaty on Outer Space, Message from the President of the United States," in Treaty on Outer Space, Hearings Before the Committee on Foreign Relations, United States Senate, Ninetieth Congress, First Session, 7, 13 March and 12 April 1967, U.S. Government Printing Office, Washington, D.C., 105–6, cited in Nancy Gallagher and John D. Steinbruner, *Reconsidering the Rules for Space Security* (Cambridge, Mass.: American Academy of Arts and Sciences, 2008).

8. Defining "peaceful" as "nonmilitary" proved problematic, as strict interpretation meant the military was unable to use space assets for such purposes as communications, weather monitoring, or reconnaissance. In May 2008, the Japanese parliament voted to revise the law which until that time had prevented Japanese use of space for military purposes, thus freeing Japan from that bind.

9. Hans-Joachim Heintz, "Peaceful Uses of Outer Space and the Law," paper presented at Space Use and Ethics Conference, Darmstadt, Germany, 3–5 March 1999. http://www.inesap.org/bulletin17/bul17art22.htm.

10. Gallagher and Steinbruner, *Reconsidering the Rules*, 11.

11. See Mark W. Davis, "Reagan's Real Reason for SDI," *Policy Review*, 1 October 2000; Lou Cannon, "*Reagan's Big Idea; How the Gipper Conceived Star Wars,*" *National Review*, 22 February 1999.

12. Frances Fitzgerald, *Way Out There in the Blue: Reagan, Star Wars and the End of the Cold War* (New York: Simon and Schuster, 2001), 191.

13. Ibid., 206.

14. Hal G. P. Colebatch, "James Patrick Baen, 1943–2006," *American Spectator Online*, 10 January 2007.

15. http://www.ronaldreagan.com/sdi.html.

16. http://www.pbs.org/newshour/debatingourdestiny/84debates/2prez3 .html.

17. Frank J. Gaffney, Jr., "U.S. Must Move to Full Missile Defense," *Human Events Online*, 6 October 2006.

18. Seiitsu Tachibana, "Bush Administration's Nuclear Policy Seeks Omnipotence," *Peace Research* 34, no. 2 (November 2002): 35.

19. Geoffrey Smith, "Who Won the War?" *National Interest* 79 (Spring 2005): 119–125.

20. Davis, "Reagan's Real Reason for SDI."

21. http://www.ronaldreagan.com/sdi.html.

22. Jeffrey Hart, "A Surprising Poll on Star Wars," *Washington Times*, 9 August 1985.

23. "Big Ifs for Star Wars," *Time*, 4 March 1985. http://www.time.com/ time/magazine/article/0,9171,961937,00.html.

24. Viktor Shlenov, "Norway's Decision against 'Star Wars' Involvement 'Symptomatic,'" BBC Summary of World Broadcasts, 22 April 1985.

25. Jeffrey Simpson, "NATO and Star Wars," *Globe and Mail* (Canada), 12 January 1985.

26. "Europe is Reluctant to Reach for the Stars," *Economist*, 16 February 1985, 57.

27. Nanette Brown, *The Strategic Defense Initiative and European Security: A Conference Report* (Santa Monica, Calif.: Rand Corporation, 1986), 5.

28. Walter Andrews, "'Star Wars' Plans Impossible Until Deployment," *United Press International*, 26 September 1987.

29. Donald Baucom, "Missile Defense Milestones," http://www.fas.org/ spp/starwars/program/milestone.htm.

30. Laura Grego, "A History of Anti-Satellite Programs," Union of Concerned Scientists. http://www.ucsusa.org/global_security/space_weapons/a-history-of-asat-prog rams.html.

31. David J. Scheffer, "Nouveau Law and Foreign Policy," *Foreign Policy* 76 (Autumn 1989): 50–55.

32. George H. W. Bush, Address on Administration Goals before a Joint Session of Congress, U.S. Capitol, Washington, D.C., 9 February 1989, http://www .cspan.org/executive/transcript.asp?cat = current_event&code = bush_admin& year = 1989 (accessed 19 January 2008); *New York Times*, "Transcript of President's Address to a Joint Session of the House and Senate," *New York Times*, 10 February 1989.

33. Andrew Rosenthal, "Tower Declares 'Star Wars' Shield Can't Be Complete," *New York Times*, 27 January 1989.

34. Andrew Rosenthal, "Missile Shield Must Be Balanced Against Other Goals, Cheney Says," *New York Times*, 29 March 1989.

35. "Star Wars Goal Cut, Quayle Says," *Los Angeles Times*, 7 September 1989.

36. "High-Tech Weaponry Shows Its Teeth in Test of Battle," *Los Angeles Times*, Part P, late final desk, 18 January 1991, 3.

37. Les Aspin, "Three Propositions for a New Era Nuclear Policy" (commencement address, Massachusetts Institute of Technology, Cambridge, Mass., 3 June 1992).

38. http://www.fas.org/spp/starwars/program/milestone.htm.

39. *Air Force Doctrine Document 4, Space Operations Doctrine*, 10 July 1996, 8.

40. Ibid.

41. Ibid.

42. Ibid.

43. Ibid.

44. See DoD Directive 3100.10, http://www.dtic.mil/whs/directives/cor res/html/310010.htm.

45. http://www.fas.org/spp/military/docops/usspac/lrp/ch02.htm#intro duction.

46. Michael Dobbs, "The Missile Threat: An Intelligence Turnabout How Politics Helped Redefine Threat," *Washington Post Foreign Service*, 14 January 2002, A01.

47. Joseph Cirincione, "Assessing the Ballistic Missile Threat," Subcommittee on International Security, Proliferation, and Federal Services, Committee on Governmental Affairs, United States Senate, 9 February 2000. http://www.senate.gov/~govt-aff/020900_cirincione.htm.

48. Charges that National Intelligence Estimates (NIE) are unduly influenced by politics with analysts pressured to follow lines of analysis consistent with political policy decisions have been heard throughout the George W. Bush administration, especially with regard to Iraq. When compared to the 2005 NIE, the dramatic change in the 2007 NIE assessment of the Iranian nuclear program is considered evidence of a reduction of these political pressures.

49. Frederick II, *Frederick the Great on the Art of War*, ed. Jay Luvaas (New York: Da Capo Press, 1999), 120.

50. Joseph Cirincione. http://www.senate.gov/~govt-aff/020900_cirincione.htm.

51. Heritage Foundation Lecture 614, 15 May 1998.

52. "Missile Defense, The Stakes Couldn't Be Higher," 8 September 1998. http://www.heritage.org/Press/Commentary/ed090898b.cfm.

53. Brian Knowlton, "Battle on Missile-Defense Funds Heats Up," *International Herald Tribune*, 10 September 2001.

54. BBC News Online, "Russia Condemns U.S. 'Star Wars,'" 4 February 2001, http://news.bbc.co.uk/1/hi/world/europe/1152711.stm.

55. Knowlton, "Battle on Missile-Defense Funds."

56. Robert Burns, "Rumsfeld Assures Russia over Arms, *New York Times*, 3 February 1991.

57. Report of the National Missile Defense Independent Review Team, 13 June 2000, http://www.armscontrol.org/act/2000_07-08/welchjulaug.asp.

58. Department of Defense, "Missile Defense Test Yields Successful 'Hit to Kill' Intercept," *American Forces Press Service*, Washington, D.C., 23 June 2006; Baker Spring, "Criticizing Success? The Test of the Long Range Missile Defense System," *Heritage Foundation WebMemo*, 16 October 2004; Bradley Graham, "U.S. Missile Defense Test Fails: Latest Setback in Pacific Fuels Doubts About System's Future," *Washington Post*, 16 December 2004, A05; Thom Shanker, "Key Test for U.S. Missile Defense Comes Amid Debate," *International Herald Tribune*, 23 May 2007. For a technical analysis of missile-defense tests through 2004, see Union of Concerned Scientists, "Technical Realities: An Analysis of the 2004 Deployment of a U.S. National Missile Defense System." http://www.ucsusa.org/glo bal_security/missile_defense/technical-realities-national-missile-defense-deploy ment-in-2004.html.

59. Acceptance speech of George W. Bush at the Republican National Convention, 3 August 2000, http://www.cnn.com/election/2000/conventions/ republican/transcripts/bush.html.

60. "Modest Support for Missile Defense, No Panic on China," Pew

Research Center for the People and the Press, 15–28 May 2001. http://people-press.org/reports/print.php3?PageID = 53.

61. "RNC Poll Results: Over 75% of Voters Favor Missile Defense," Press Release, Republican National Committee, 16 July 1998. http://www.fas.org/news/usa/1998/07/index.html. See also http://www.uninfo.state.gov/topical/pol/arms/stories/00071801.htm.

62. See Bloomberg News Poll conducted by Princeton Survey Research Associates, 31 July to 5 August 2001; *Newsweek*, conducted by Princeton Survey Research Associates, 3–4 May 2001; and others at http://www.pollingreport .com/defense.htm.

63. Director of Central Intelligence, "Foreign Missile Developments and the Ballistic Missile Threat Through 2015," National Intelligence Council, Washington, D.C., December 2001, 7.

64. Michael Cabbage, "Star Power Helps Tout Missile Defense," *Orlando Sentinel*, 19 October 2004.

65. William J. Broad, "From the Start, the Space Race Was an Arms Race," *New York Times*, 25 September 2007.

66. http://www.dtic.mil/doctrine/jel/new_pubs/jp3_14.pdf.

67. http://www.af.mil/library/posture/AF_trans_flight_plan-2003.pdf.

68. U.S. Air Force, *Counterspace Operations, Air Force Doctrine Document 2-2.1*, 2 August 2004, 1–66.

69. Joan Johnson-Freese, "Strategic Communication with China: What Message About Space?" *China Security* 2 (2006): 37–57.

70. U.S. Air Force, *Counterspace Operations*, 55.

71. Joan Johnson-Freese, "The New U.S. Space Policy: A Turn Toward Militancy?" *Issues in Science & Technology* 23, no. 2 (Winter 2007): 33–36.

72. National Space Based—PNT Executive Committee, "U.S. Space-Based Positioning, Navigation, and Timing Policy," updated 17 August 2006, http://pnt.gov/policy (accessed 16 November 2006); U.S. Geologic Survey, "U.S. Commercial Remote Sensing Policy," Washington, D.C., 2003; U.S. Space Transportation Policy, Washington, D.C., 6 January 2006; Office of the Press Secretary, *President Bush Announces New Vision for Space Exploration Policy, Fact Sheet: A Renewed Spirit of Discovery*, White House, Washington, D.C., 14 January 2004.

73. Dwayne Day, "Not Really Lost in Space: The New National Space Policy," *Space Review*, 13 November 2006.

74. An earlier, unrelated study addressed the need for space professionals as well. See George Abbey and Neal Lane, *United States Space Policy: Challenges and Opportunities* (Cambridge, Mass.: American Academy of Arts and Sciences, 2005).

75. Gregory Kulacki and David Wright, "A Military Intelligence Failure: The Case of the Parasite Satellite," 16 August 2004. http://www.ucsusa.org/global_security/china/a-military-intelligence-failure-the-chinese-parasite-satel lite.html.

76. http://www.america.gov/st/space-english/2006/October/2006102510 2809lcnirel lep0.5205347.html.

77. United States Senate, "S.1547-FY08 Defense Authorization Bill." Washington, D.C., 9 July 2007.

78. A. Wess Mitchell, "The Polish Lesson: America Must Give Something in Return for Support," *Christian Science Monitor*, 18 January 2008.

79. "Physicists Challenge U.S. Missile Claims," *USA Today*, 27 September 2007.

80. Ibid.

81. Philip Coyle and Victoria Samson, "Missile Defense Malfunction: Why the Proposed U.S. Missile Defenses in Europe Will Not Work," *Ethics and International Affairs* 22 (Spring 2008): 3–24.

82. See Pavel Podvig and Hui Zhang, *Russian and Chinese Responses to U.S. Military Plans in Space* (Cambridge, Mass.: American Academy of Arts and Sciences, 2008).

83. Theresa Hitchens, "Statement," U.S. Congress, House, Committee on House Oversight and Government Reform, Subcommittee on National Security and Foreign Affairs, Weapons in Space, 23 May 2007, 7.

84. Senator Jon Kyl, "China's Anti-Satellite Weapons and America's National Security," Heritage Foundation Lecture 990, 29 January 2007.

85. Terry Everett, "Arguing for a Comprehensive Space Protection Strategy," *Strategic Studies Quarterly* 1 (Fall 2007): 21.

86. http://www.afspc.af.mil/library/speeches/speech.asp?id = 318.

87. See "Space Experts Meet to Address Warfighter Needs," DoD USAF Press Release, 4 September 2007.

88. "DOD Cuts Funding for Operationally Responsive Space Across POM," *Inside the Pentagon*, 6 November 2008.

89. Elaine M. Grossman, "Is China Disrupting U.S. Satellites?" *Inside Defense*, 13 October 2006. http://www.military.com/features/0,15240,116694,00.html.

Chapter 3. Space Weapons

1. Dwayne Day, "A Look at . . . Spy Satellite and Hollywood," *Washington Post*, 2 July 2000, B03.

2. "'The Sum of All Fears' Uses High-Resolution IKONOS Satellite Imagery to Create Hollywood Magic," *PRNewswire*, 31 May 2002. http://www.spaceref.com/news/viewpr.html?pid = 8537 (accessed 5 August 2008).

3. Karl P. Mueller, "Totem and Taboo: Depolarizing the Space Weapon Debate," in *Space Weapons: Are They Needed?* ed. John Logsdon and Gordon Adams, 1–50 (Washington, D.C.: George Washington University, 2003).

4. David Wright, Laura Grego, and Lisbeth Gronlund, *The Physics of Space Security: A Reference Manual* (Cambridge, Mass.: Union of Concerned Scientists, 2005).

5. Ibid., xi.

6. Rick Atkinson, "When 'Physics Gets in the Way,'" *Washington Post*, 2 October 2007, 13.

7. John Steinbruner and Nancy Gallagher, "Reconsidering the Rules for Space Security," *CISSM Working Paper*, September 2007, 4.

8. Wright, Grego, and Gronlund, *The Physics of Space Security*, 1.

9. Steinbruner and Gallagher, "Reconsidering the Rules," *CISSM Working Paper*, 4.

10. Wright, Grego, and Gronlund, *The Physics of Space Security*, 15.

11. Steinbruner and Gallagher, "Reconsidering the Rules," *CISSM Working Paper*, 4.

12. Wright, Grego, and Gronlund, *The Physics of Space Security*, 15.

13. Steven Kosiak, "Arming the Heavens: A Preliminary Assessment of the Potential Cost and Cost-Effectiveness of Space-Based Weapons," October 2007. http://www.csbaonline.org/2006–1/index.shtml.

14. In Strategic Defense Initiative days it was called the "post boost" phase.

15. National Policy on Ballistic Missile Defense Fact Sheet, 20 May 2003. http://www.whitehouse.gov/news/releases/2003/05/20030520-15.html (accessed 4 January 2008).

16. Missile Defense Agency, Historical Funding for MDA FY85–07, Washington, D.C., Department of Defense, http://www.mda.mil/mdalink/pdf/hist-funds
.pdf (accessed on 31 October 2008).

17. General Accounting Office, Defense Acquisitions: Assessment of DoD Efforts to Enhance Missile Defense Capabilities and Oversight, GAO-08–506T, 26 February 2008.

18. Ibid.

19. Joseph Cirincione, "The Incredible Shrinking Missile Threat," *Foreign Policy* 166 (May–June 2008): 68–73.

20. George Orwell. http://www.netcharles.com/orwell/essays/asiplease 1944-01.htm.

21. William J. Broad, "MIT Studies Accusations of Lies and Cover-Up of Serious Flaws in Antimissile System," *New York Times*, 2 January 2003.

22. George N. Lewis and Theodore A. Postol, "Video Evidence on the Effectiveness of Patriot During the 1991 Gulf War," *Science and Global Security* 4, no. 11993: 1–63, http://princeton.edu/%7eglobsec/publications/pdf/4_1lewis
.pdf; George N. Lewis and Theodore A. Postol, "An Evaluation of the Army Report 'Analysis of Video Tapes to Assess Patriot Effectiveness,'" 31 March 1992 (A Study Performed In Response to a Request by Congressman John Conyers, Jr., Chairman of the House Government Operations Committee, September 1992). http://www.fas.org/spp/starwars/docops/pl920908.htm.

23. See results of ITF-3, Chronology of Missile Defense Tests, Union of Concerned Scientists, 2 October 1999. http://www.ucsusa.org/global_security/missile_defense/chronology-of-missile-defense-tests.html.

24. Matt Kelley, "Missile Intercept Test Will Succeed Regardless of Outcome, Pentagon Says," *Associated Press*, 1 December 2001.

25. "General: 'Glitch' Caused Missile Defense Test Failure," *Cable News Network*, 13 January 2005.

26. David Stout and John H. Cushman, Jr., "Defense Missile for U.S. System Fails to Launch," *New York Times*, 16 December 2004.

27. Rebecca Christie, "DoD: U.S. Has 'Better Than Zero' Chance at Missile Intercept," *Dow Jones News*, 21 July 2005.

28. CRS Report, *Kinetic Energy Kill for Ballistic Missile Defense: A Status Overview*, 5 January 2007.

29. Major Laura Kenney, "Missile Defense System Goes Operational as North Korea Goes Ballistic," *Air Defense Artillery* (October–December 2006): 38–39.

30. Joan Johnson-Freese and Thomas M. Nichols, "Space Security and the New Nuclear Triad," *Brown Journal of World Affairs* 14, no. 1 (Winter–Spring 2007): 159–72.

31. Council for a Livable World, "The Illusion of Operational Readiness of National Missile Defense," 7 July 2006. http://clw.org/policy/missiledefense/resources/clippings/illusion_ofoperational—readiness.

32. Thom Shanker, "Missile Defense is Up and Running, Military Says," *New York Times*, 3 October 2007.

33. See http://www.cdi.org/program/issue/document.cfm?DocumentID= 1984&IssueID = 79&StartRow = 1&ListRows = 10&appendURL = &Orderby = DateLastUpdated&ProgramID = 68&issueID = 79; http://www.mda.mil/mda

Link/html/milstone.html; http://www.missiledefenseadvocacy.org/news/arti cle.php?cat=bydate&articleid=734.

34. http://www.mda.mil/mdaLink/html/milstone.html.

35. http://www.missiledefenseadvocacy.org/news/article.php?cat=bydate &articleid=734.

36. http://www.cdi.org/program/issue/document.cfm?DocumentID=19 84&IssueID=79&StartRow=1&ListRows=10&appendURL=&Orderby=Date LastUpdated&ProgramID=6&issueID=79.

37. Victoria Samson, "Missile Defense by the Numbers." http://www.cdi .org/program/document.cfm?DocumentID=4117&StartRow=1&ListRows= 10&appendURL=&Orderby+D.DateLastUpdated&ProgramID6&from_page =index.cfm.

38. Ibid.

39. "Classified Report Details Difficulties with Boost-Phase Intercept Mission: Countermeasures Seen as Real Hurdle," *Inside the Pentagon*, 13 December 2007.

40. http://www.missilethreat.com/missilesoftheworld/id.145/missile_de tail.asp.

41. Peter Huessey, "America Becomes Safer: Progress Made on Missile Defense," *Washington Times*, 18 October 2007, 19.

42. Ibid.

43. Brian R. Green, Memorandum on Key DoD Message for Public Discussion on Space Protection, 25 January 2008, 3.

44. Theresa Hitchens, Victoria Samson, and Sam Black, "Space Weapons Spending in the FY 2008 Defense Budget," 21 February 2007. http://www .cdi.org.

45. Michael Goldfarb, "The Rods from God: Are Kinetic-Energy Weapons the Future of Space Warfare," *Weekly Standard*, 8 June 2005. http://www.weekly standard.com/Content/Public/Articles/000/000/005/7000klkt.asp.

46. Wright, Grego, and Gronlund, *The Physics of Space Security*, 89–96; Nick Wadhams, "Scientists Warn Against Weaponizing Space," *Space.com*, 20 May 2005. http://www.space.com/news/ap_050520_space_weapons.html.

47. "The Race of the Space Warriors," *New Zealand Herald*, 23 September 2006.

48. "China's ASAT Test and American National Security," remarks by Senator Kyl at the Heritage Foundation, 29 January 2006. http://www.globalsecurity .org/space/library/news/2007/space-070129-kyl01.htm.

49. Michael Bruno, "Space-Based Test Bed Falls Again as Spending Rejected," *Aerospace Daily & Defense Report*, 4 October 2007, 1.

50. Ibid., 1.

51. James Oberg, "The War of Words over War in Space," 16 April 2004. http://www.msnbc.msn.com/id/4732874.

52. Ibid.

53. Hitchens, Samson, and Black, "Space Weapons Spending."

54. Elaine M. Grossman and Keith J. Costa, "Small, Experimental Satellite May Offer More Than Meets the Eye," *Inside the Pentagon*, 4 December 2003. http://www.globalsecurity.org/org/news/2003/031204-asat.htm.

55. The weight of the vehicle, plus fuel.

56. Jeremy Singer, "U.S. Air Force to Boost ANGELS Size, Mission," *Defense News*, 26 November 2007, 20.

57. Bucky McMahon, "BIG FREAKIN' LASER BEAMS in Space," *Esquire*, 1 December 2006, 196.

58. Ibid.

59. See Taylor Dinerman, "Pete Worden: The New Guy at Ames," *Space Review,* 1 May 2006. http://www.thespacereview.com/article/612/1.

60. Simon Worden, "High Anxiety," *Bulletin of the Atomic Scientists,* May–June 2006, 22.

61. Ibid.

62. "'Death Stars' and Other Bogeymen," *Washington Times,* 29 May 2005, B02.

63. Ibid.

64. James Oberg, "Space Weapons: Hardware, Paperware, Beware," *Space Review,* 13 November 2006.

65. Dwayne Day, "General Power vs Chicken Little," *Space Review,* 23 May 2005. http://www.thespacereview.com/article/379/1.

66. Ibid.

67. Ibid.

Chapter 4. Strategic Communications

1. Walter Russell Mead, *Power, Terror, Peace, and War* (New York: Alfred A. Knopf, 2004), 4–5.

2. "Global Unease with Major World Powers," 27 June 2007. http://www.pewglobal.org.

3. Ibid.

4. Francis Fukuyama, "The Fall of America, Inc." *Newsweek,* 13 October 2008.

5. Pew Global Attitudes Project, "U.S. Image up Slightly, but Still Negative," 23 June 2005, cited in "Poll: In Wake of Iraq War, Allies Prefer China to U.S.," 24 June 2005. http://www.cnn.com/2005/US/06/23/poll.america.ap.

6. "Global Unease." See also "Soft Power in Asia 2008," Chicago Council on Global Affairs and the East Asia Institute. http://e-chronicle.the chicago-council.org.

7. Zhang Hui, "Space Weaponization and Space Security: A Chinese Perspective," *China Security* 2 (Spring 2006): 24.

8. Some material in this section was originally presented in Joan Johnson-Freese, "Strategic Communication with China: What Message About Space?" *China Security* 2 (Spring 2006): 37–57.

9. Referenced by Christopher R. Hill, Assistant Secretary for East Asian and Pacific Affairs, Testimony before the Senate Foreign Relations Committee, Subcommittee on East Asian and Pacific Affairs, Washington, D.C., 7 June 2005. http://www.state.gov/p/eap/rls/rm/2005/47334.htm.

10. http://www.state.gov/r/pa/prs/ps/2005/57822.htm.

11. John D. Negroponte, Deputy Secretary of State, Press Roundtable in China, Press Section Program Room, U.S. Embassy, Beijing, China, 17 January 2008.

12. DoD News Briefing with Secretary Gates and Gen. Cartwright from the Pentagon Defense Department Documents and Publications, 21 December 2007.

13. Ibid.

14. "Giving China a Bloody Nose: China Bashing," *Economist,* 6 August 2005, 53; Bates Gill and Robin Niblett, "Divergent Paths Hurt U.S. and Europe: Dealing with China," *International Herald Tribune,* 6 September 2005; Sheila McNulty, "Chevron Chief Regrets Taint of Xenophobia," *Financial Times* (London), 11 August 2005.

15. Stephen Glain, "Why America's Point Man on China Is Running into a Wall," *Newsweek*, 17 December 2007.

16. Craig Covault, "Space Probes: China's Military Secrecy Clouds Its Value as Exploration Partner to Moon and Beyond," *Aviation Week & Space Technology*, 5 May 2008, 28–30.

17. Richard Fisher, Statement before Committee on House Armed Services, 27 July 2005.

18. It should be noted too that part of the problem is clearly political. Communication and information-sharing issues are less common with businesses, even U.S. businesses, and among non-U.S. entities. European Union officials, for example, state that even on sensitive issues like nuclear affairs, communication and information sharing are far less an issue than their American counterparts claim they encounter.

19. The report can be found at http://www.house.gov/coxreport. Though the findings have become urban legend, they have been widely repudiated by experts. See Alastair Iain Johnston, W. K. H. Panofsky, Marco Di Capua, and Lewis R. Franklin, "The Cox Committee Report: An Assessment," December 1999. http://www.carnegieendowment.org/pdf/npp/coxfinal3.pdf.

20. Union of Concerned Scientists, "Significant Errors in Testimony on China's Space Program, May 2008, http://devucs.wsm.ga3.org/.../international_information/us_china_relations/significant-errors-in.html.

21. "A Different View of China's ASAT Test," 13 November 2007. http://www.carnegieendowment.org/events/index.cfm?fa = eventDetail&id = 1074&&prog = zch.

22. James Mulvenon, "Rogue Warriors? A Puzzled Look at the Chinese ASAT Test," *China Leadership Monitor* 20 (Winter 2007): 1. http://www.media.hoover.org/documents/clm20jm.pdf.

23. Ibid, 6.

24. "A Different View of China's ASAT Test," 13 November 2007. http://www.carnegieendowment.org/events/index.cfm?fa = eventDetail&id = 1074&&prog = zch.

25. Ibid.

26. Some material in this section was originally presented in Joan Johnson-Freese, "The New U.S. Space Policy: A Turn Toward Militancy?" *Issues in Science and Technology* 23, no. 2 (Winter 2007).

27. Terry Everett, "Needed: Strategy for Space Protection," *Washington Times*, 11 January 2008, 19.

28. http://www.dtic.mil/whs/directives/corres/pdf/310010p.pdf.

29. Report of the Commission to Assess United States National Security Space Management and Organization, 2001, 17, 18.

30. United Nations General Assembly, "Prevention of an Arms Race in Outer Space," A/RES/54/53, Fifty-Fourth Session, New York, 31 December 1999.

31. United Nations General Assembly, "Prevention of an Arms Race in Outer Space," A/RES/58/36, Sixtieth Session, New York, 12 October 2005.

32. "Eutelsat Takes Steps to Use Chinese Launch Services," *Wall Street Journal*, 28 April 2008, B3.

33. Bronwen Maddox, "America Wants It All—Life, the Universe, and Everything." http://www.timesonline.co.uk/article/0,,30809-2410592,00.html.

34. Ehsan Ahrari, "U.S. Turns Space into Its Colony," *Asia Times* (Hong Kong), 20 October 2006. http://www.atimes.com/atimes/Front_Page/HJ20Aa02.html.

35. Presentation by John Logsdon, International Cooperation, Competition, and the New National Space Policy, a seminar sponsored by the Center for Space Policy and Strategy, 24 January 2007. http://www.gwu.edu/~spi/Semi nar_Presentations_24Jan07.ppt.

36. Interviewed by Frank Sietzen, Jr., in *Aerospace America*, 14–16 February 2008.

37. Eun Kyung Kim, "Nelson: Russia's Actions Could Hurt U.S. Space Program," *Florida Today*, 13 August 2008.

38. Robert Block, "Russian Invasion Threatens Space Station," *Orlando Sentinel*, 12 August 2008.

39. Brian Berger, "Obama Backs NASA Waiver, Possible Shuttle extension," SPACE.com, 23 September 2008. http://www.usatoday.com/tech/science/space/2008-09-23-obama-nasa-shuttle_N.htm.

40. Zhong Jing, "China and Space Security," in *Collective Security in Space*, ed. John M. Logsdon and James Clay Moltz, 77 (Washington, D.C.: George Washington University, January 2008).

41. RIA Novosti, "Russia to Raise Space Funding 13%, Build New Space Center," 21 January 2008. en.rian.ru/russia/20080121/97438434.html.

42. Rose Monacelli, "Russian Dream of Space Dominance Hampered," *ISCIP Analyst* 14 (April 2008).

43. The history of US-193 itself is interesting and curious. It was built on a contract to Boeing, which had never built a spy satellite before, and had problems throughout development.

44. John Schwartz, "Satellite Spotters Glimpse Secrets, and Tell Them," *New York Times*, 5 February 2008, 1.

45. "U.S. Tracks Spy Satellite Falling to Earth," *Agence France-Presse*, 26 January 2008.

46. DoD News briefing with Deputy National Security Advisor Jeffrey, Vice Chairman, General Cartwright, and NASA Administrator Mike Griffin. http://www.defenselink.mil/transcripts/transcript.aspx?transcriptid=4145.

47. Ten out of eleven tests of the SM-3 tests were successful according to the Global Security website. See http://www.globalsecurity.org/space/systems/sm3-test.htm.

48. After the fact, requests for the data were filed under the Freedom of Information Act by the Union of Concerned Scientists.

49. http://chemphys.gcsu.edu/msds/302-01-2.htm.

50. Marc Kaufman and Josh White, "Satellite Fuel's Risks Are Disputed," *Washington Post*, 21 February 2008, 3.

51. Ibid.

52. http://www.aero.org/capabilities/cords/reentry-overview.html.

53. http://www.globalsecurity.org/space/library/news/1998/fact02.htm.

54. http://blogs.physicstoday.org/newspicks/2008/02/experts_query_pen tagons_explan.html.

55. The term "shootdown" is used descriptively only. Technically, the satellite was coming down anyway.

56. "Aim High," *National Review Online*, 19 February 2008. http://article.nat ionalreview.com/?q=YmEwY2FkOGM1MzhlMzc1ODU5NWRmODk2ODUzNW JjYWY=.

57. Yury Zaitsev, "Outside View: ASAT Weapons—Part 2," reprinted from RIA Novosti in *UPI Outside View Commentator*. http://www.upi/Internat ional_Security/Industry/Analaysis/2008/02/25/outside_view_as.

58. Traci Watson, "China Seeks Data from Downing of U.S. Satellite," *USA Today*, 22 February 2008, 2.

59. Thom Shanker, "An Errant Satellite Is Gone, but Questions Linger," *New York Times*, 22 February 2008.

60. Mehran Derakhshandeh, "Satellite Shootdown Rattles China, Russia," *Tehran Times*, 26 February 2008.

61. Sreeram Chaulia, "Should India Also Develop Satellite-Killing Capability?" *Thaindian News*, 2 March 2008.

62. Gail Collins, "Look, Up in the Sky!" *New York Times*, 21 February 2008.

63. "Satellite Strike Shows Missile Defense Works: Gates," *Space Daily*, 21 February 2008. http://www.spacedaily.com/reports/Satellite_strike_shows_US_missile_defense_works_Gates_999.html.

64. Greg Miller, "Missile's Bull's Eye on Satellite Echoes Far, Experts Say," *Los Angeles Times*, 22 February 2008.

65. Marc Kaufman and Josh White, "Spy Satellite Downing Shows a New U.S. Weapon Capability," *Washington Post*, 22 February 2008, A03.

66. Warren Ferster, "U.S. Will Try to Destroy Crippled Satellite," *Space News*, 14 February 2008, http://www.space.com/news/080214-sn-destroy-spysat.html (accessed 19 March 2008).

67. House Armed Services Committee statement in support of "Engage Non-responsive U.S. Satellite," 14 February 2008.

68. Riki Ellison, "Out of Space," Missile Defense Advocacy Alliance Blog, 21 February 2008, http://www.missiledefenseadvocacy.org/BLOG.aspx?blogID = 2.

69. Kaufman and White, "Spy Satellite's Downing," 3.

70. Hearing on United States Strategic Posture and the Fiscal Year 2009 Budget Request for Strategic Programs. http://www.armedservices.house.gov/apps/list/speech/armedsvc_dem/tauschero s0 22708.shtml.

71. Kaufman and White, "Spy Satellite's Downing," 3.

72. *People's Daily*, 21 February 2008.

73. Michio Kaku, *Physics of the Impossible* (New York: Doubleday, 2008).

74. Quoted in James Randerson, "China Accuses U.S. of Double Standards over Satellite Strike," *Guardian* (London), 21 February 2008. http://guardian.co.uk/science/2008/feb/21/spaceexploration.usa/print

75. Report of the Defense Science Board Task Force on Strategic Communications, January 2008, x–xi.

76. Brian R. Green, Cover Letter to Memorandum on Key DoD Message for Public Discussion on Space Protection, 25 January 2008, 2, 1.

77. Ibid., 3.

Chapter 5. Diplomacy and Arms Control

1. "Report of the Commission to Assess United States National Security Space Management and Organization," Washington, D.C., 11 January 2001, 17–18. The Space Commission was created pursuant to the National Defense Authorization Act for Fiscal Year 2000 to assess the organization and management of space activities that support U.S. national security interests.

2. U.S. National Space Policy, Washington, D.C., 31 August 2006, 2. http://www.globalsecurity.org/space/library/policy/national/us-space-policy_060831.htm.

3. "Air Force Space Command, Strategic Master Plan: FY 04 and Beyond," 5 November 2002, 3.

4. James Clay Moltz, "Breaking the Deadlock on Space Arms Control," *Arms Control Today* 32 (April 2002): 3–9; James Clay Moltz, *The Politics of Space Security: Strategic Restraint and the Pursuit of National Interests* (Palo Alto, Calif.: Stanford University Press, 2008).

5. Moltz, "Breaking the Deadlock," 4.

6. Lieutenant Colonel Bruce M. DeBlois, "Space Sanctuary: A Viable National Strategy," *Airpower Journal* 12, no. 4 (Winter 1998): 46.

7. Major Howard D. Belote, "The Weaponization of Space: It Doesn't Happen in a Vacuum," *Aerospace Power Journal* 14, no. 1 (Spring 2000): 46–52.

8. Lt. Col. Christopher M. Petras, USAF, "The Debate over the Weaponization of Space—A Military-Legal Conspectus," *Annals of Air and Space Law*, Institute and Centre of Air and Space Law, McGill University, Montreal, Canada, 2003, 206, cited in Theresa Hitchens, "Safeguarding Space: Building Cooperative Norms to Dampen Negative Trends," *Disarmament Diplomacy* 28 (Winter 2005): 171–217.

9. Capt. David C. Hardesty, "Space-Based Weapons: Long-Term Strategic Implications and Alternatives," *Naval War College Review* 58, no. 2 (Spring 2005): 46.

10. Andrew T. Park, "Incremental Steps for Achieving Space Security: The Need for a New Way of Thinking to Enhance the Legal Regime for Space," *Houston Journal of International Law*, 22 September 2006, 874.

11. "United Nations Committee on the Peaceful Uses of Outer Space: History and Overview of Activities." http://www.unoosa.org/oosa/COPUOS/Cop_overview.html.

12. United Nations Declaration of Legal Principles Governing the Activities of States in the Exploration and Use of Outer Space, *United Nations Treaty Series* 610 (October 1967). http://www.unoosa.org/oosa/SpaceLaw/lpos.html.

13. Park, "Incremental Steps," 876–77.

14. Philip Ball, "Time to Rethink the Outer Space Treaty," *Nature News*, 4 October 2007, 1038. http://www.nature.com/news/2007/071004/full/news.2007.142.html.

15. Cited in Ball, "Time to Rethink."

16. Conference on Disarmament. Treaty on the Prevention and Placement of Weapons in Outer Space, the Threat or Use of Force Against Outer Space Objects, treaty draft, Geneva, Switzerland, 12 February 2008.

17. See Hui Zhang, "FMCT and PAROS: A Chinese Perspective," INESAP, Bulletin 20, Prevention of an Arms Race in Space. http://www.inesap.org/bulletin20/bul20art06.htm.

18. David Wright, "Space Debris from Antisatellite Weapons," *Bulletin Online*, 2 October 2007. http://www.thebulletin.org/web-edition/features/space-debris-antisatellite-weapons.

19. Inter-Agency Space Debris Coordination Committee (IADC). http://www.iadc-online.org/index.cgi?item=docs_pub.

20. Section 5.2.3 IADC Space Debris Mitigation Guidelines, IADC-02–01. http://www.iadc-online.org/index.cgi?item=docs_pub.

21. For additional information on the debris situation, see David Wright, "Space Debris," *Physics Today* 60 (October 2007): 35. http://www.ucsusa.org/global_security/space_ns/space-debris-from-anti-satellite-weapons.html.

22. United Nations Office at Geneva, "Disarmament: An Introduction to the Conference." http://www.unog.ch/80256ee600585943/(httppages)/bf18abfefe5d344dc1256f3100311c e9? (accessed 16 March 2008).

23. Stephen G. Rademaker, "The Conference on Disarmament: Time is Running Out," *Arms Control Today* 36, no. 10 (December 2006): 13–16. Rademaker, along with Ambassador Paul Meyer, Canada's permanent representative to the United Nations for disarmament, and Michael Krepon, codirector of the Henry L. Stimson Center, each provided their perspectives on the Conference on Disarmament through articles in the December 2006 issue of *Arms Control Today*. Their perspectives for the most part still represent the issues confronting the Conference on Disarmament in 2008.

24. Ibid., 13.

25. Ibid., 15.

26. "Conference on Disarmament Hears Statements from Seventeen States on Prevention of an Arms Race in Outer Space," 13 February 2007. http://www.unog.ch/80256edd006b9c2e/(httpNewsByYear_en)/d619655055a00c6e c125728100547de3.

27. Statement by Ambassador Christine Rocca, 15 February 2008. http://www.unog.ch/80256edd006b8954/(httpassets)/de7eeeeb629d982fc12573f0004 a1e07/$file/Statement + by + Ambassador + Rocca.pdf.

28. Charles J. Hanley, "Satellite Strike Makes Space Treaty More Elusive; Less Formal 'Code' Promoted," *Canadian Press*, 25 February 2008. http://cana dianpress.google.com/article/aleqm5ipwilgcjarwhfylaatjb_wj4g0za.

29. Paula A. DeSutter, "Is An Outer Space Arms Control Treaty Verifiable?" remarks to the George C. Marshall Institute, 4 March 2008. http://state.gov/t/ vci/rls/rm/101711.htm.

30. Ibid.

31. Jeff Keuter, "USA Today's Editorial on Weapons in Space and the Marshall Institute Response," Marshall Institute, 21 February 2008. http://www.mar shall.org/article.php?id = 578 (accessed 25 March 2008).

32. Ambassador Paul Meyer, "The Conference on Disarmament: Getting Back to Business," *Arms Control Today* 36 (December 2006): 16.

33. Ibid.

34. Côte d'Ivoire abstained as well, though later the Côte d'Ivoire representative said he had intended to vote "yes."

35. Meyer, "The Conference on Disarmament," 17.

36. Michael Krepon, "The Conference on Disarmament: Means of Rejuvenation," *Arms Control Today* 36 (December 2006): 22.

37. See Agreement Between the Government of the United States of America and the Government of the Soviet Socialist Republics on the Prevention of Incidents on and Over the High Seas, TIF, 1 January 1973, Department of State publication 8697, Washington, D.C.: U.S. Government Printing Office, 1973, 247, http://www.state.gov/t/ac/trt/4791.htm; Proliferation Security initiative, U.S. Department of State, Bureau of Nonproliferation, 31 May 2003, http://www.state.gov/t/isn/c10390/htm (accessed 18 March 2008); International Code of Conduct Against Ballistic Missile Proliferation, http://www.nti .org/db/china/icoc.htm (accessed 24 April 2008); Sharon Squassoni, Proliferation Security Initiative (PSI), Congressional Research Service Report for Congress, Order Code RS21881, updated 14 September 2006, http://www.fas.org/ spg/crs/nuke/RS21881.pdf.

38. Henry L. Stimson Center, Research Programs: Space Security Program. http://www.stimson.org/space/?SN = WS200702131213 (accessed 16 March 2008).

39. Geoffrey Forden, "How China Loses the Coming Space War," *WIRED*,

10 January 2008, part 1. http://blog.wired.com/defense/2008/01/inside-the-chin.html.

40. Henry L. Stimson Center, "Model Code of Conduct for Space-Faring Nations," Stimson Center, Washington, D.C., 24 October 2007. http://www .stimson.org/pub.cfm?ID = 575.

41. Stimson Center, "Model Code," 2–3.

42. http://www.stimson.org/space/?SN + WS200701191170.

43. His statement: "L'une d'entre elles, qui mérite d'être explorée plus avant, serait celle d'un code de 'bonne conduite' ou de 'bonnes pratiques.' Les Européens doivent avoir toute leur part dans cette réflexion. Nous devons également être davantage en mesure de tirer pleinement partie des technologies spatiales afin de renforcer la sécurité dans les relations internationales." M. Philippe Douste-Blazy, Closing Address, Space Policy Symposium, Toulouse, France, 17 November 2006. https://pastel.diplomatie.gouv.fr/editorial/actual/ael2/bulle tin.asp?liste = 2 0061120.html.

44. "China's ASAT Test: Irresponsible and Against International Norms," *Aviation Week & Space Technology* 166, no. 5 (29 January 2007): 74.

45. "A New Arms Race in Space?" *Economist* 382 (January 2007): 10–11.

46. Elaine M. Grossman, "Is China Disrupting U.S. Satellites?" *Inside Defense.com*, 13 October 2006.

47. U.S. Senate, Advance Questions for General Kevin P. Chilton, USAF Nominee for Commander, United States Strategic Command, Armed Services Committee, Washington, D.C., 27 September 2007, 15.

48. Vladimir Isachenkov, Associated Press, "Russia Warns Against Deploying Space Weapons," 27 September 2007.

49. Steven Kull, John Steinbruner, Nancy Gallagher, Clay Ramsay, and Evan Lewis, "Americans and Russians on Space Weapons," WorldPublicOpinion.org and Advanced Methods of Cooperation Security Program, CISSM, 24 January 2008.

50. Council for a Livable World, "2008 Presidential Candidates' Responses to Seven Key National Security Questions," 16 August 2007. http://www.clw .org/elections/2008/presidential/2008_presidential_candidates_questionnaire_ responses/ (accessed 4 April 2008).

Chapter Six. Globalizing Space

1. Saul Hansell, "Verizon and AT&T Win Big in Auction of Spectrum," *New York Times*, 21 March 2008, 3.

2. Thomas L. Friedman, *The Lexus and the Olive Tree* (New York: Anchor Books, 2000), 331.

3. Thomas P. M. Barnett, *The Pentagon's New Map* (New York: Putnam Books, 2004), 122.

4. Immanuel Wallerstein, for example, in his seminal work *The World System* (3 vols., 1974–89), talks about core, periphery, and the semiperiphery countries. See *The Modern World-System, Vol. I: Capitalist Agriculture and the Origins of the European World-Economy in the Sixteenth Century* (New York: Academic Press, 1974); *The Modern World-System, Vol. II: Mercantilism and the Consolidation of the European World-Economy, 1600–1750* (New York: Academic Press, 1980); *The Modern World-System, Vol. III: The Second Great Expansion of the Capitalist World-Economy, 1730–1840s* (San Diego: Academic Press, 1989).

5. http://www.navy.mil/maritime/MaritimeStrategy.pdf.

6. Taylor Dinerman, "Space and the 2,000 Ship Navy," *Space Review,* 7 January 2008, http://www.thespacereview.com/article/1031/1.

7. Simon P. Worden and Joan Johnson-Freese, "Globalizing Space Security," *Joint Forces Quarterly* 33 (Winter 2002–2003): 66–67.

8. See, for example, Theresa Hitchens, "Space Sustainability," presentation at CSIS, *Can We Keep Space from Becoming a Shooting Gallery,* 21 July 2008.

9. Schriever Air Force Base, "Global Positioning System," http://www.schriever.af.mil/gps/ (accessed 13 April 2008).

10. Bill Gertz, "Inside the Ring," *Washington Times,* 28 March 2008, 8.

11. Tom Roeder, "Air Force Concerned About Holes in Space Defense," *Colorado Springs Gazette,* 13 April 2008. http://www.gazette.com/articles/space_35247___article.html/air_concerned.html.

12. Department of Defense, *Military Power of the People's Republic of China,* 2007, 21. http://www.defenselink.mil/pubs/pdfs/070523-China-Military-Power-final.pdf.

13. Roeder, "Air Force Concerned."

14. John Schwartz, "Thrillionaires: The New Space Capitalists," *New York Times,* 14 June 2005, F1.

15. Brad Lemley, "Shooting the Moon," *Discover* 26, no. 9 (September 2005): 28.

16. John Schwartz, "Entrepreneur Unveils New Tourist Spacecraft," *New York Times,* 23 January 2008, http://www.nytimes.com/2008/01/23/science/space/23cnd-spaceship.html.

17. William B. Scott and Michael J. Coumatos, *Space Wars: The First Six Hours of World War III* (New York: Tor Books, 2008).

18. William B. Scott and Michael J. Coumatos, "Would China Start a War in Space?" *Aviation Week & Space Technology,* 7 January 2008, 62.

19. Yong Deng and Thomas G. Moore, "China Views Globalization: Toward a New Great-Power Politics?" *Washington Quarterly* 27, no. 3 (Summer 2004): 117–36.

20. "Pentagon: Iranian Rocket Likely a Failure," *United Press International,* 18 August 2008, http://www.upi.com/Top_News/2008/08/18/Iran_launches_telecommunications_satellite/UPI-50941219062447/.

21. "U.S. Now Believes North Korea Launched a Satellite After All," *CNN.com,* 14 September 1998.

22. Lewis Page, "Iran Fires Rocket 'Into Space,' Plans Satellite for '09," *Register* (London), 5 February 2008, http://www.theregister.co.uk/2008/02/05/iran_rocket_launch_satellite_plans.

23. Bruce W. MacDonald, "China, Space Weapons, and U.S. Security," Council on Foreign Relations, Council Special Report 38, September 2008, 3.

24. Michael Krepon, "What Next for U.S. Space Diplomacy?" http://www.stimson.org/pub.cfm?ID=696.

25. MacDonald, "China, Space Weapons, and U.S. Security," 17.

26. Ibid., 24–25.

27. Dr. S. Peter Worden, private interview, 30 March 2008.

28. Ibid.

29. Colin Powell, "U.S. Forces: Challenges Ahead," *Foreign Affairs* 71, no. 5 (Winter 1992): 32–45.

30. Jim Wolf, "Top U.S. Contractors Say Ready for Space-Arms Studies," *Reuters,* 10 April 2008, http://uk.reuters.com/article/governmentFilingsNews/IdUKN1030405620080410.

31. John R. Bolton, "Should We Take Global Governance Seriously?" *Chicago Journal of International Law* 1 (Fall 2000): 206, cited in Charles A. Kupchan and Peter L. Trubowitz, "Dead Center: The Demise of Liberal Internationalism in the United States," *International Security* 32 (Fall 2007): 25.

32. See Theresa Hitchens and David Chen, "Forging a U.S.-Sino 'Grand Bargain' in Space," *Space Policy* 24, no. 23 (August 2008): 128–31.

33. See "Space Competitiveness," *Economist*, 10 April 2008, http://www.economist.com/markets/indicators/displaystory.cfm?story_id=11019607.

34. The study is based on two reports: "Authoritative Guide to Global Space Activity," released by the Space Foundation of Colorado Springs, Colorado and "2008 Space Competitiveness Index" issued by the Futron Corporation of Bethesda, Maryland. See "India and China Set to Reduce U.S. Dominance in Space Activity," 19 April 2008. http://in.news.yahoo.com/ani/20080419/r_t_ani_sc/tsc-india-and-china-set-to-reduce-us-dom-f32bc39.html (accessed 23 April 2008).

35. See Joan Johnson-Freese, *Space as a Strategic Asset* (New York: Columbia University Press, 2007), chapter 6.

Index

Acknowledgments

I wrote this book with the fervent hope that change is the in the air. In classes at both the Naval War College and Harvard Summer and Extension School, I speak with students about the tools of foreign policy through the acronym DIME, which stands for Diplomacy, Information, Military, and Economics. Lately, the United States has overly emphasized the "M," to the near exclusion of all others, in general and regarding space specifically. Fundamentally, this book argues for a more balanced approach.

I would like to thank Rear Admiral Jake Shuford, the President of the Naval War College from 2004 to 2008, for his commitment to academic freedom and for fostering an environment of intellectual curiosity at the Naval War College such that faculty are inspired to write books on topics such as this. He is a warrior and a scholar with more energy than anyone I have ever known.

I would also like to thank Harvard Extension School for its support in providing a research assistant from 2007 to 2008. Amy Hull worked on this project not only when Harvard paid her to do so—but when the money ran out and she just volunteered to keep going because she was interested. I am confident she has a bright future ahead of her.

Alice Juda at the Naval War College Library is always able to find a needle in a haystack, and I have asked her to do so many times. Without the willing assistance of professional research librarians like Alice, authors like me would be stymied. Thank you, Alice.

A number of men and women, colleagues and friends, experts and lay readers, have read various draft chapters and portions of the book and I owe each a debt of gratitude.

Jim Vedda read early drafts and provided valuable feedback. He is one of the few individuals I know equally comfortable in both the policy and technical worlds. His ideas on defining space weapons were especially helpful.

Everyone needs an English teacher as a friend, and mine is Paul Midura. He is also a whiz with quotations. I appreciate both his help and his friendship.

Many others also offered constructive advice and criticism, as well as support and encouragement. To Vic Budura, Theresa Hitchens, Christine Laudon, Gene Milowicki, Tom Nichols, Bonnie Watson, and David Wright, I offer my thanks, although all interpretations are mine.

Bill Finan, my editor at University of Pennsylvania Press, made this project enjoyable through his professionalism and support. I hope we can work together again.

It is impossible to thank all the space professionals whom I have talked with and learned from, even when I do not agree with them. I am very proud to be part—even a peripheral part—of the space adventure.